D0950248

THE ABCs OF BRIDGE

BILL ROOT BRIDGE BOOKS
All Published by Crown Publishers, Inc.

Modern Bridge Conventions
(coauthor Richard Pavlicek)

Commonsense Bidding

How to Play a Bridge Hand

How to Defend a Bridge Hand

THE
ABCs
OF BRIDGE

by **William S. Root**

Patricia L. Magnus, Editor

Three Rivers Press
New York

Copyright © 1998 by William S. Root

Published by Three Rivers Press, a division of Crown Publishers, Inc. 201 East 50th Street, New York, New York 10022. Member of the Crown Publishing Group.

Random House, Inc. New York, Toronto, London, Sydney, Auckland

www.randomhouse.com

THREE RIVERS PRESS and colophon are trademarks of Crown Publishers, Inc.

Printed in the United States of America

Typeset by Patricia L. Magnus
Caricatures by Tom Donnelly

Library of Congress Cataloging-in-Publication Data
Root, William S.
        The ABCs of Bridge / William S. Root — 1st ed.
        1. Contract bridge. 2. Contract bridge—Bidding I. Title
     GV1282.3.K5725   1988
     795.41'5—dc21   98-8096
                                                                              CIP
ISBN 0-609-80162-7

10 9 8 7 6 5 4 3 2 1

First Edition

CONTENTS

PART TWO—THE PLAY

PART THREE—THE DEFENSE

INTRODUCTION

WELCOME TO THE WONDERFUL GAME OF BRIDGE; a game which can be enjoyed on many levels. It is played competitively by the experts in world-wide competition, and socially by those who have very little knowledge of the game. Please study this book with me and learn the essentials; something about scoring; and enough about the bidding, play and defense to get started.

"How the Game is Played" covers the regulations, procedures, definitions of terms, (etc.), that you should learn before you start to play. If you consider yourself beyond the beginner stage and believe you already know how the game is played, you may start reading Part One. Information about scoring, rules and bridge terms can be found in the Appendix and Glossary at the end of the book.

This book is for those who want to play bridge but are afraid the game is too difficult. It is also for those who played bridge in the past, but need a refresher because they have not had time to play in recent years.

Practice is important, but you must have a few ideas in your head before you get started. If you are lucky, you have friends who will play bridge with you. Your friends will be a lot more tolerant if you have read this book first.

Bridge has been a major part of my life. For many years I have enjoyed teaching and sharing my love of the game with thousands of students who now consider bridge an important part of their lives. Remembering their plight when they were beginners has inspired me to write this book.

So lend me your mind and I will get you started. Before looking into the Table of Contents, here are a few words about the history of bridge.

HISTORY: People, primarily Englishmen, have been playing variations of bridge since the 16th century—Whist, Bridge, Auction Bridge and Plafond. "Contract Bridge," the game that is played today, was first evolved by Harold S. Vanderbilt, of the famous family, while playing bridge with friends on a cruise through the Panama Canal in 1925. Vanderbilt compiled a scoring table that added challenge, competition and excitement to the game. Today, bridge is the most popular card game in the world.

Bill Root

THE ABCs OF BRIDGE

THE ABC OF BRIDGE

HOW THE GAME IS PLAYED

Bridge is a partnership game. It consists of two parts—the "bidding" and the "play."

Once partnerships have been determined and the cards dealt, the four players pick up their 13 cards (their "hands") and sort them into suits (it is helpful and customary to alternate red and black suits).

Then the bidding (the "auction") begins.

THE BIDDING

Bidding is an estimation by two partners as to how many "tricks" their combined hands can win in the play. A trick consists of a card from each of the four hands and the play period consists of 13 tricks. How tricks are won will be explained shortly, but bidding comes first.

The dealer has the first chance to bid. After evaluating his hand (as will be described in Chapter One), he either "passes" or makes the "opening bid" by mentioning a number from one to seven together with one of the four suits or "notrump" (an offer to play without a trump suit). If the dealer passes, the next player in rotation (clockwise) has a chance to start the bidding or pass, and so on until somebody opens the bidding or all four players pass. When nobody opens the bidding, the cards are thrown in and a new hand is dealt (but there is no redeal at duplicate bridge). Once the bidding has been opened, each player in his turn (clockwise) has a chance to make a "higher" bid or pass. The suits and notrump have rank in the bidding—notrump (high), spades, hearts, diamonds and clubs (low). For example, if the last bid was two hearts, the lowest possible bids in each denomination are two spades, two notrump, three clubs, three diamonds and three hearts. See the "bidding ladder" on page six. The bidding continues until there are three consecutive passes, at which time the bidding is over. A player may pass any time it is his turn to bid, *but by passing he does not forfeit his right to bid later in the auction.*

The number of tricks a bid calls for is determined by adding the number of the bid to a "book" of six. For example, a bid of one heart is an offer to make seven tricks (six and one) with hearts as the trump suit, while a bid of three clubs is an offer to make nine tricks—six and three—with clubs as the trump suit.

Here is a practice deal. Suppose East deals these four hands.

North
♠ 7 6 3
♡ Q 9 5 2
◊ K 10 8
♣ K 9 4

West
♠ A K Q 10 9
♡ 4
◊ J 6 5 3 2
♣ Q 7

East (Dealer)
♠ 8 5 2
♡ J 7 6
◊ 9 4
♣ J 10 8 5 3

South
♠ J 4
♡ A K 10 8 3
◊ A Q 7
♣ A 6 2

West	North	East	South
—	—	Pass	1♡
1♠	2♡	Pass	4♡
Pass	Pass	Pass	

This diagram shows the typical way that bridge hands and bidding are displayed in bridge books, newspapers, etc. The four players are given geographical names—West, North, East and South.

(Throughout the book abbreviations are used to describe the cards, for example: ♡A = the ace of hearts; ◊K = the king of diamonds; ♣7 = the seven of clubs. Abbreviations are also used to describe the bids, for example: 1♠ = a bid of one spade; 4◊ = a bid of four diamonds, etc. Also, an "x" will sometimes be used to represent an insignificant low card; for example, ♠A Q x x x = five spades headed by the ace and queen. All aces, kings, queens, jacks and tens are called "honor cards.")

This is just a practice deal to acquaint you with bidding procedures, but the meaning of each bid is explained as follows.

Since East was the dealer he had the first chance to bid and passed because he had a very poor hand. The bidding continued in a clockwise rotation, and since South had more than his share of the high cards, he opened the bidding. Most opening bids are made at the one-level, and in this case South bid 1♡ as an offer to win seven tricks and make hearts trump (because he had length in that suit).

West "overcalled" 1♠ because he had a long and strong spade suit. Note that West could bid spades at the one-level because spades rank higher than hearts. If his long suit had been clubs or diamonds, he would have had to bid at the two-level, or higher.

North "raised" his partner's suit by bidding 2♡ to show three or more cards in the suit. A good trump suit is one in which the combined hands have "length," at least eight cards. Once his suit has been raised, South should be content to make hearts the trump suit—he knows his side has at least eight hearts, leaving at most five for his opponents. His only remaining problem is how high to bid.

You may be wondering why South bid 4♡, which requires ten tricks, when he could have passed 2♡, which requires only eight tricks. It often pays to be daring and bid to high contracts because high-scoring "bonuses" are awarded for *bidding and making* games and slams.

The minimum game contracts are:
    3NT   4♠   4♡   5♢   5♣

The small slam contracts are:
    6NT   6♠   6♡   6♢   6♣

The grand slam contracts are:
    7NT   7♠   7♡   7♢   7♣

Note that ten tricks are needed to score a game in spades or hearts, while 11 are needed in diamonds and clubs. Spades and hearts are called the "major suits," while diamonds and clubs are called the "minor suits."

Should you take a chance and bid to a game or slam and risk a minus score, or should you stop bidding below game (called a "part-score," or "partial") and take a small but sure profit? The answer, roughly speaking, is you should gamble and bid a game or a small slam if you think you are a favorite to make it; but it is unwise to bid a grand slam unless you have figured out in advance how you are going to win all 13 tricks. DECIDING HOW HIGH TO BID, AND WHETHER TO PLAY THE HAND IN A PARTICULAR TRUMP SUIT OR IN NOTRUMP, ARE THE TWO OBJECTIVES OF BIDDING. But remember, bidding is not an exact science, it is an estimation of probabilities. When you make a bid, you are making a bet and you will not win every time; you must take chances if you want to be a winning player.

Memorize the following and you are on your way.

THE BIDDING LADDER

7NT (high)		**3NT**	GAME
7♠		3♠	
7♡	GRAND SLAM	3♡	
7♢	(13 tricks)	3♢	
7♣		3♣	
6NT		2NT	
6♠		2♠	
6♡	SMALL SLAM	2♡	
6♢	(12 tricks)	2♢	
6♣		2♣	
5NT		1NT	
5♠		1♠	
5♡		1♡	
5♢	GAME	1♢	
5♣	GAME	1♣ (low)	
4NT		Pass	
4♠	GAME		
4♡	GAME		
4♢			
4♣			

RANK OF CARDS

Ace (high)		9	
King	HONOR	8	
Queen	CARDS	7	
Jack		6	SPOT
Ten		5	CARDS
		4	
		3	
		2 (low)	

RANK OF SUITS

Notrump (high)
Spades
Hearts
Diamonds
Clubs (low)

THE PLAY

The bidding is over and the play period begins after three consecutive passes. The last bid made becomes the "contract." The player who *first* bid the "denomination" of the contract (notrump, spades, hearts, diamonds or clubs) becomes the "declarer." The partner of the declarer becomes the "dummy."

The player to declarer's left makes the opening lead by placing any card from his hand face up in the center of the table. Then the dummy spreads his entire hand (also called the dummy) face up on the table, neatly arranged in suits with the trump suit on his right (declarer's left). It is also helpful if the dummy alternates colors; for example, if hearts are trumps, dummy places the hearts to his right, then spades, diamonds, clubs. Declarer plays all of the cards from both hands for his side. After planning his play, declarer plays a card from dummy. Then, in a clockwise manner, right-hand opponent and declarer play a card to complete the first trick. The player who wins the trick leads to the next, and so on until all 13 tricks have been played.

The declarer's goal is to win the number of tricks he contracted for in the bidding. The two defenders' goal is to stop him—to beat the contract by one or more tricks. The outcome of every deal depends on how many tricks are won by each side in the play. If you win the number of tricks required by your contract, you win points; if you win fewer than are required, you lose points. So do not try to win more tricks than you need ("overtricks") if doing so jeopardizes your contract. The reward for making a contract is sizable—especially if it is a game or slam—while the reward for making overtricks is trivial.

Soon we will play the practice deal in 4♡, but first:

HOW TRICKS ARE WON

When all four players "follow suit," the player who plays the highest card wins the trick. For example:

North (dummy)
♠ J

West (defender)   East (defender)
♠ 5   ♠ K

South
♠ 2 (declarer)

West leads the ♠5, the ♠J is played from dummy, East plays the ♠K and South the ♠2. East wins the trick because he played the highest spade. After gathering in the four cards and turning them face down on the table, East leads any card in his hand to the next trick.

Each player must *follow suit* if he can—that is, he must play a card of the same suit that was led. If he has no more cards in the led suit, he may "discard" (play a card from some other suit). For example:

North (dummy)
♡ 9

West (defender   East (defender)
♣ 8   ♣ 2

South (declarer)
♣ 7

East leads the ♣2, South plays the ♣7, West the ♣8 and the ♡9 is played from dummy. West wins the trick because he played the highest club. The ♡9 was discarded since dummy had no clubs.

The bidding determines whether the hand is played with a trump suit, or in notrump. The trump suit is the most powerful of all. Any trump, even the two-spot, ranks higher than any card in any other suit.

In the following illustration, diamonds are trump:

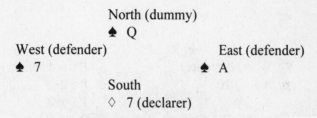

West leads the ♠7, the ♠Q is played from dummy, East plays the ♠A and South the ◇7. South wins the trick by trumping (more commonly called "ruffing"). Remember though, that a player is not allowed to ruff unless he is "void" (has no cards) in the suit that was led. If he is void in that suit, he may ruff or discard, as he chooses.

When a trick contains two or more trumps, it is won by whomever plays the highest trump. For example, diamonds are again trumps:

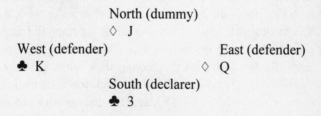

South leads the ♣3, West plays the ♣K, declarer ruffs in dummy with the ◇J, and East "overruffs" with the ◇Q. East wins the trick. East is not required to overruff, he may discard if he chooses. The simple rule to remember is: *A player may lead any card in his hand; the other three players in their turn must follow suit if possible; if they*

cannot follow suit they may play any card in their hand (ruff or discard), as they choose.

PRACTICE DEAL

Now back to the play of the practice deal in a 4♡ contract:

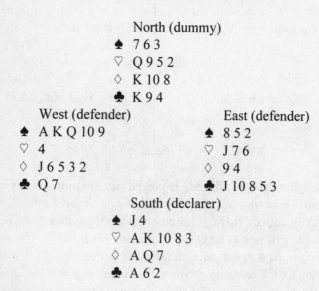

North (dummy)
♠ 7 6 3
♡ Q 9 5 2
◇ K 10 8
♣ K 9 4

West (defender)
♠ A K Q 10 9
♡ 4
◇ J 6 5 3 2
♣ Q 7

East (defender)
♠ 8 5 2
♡ J 7 6
◇ 9 4
♣ J 10 8 5 3

South (declarer)
♠ J 4
♡ A K 10 8 3
◇ A Q 7
♣ A 6 2

West's opening lead is the ♠K, and it wins the trick when all other players follow suit with low spades. As each trick is won, a player from the winning side gathers the four cards together and turns them face down on the table in front of him. After taking the first trick, West leads the ♠A and wins the second trick when the other three players follow suit. West loses the third trick when he leads the ♠Q and declarer ruffs with the ♡3. Declarer has the ten tricks he needs to make his contract (five hearts, three diamonds and two clubs), but he must play the ace, king and queen of trumps before cashing his diamond winners. Note that East has three trumps and only two diamonds; if declarer leads the third round of diamonds before drawing three rounds of trumps, East can set the contract by ruffing the third diamond.

The key play: Drawing three rounds of trumps before cashing the high cards in the other suits.

DOUBLES AND REDOUBLES

Before continuing, a few words about "doubles" and "redoubles." Any player in his turn may double, *provided the last bid was made by one of his opponents.* A player doubles when he thinks his opponents have bid too high and will be unable to win enough tricks to make their contract. If the doubler "sets" (defeats) the contract, he wins more points than he would if he had not doubled; if he does not set the contract, he loses more. (A declaration of double sometimes has an artificial meaning, such as a "takeout double"— you will read about this important strategy in Chapter Nine.)

Any player, in his turn, may redouble, *but only when his right-hand opponent has just said double, or, more rarely, when a double by his left-hand opponent is followed by two passes.* A player redoubles when he thinks his contract cannot be set, and this further increases the number of points that will be won or lost. (Redouble may also be used to show high-card strength; see Chapter Ten.)

WHAT HAPPENS NOW

When one deal is completed, the score is entered and the next player in turn (clockwise) deals. This procedure continues until a "rubber" ends, at which time the scores are totaled and the score for each player is entered on a score sheet. Partners are determined for the next rubber—usually by cutting the cards.

There are two popular types of bridge (other than duplicate bridge), "Chicago" and "rubber." "Chicago" is the better game and the one I recommend that you play. Chicago Bridge consists of four played deals, one dealt by each player. (You can look in the Appendix to see the procedures for playing Chicago and how to score it. It is unnecessary to learn how to score before you begin to play, but you should refer to the scoring chart when your curiosity is aroused, or when it is suggested that you do so in the following pages. The scoring of any game dictates the strategy, so you must learn to score eventually.)

Part One is on bidding, Part Two is on how to play a hand, and Part Three covers defense. But the more you know about how hands are played, the more you will understand what you read in the chapters on bidding. Therefore, I have included "practice deals" throughout the book. It is also appropriate to read any portion (or all) of the parts on play and defense before reading all of the chapters on bidding. IT WOULD BE A GOOD IDEA TO READ THE FIRST EIGHT PAGES OF PART TWO ON HOW TO PLAY SUIT COMBINATIONS NOW.

If you encounter any bridge terms that you do not understand, look them up in the Glossary.

PART ONE

THE BIDDING

THE FOLLOWING TEN CHAPTERS
COVER WHAT EVERY BRIDGE PLAYER
SHOULD KNOW ABOUT BIDDING.

CHAPTER ONE

HOW TO VALUE YOUR HAND

The first step when you pick up your cards is to place a value on your hand. Then, in turn, make a bid (or pass) to describe it. As the bidding proceeds, you and your partner exchange information in an effort to predict how many tricks the combined hands can win in the play. In most cases it is difficult (or impossible) to judge how many *tricks* a hand can win, so the method of evaluation used by practically all bridge players is to count "points."

THE POINT-COUNT SYSTEM

There are three ways to win tricks: with high cards, with low cards in a long suit, and with trumps. Points are counted as follows:

High-card points:
Each ace counts four points
Each king counts three points
Each queen counts two points
Each jack counts one point

Each suit contains ten high-card points; therefore, a deck contains 40 high-card points. A hand containing ten high-card points is an "average hand."

Almost everyone agrees with this method of counting points for high cards, but there is a variety of ways to count "distributional points," and all authorities do not agree as to which is best. The following is one of the most popular and the one I recommend because of its simplicity. If you play with others who use a different method for counting points, you will have no difficulty. Just count your points as described below and bid as though your partner is doing the same thing.

Long cards: A suit containing four or more cards has trick-taking potential because of its length. For example: If you hold A K Q 2 opposite 5 4 3, after the ace, king and queen have been played you can win a trick with the two if the missing six cards divide 3-3. Similarly, if you hold A K Q 3 2 opposite 6 5 4, after the ace, king and queen have been played you can win tricks with the three and the two if the missing five cards divide 3-2.

Although a four-card suit may produce a trick with its long card, no points are counted for it. It is the five-card and longer suits that have good trick-taking potential. It is better if a long suit is headed by high cards. However, for practical purposes in bidding, count points for long suits regardless of the strength of the suit, as follows:

Long-card points
Each five-card suit counts one point
Each six-card suit counts two points
Each seven-card suit counts three points

In other words, count one point for each additional card over four in any suit.

Test Yourself
How many points are counted (for high cards and long cards together) in each of the following hands?

(1) ♠ A K 9   (2) ♠ —
     ♡ A J 10 8 6   ♡ K 2
     ◇ 7 4   ◇ K Q 9 8 7 5
     ♣ Q 7 5   ♣ A 8 6 5 3

(3) ♠ Q J 10 5   (4) ♠ K J 3 2
     ♡ 6 4   ♡ K Q J 6 5
     ◇ A Q J 10   ◇ A 2
     ♣ K 9 7   ♣ K 3

Solutions
(5)   15 points, 14 for high cards and one for the five-card heart suit.

(6) 15 points, 12 for high cards, two for the six-card diamond suit and one for the five-card club suit.
(7) 13 points, all for high cards.
(8) 18 points, 17 for high cards and one for the five-card heart suit.

Trumps (short suits): Since you cannot trump (ruff) a trick if you have any cards in the suit that was led, the method for valuing trumps is to count points for short suits. Logically, the time you are likely to win tricks by ruffing is when you have a good trump fit—eight or more cards between your hand and partner's. Therefore, *add extra points for short suits any time you raise your partner's suit with four-card support (sometimes with three-card support), or when your partner has raised your suit.* In other words, *both* partners count points for short suits when a good trump suit has been found, as follows:

Short-suit points
A void (no cards in a suit) counts three points
A singleton (one card in a suit) counts two points
A doubleton (two cards in a suit) counts one point

It is better to have four-card support for partner's suit than just three cards. Although you usually need at least four trumps to raise a minor suit, it is common practice to raise a major with just three. When you raise a suit with just three trumps, count points for short suits and deduct one point from the total. For example, if your short suit is a singleton, count it as one point rather than two.

Test Yourself

(5) ♠ Q 9 8 2   Your partner opens with 1♠.
     ♡ 7   How many points do you
     ◇ A 7 5   have?
     ♣ 10 8 6 4 3

(6)   ♠ A J 7 4 3   You open with 1♠ and your
       ♡ A 9 8 6 5   partner raises to 2♠. How
       ◇ K 10 4   many points do you have?
       ♣ —

Solutions

(5)   Nine points. You started with seven (six in high cards plus one
       for the five-card club suit), but you add two more for the
       singleton heart after partner bids 1♠.

(6)   17 points. You started with 14 points (12 in high cards and one
       for each of the five-card suits), but add three more for the void
       in the club suit after partner has raised your suit.

The objectives of bidding are *to decide how high to bid, and to
decide whether to play the contract in a trump suit or notrump.* A
large bonus is awarded for bidding and making a game, and an
additional large bonus for bidding and making a slam. When the
combined hands have the required point count, you should bid a game
or a slam in the trump suit of your choice (or notrump) in order to
increase the amount that you win.

POINT-COUNT REQUIREMENTS
FOR GAMES AND SLAMS

You need in the combined hands to bid:

3NT, 4♡ or 4♠	26 points
5♣ or 5◇	29 points
Any small slam (six bid)	33 points
Any grand slam (seven bid)	37 points

The "magic numbers" to remember during the bidding are 26
points for game and 33 points for slam. If the combined hands have
fewer than 26 points stop bidding in a part-score; with 26-32, bid a
game; and with 33 or more, bid a slam.

An exception is when you plan to bid a game in a minor suit. You
need 29 points to bid a minor-suit game, but only 26 to bid game in
notrump or a major suit. If your intention is to bid a game, you should
seek contracts of 4♡, 4♠ or 3NT before settling for 5♣ or 5◇.

The point-count requirement to bid a small slam is the same whether played in notrump, a major suit or a minor suit, and the same is true of grand slams. But it is usually safer to bid a slam in a good trump suit (major or minor) rather than in notrump.

QUICK TRICKS
(Sometimes Called Defensive Tricks or Honor Tricks)

Quick tricks are high cards that can be expected to win a trick the first or second time that suit is led. Sometimes it is better to estimate the trick-taking value of your hand by counting your quick tricks, rather than your points. The situations where counting quick tricks is better will be explained in later chapters. For now, familiarize yourself with the following quick-trick table:

Ace-king in the same suit	two quick tricks
Ace-queen in the same suit	one and one-half quick tricks
An ace, or king-queen in the same suit	one quick trick
A king plus at least one lower card in a suit	one-half quick trick

Test Yourself

How many quick tricks are in each of the following hands?

(7) ♠ K Q 9   (8) ♠ A K 2
     ♡ A J 3   ♡ K Q 6
     ◇ Q 7 5 2   ◇ A Q 4 3
     ♣ Q 8 4   ♣ 10 7 3

Solutions

Hand (7) has two quick tricks (one for the ♠K Q and one for the ♡A), while hand (8) has four and one-half—two for the ♠A K, one for the ♡K Q, and one and one-half for the ◇A Q.

WHEN YOU HAVE A CLOSE DECISION

Although the point-count system is a good guideline to help you place a value on your hand, it does not always describe a hand accurately. As the bidding proceeds you may be faced with a close decision (for example, you learned from your partner's bidding that the combined hands have about 25 points and you do not know whether to stop bidding in part-score or to take a chance and bid a game). In such cases it pays to reexamine your points. If you like their quality, add a point or two and take an aggressive view; if you dislike their quality, subtract a point or two and take a pessimistic view. Here are a few pointers for you to mull over when you are faced with a close decision. Look them over, but do not worry about memorizing them yet.

* An ace is slightly undervalued at four points. With an abundance of aces, take an aggressive view.
* It is better to have honor cards together in the same suit. For example: the queen in A Q 2 is better than the queen in Q 3 2; the jack in A K J is better than the jack in J 3 2.
* Honor cards in your long suits increase your chances of winning tricks with low cards. For example:

  ♠ AQxxx   ♡ xx   ◇ xx   ♣ KQxx is better than
  ♠ xxxxx   ♡ AQ   ◇ KQ   ♣ xxxx

* Although no points are counted for tens and nines, they may be of value; especially when they are in a suit with honor cards. For example, K 10 9 8 is better than K 7 6 5.
* Unguarded honor cards such as: a singleton king, queen or jack; or a doubleton queen or jack, are of dubious value unless they are in a suit bid by partner.
* When your partner will be declarer at a trump contract and his bidding has shown that he has one very long suit, or two long suits, only "quick tricks" in his short suits will be of value; stray queens and jacks in his short suits are usually worthless. For example, if partner has bid spades and hearts, demote the value of a queen or jack in clubs or diamonds.

PLEASE NOTE: Do not waste your time reexamining your points when the decision of how high to bid is clear. For example, if you have found a good trump suit and the combined hands have enough points to bid a game, bid it directly. It is only when you are not sure whether to stop bidding in a part-score, to bid a game, or to bid a slam, that reexamining your point count is worthwhile.

PRACTICE DEAL

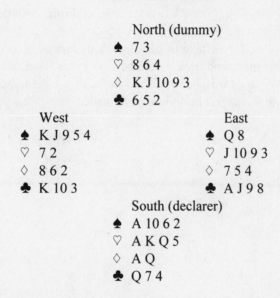

North (dummy)
♠ 7 3
♡ 8 6 4
◇ K J 10 9 3
♣ 6 5 2

West
♠ K J 9 5 4
♡ 7 2
◇ 8 6 2
♣ K 10 3

East
♠ Q 8
♡ J 10 9 3
◇ 7 5 4
♣ A J 9 8

South (declarer)
♠ A 10 6 2
♡ A K Q 5
◇ A Q
♣ Q 7 4

South winds up as the declarer in 3NT. It is too early to discuss how these hands should be bid, but note that the combined hands do have the 26 points required to bid game (South has 21 and North five—one for the five-card diamond suit).

West's opening lead is the ♠5 (the *fourth-highest* card from a long suit is often the best opening lead against a 3NT contract). After the opening lead the dummy spreads his hand face up on the table. Then, *before playing a card from dummy,* the declarer counts his tricks and plans his play. He has nine winners (one spade, three hearts and five diamonds), enough to make his contract. His play from dummy on the first trick is a low spade, and East plays the ♠Q—"third hand high." Note that if East mistakenly played the ♠8, declarer could win the first trick with the ♠10. After winning the first trick with the ♠A and cashing the ◇A, declarer leads the ◇Q and *overtakes it with dummy's ◇K*. While the lead is in the dummy, he cashes three more diamond tricks and then the three top hearts. Note that there was a chance to win a tenth trick with the fourth heart in declarer's hand if the missing six hearts divided 3-3, but as you can see they did not.

The key plays: Cashing the ◇A first (as a general rule, cash the high cards in the short hand first), and then overtaking the ◇Q with the ◇K. If declarer makes the mistake of playing the diamonds in any other way, the second diamond trick would be won in his hand. Since the dummy has no entry cards, he would be limited to two diamond tricks and go down in a contract he should have made.

CHAPTER TWO

OPENING BIDS

This chapter includes opening bids of 1NT and 2NT, as well as suit bids at the one-level. Other opening bids will be covered in Chapter Seven.

OPENING NOTRUMP BIDS

Some opening bids describe a hand more accurately than others and the most descriptive are opening notrump bids. An opening bid of 1NT or 2NT shows a "balanced hand" within a three-point range.

Balanced hand: A balanced hand is one that contains no voids, no singletons and not more than one doubleton. The possible distributions are 4-3-3-3, 4-4-3-2 or 5-3-3-2.

Stopper: A stopper is a combination of cards that can win a trick in a suit led by the opponents. High cards and/or length in a suit form stoppers. For example, Q J 10 is a definite stopper, Q 3 2 is a possible stopper, and Q x is not a stopper. For practical purposes in bidding, a suit is considered stopped when it contains at least: A, K x, Q x x or J x x x. (Although stoppers in all four suits are not required for an opening notrump bid, they are often required for later notrump bids.)

Point-count range for opening notrump bids:

$$1NT = 15, 16 \text{ or } 17 \text{ high-card points}$$
$$2NT = 20, 21 \text{ or } 22 \text{ high-card points}$$

(**NOTE:** Until recent years, the point-count requirement for opening notrump bids was higher—1NT showed 16-18, and 2NT showed 21-23, or sometimes 22-24. I tell you this in case you ever play with a partner who has not been exposed to modern bidding methods.)

What to do with the in-between hands: A balanced hand with 13-14 points (or maybe 12 points) is good enough to open the bidding, but too weak to open with 1NT. A balanced hand with 18-19 points is too strong to open with 1NT and too weak to open with 2NT. When your hand has one of these in-between point ranges, open the bidding with one of a suit with the intention of bidding notrump at your next turn (opening bidder's second bid is explained in Chapter Five). All hands with 23 points or more are opened with 2♣ (explained in Chapter Seven).

Test Yourself

As dealer, what is your opening bid on each of the following hands? If you think you should open in a suit, bid the longest one (for now). We will discuss specifics later in this chapter.

(1)	♠ A Q	(2) ♠ 10 7 4	(3) ♠ A Q 10
	♡ 6 3 2	♡ A J 10	♡ A J 9 7 6
	◇ A Q 4	◇ A K 5	◇ K 5
	♣ K J 10 7 5	♣ A K Q J	♣ J 10 2

(4)	♠ A 10 4	(5) ♠ A	(6) ♠ A 3
	♡ K Q 9	♡ J 10 7 2	♡ Q J 10 7 4
	◇ K 10 3	◇ A Q 8 5 2	◇ A Q 9 8
	♣ A Q 10 9	♣ A J 7	♣ K 2

Solutions

(5)   1NT with 17 points (16 in high cards and one for the five-card suit).

(6)   2NT with 22 high-card points.

(7)   1NT with 16 points (15 in high cards and one for the five-card suit).

(8)   1♣ with 18 high-card points; too strong to open 1NT, and too weak to open 2NT.

(9)   1◇ with 17 points (16 in high cards and one for the five-card suit). *Do not open the bidding with notrump if you have a singleton (or a void).*

(10) 1♡ with 17 points (16 in high cards and one for the five-card suit). This 5-4-2-2 distribution is not a balanced hand.

OPENING SUIT BIDS OF ONE

The most common opening bid by far is in a suit at the one-level. The first step is to count your points to see if your hand qualifies. There are 40 high-card points in a deck, so ten high-card points is an average hand. Logically, you need more than an average hand to open the bidding. Counting points for high cards and long suits, the minimum requirement to open the bidding with a suit bid of one is 13 points, or 12 points if the hand includes at least two quick tricks. In other words, pass with 12 points if you do not like the quality of your points, but do not pass with 13. To simplify the presentation throughout this book, I will refer to 13 points as the minimum requirement, but remember that some 12-point hands should be opened. The maximum point count for an opening suit bid of one is in the neighborhood of 21-22, so let us say that the range for opening a suit bid at the one-level is 13-22 points. (Hands with 23 points or more are opened with 2♣, explained in Chapter Seven.)

Test Yourself

As dealer, what would you bid, if anything, with each of the following hands?

(7) ♠ Q 7 2
     ♡ Q J 9
     ◊ Q 5 4
     ♣ A J 8 2

(8) ♠ A Q 7
     ♡ 9 8 3
     ◊ 7 6 4
     ♣ A Q 10 2

(9) ♠ K Q 2
     ♡ 7
     ◊ A 10 8
     ♣ A K Q J 6 3

(10) ♠ Q 10 9 7 6 3
     ♡ 5 2
     ◊ A 5
     ♣ A J 10

Solutions

(11) Pass with 12 points and only one quick trick.

(12) Bid 1♣ with an attractive 12 points—three quick tricks.
(13) Bid 1♣ with 21 points (two for the six-card suit).
(14) Bid 1♠ with 13 points (two for the six-card suit).

BIDDABLE SUITS

Once you decide that your hand qualifies for an opening bid of one in a suit, you must choose which suit to bid first from among your biddable suits. Requirements for an opening bid in a major suit (spades or hearts), are different than those in a minor suit (diamonds and clubs), so they are treated separately.

Biddable major suits: Years ago the minimum requirement for an opening bid in a major suit was a good four-card suit—called "four-card majors." A few partnerships still play that way, but today the most popular method by far is "five-card majors," and this is clearly the way you should play. *An opening bid of 1♡ or 1♠ shows a five-card or longer suit, but any five-card major is biddable, even 6 5 4 3 2.*

Biddable minor suits: Any four-card or longer minor suit is biddable, even 5 4 3 2. *With no five-card or longer major suit and no four-card or longer minor suit*, you may open the bidding in a three-card minor. An opening bid of 1♣ or 1◇ with a three-card suit is a common part of standard bidding methods and is sometimes referred to as the "short minor."

Test Yourself

Which of the following suits are acceptable for an opening one-bid? Answer twice: first answer if the suit is a major, second answer if the suit is a minor:

(11) A Q 7 2	(12) A 8 6 5 2	(13) 4 3 2
(14) 8 7 5 4 3	(15) A 8 5	(16) A K

Solutions

An opening bid in a major suit requires five cards or more, so only #12 and #14 are biddable major suits.

An opening bid in a minor suit requires three cards or more, so all of the above are biddable minor suits except #16; never open the bidding in a two-card suit.

WHICH SUIT TO BID FIRST
When you have more than one biddable suit:
* With just one five-card or longer suit, bid it first.
* With two five-card suits, or two six-card suits (equal length), bid the higher ranking first whether it is stronger or not.
* With no five-card (or longer) suit, bid the longer minor. With 4-3 in the minors, bid the four-card suit; with 3-2 in the minors, bid the three-card suit.
* With two four-card minors, bid 1♢ unless the clubs are much stronger.
* With two three-card minors, bid 1♣ unless the diamonds are much stronger.

Test Yourself
What is your opening bid with each of the following hands?

(17) ♠ A K Q 2   (18) ♠ J 9 6 4 2   (19) ♠ A Q J
   ♡ 7 6   ♡ A 8   ♡ 8 7
   ◇ A 9   ◇ A K 10 9 4   ◇ K 10 6 3
   ♣ 8 6 5 4 3   ♣ 3   ♣ K J 5 2

(20) ♠ K Q 5   (21) ♠ A 10 7 2   (22) ♠ 10 8 2
   ♡ A Q J 4   ♡ A Q 8 5   ♡ A Q 5 3
   ◇ J 9 2   ◇ Q 8 5   ◇ A K J
   ♣ J 7 3   ♣ A K   ♣ 9 7 4

Solutions
(17) 1♣. With just one five-card or longer suit, bid it first.

(18) 1♠. With two five-card suits, bid the higher ranking first whether it is stronger or not.

(19) 1◊. With two four-card minor suits, bid 1◊ unless the clubs are much stronger.

(20) 1♣. With two three-card minor suits, bid 1♣ unless the diamonds are much stronger.

(21) 1◊. With no five-card or longer major suit, bid the longer minor suit.

(22) 1◊. With two three-card minor suits, bid 1♣ *unless the diamonds are much stronger*.

IN REVIEW

An opening bid of 1NT shows a balanced hand with 15-17 points.

An opening bid of 2NT shows a balanced hand with 20-22 points.

An opening suit bid of one shows 13-22 points (or 12 with two quick tricks). It denies the ability to open 1NT or 2NT.

Hands with 23 points or more are opened with 2♣. See Chapter Seven.

Biddable suits for an opening bid:
* Any five-card or longer suit is biddable, even 6 5 4 3 2.
* Any four-card minor is biddable, even 5 4 3 2.
* A three-card minor suit is biddable provided you do not have four or more cards in the other minor suit, or five or more cards in either major suit. But remember that an opening notrump bid is preferable to bidding a suit if you have a balanced hand with the proper point count.

Which suit to bid first:
* With only one five-card (or longer) suit, bid it first.
* With two five-card suits, or two six-card suits, bid the higher ranking first whether it is stronger or not.

* With no five-card or longer suit, bid the longer minor suit. With two four-card minors, bid 1◇ unless the clubs are much stronger. With two three-card minors, bid 1♣ unless the diamonds are much stronger.

PRACTICE DEAL

Contract: 3NT
Opening Lead: ♡Q

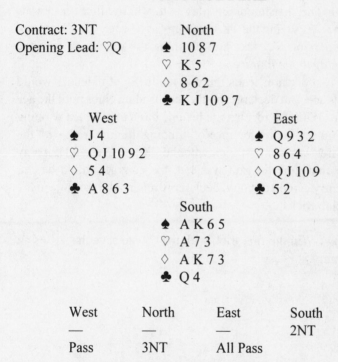

North
♠ 10 8 7
♡ K 5
◇ 8 6 2
♣ K J 10 9 7

West
♠ J 4
♡ Q J 10 9 2
◇ 5 4
♣ A 8 6 3

East
♠ Q 9 3 2
♡ 8 6 4
◇ Q J 10 9
♣ 5 2

South
♠ A K 6 5
♡ A 7 3
◇ A K 7 3
♣ Q 4

West	North	East	South
—	—	—	2NT
Pass	3NT	All Pass	

The bidding: South's 2NT opening bid shows a balanced hand with 20-22 points. With a balanced hand and eight points (seven in high cards and one for the five-card club suit), North knows the combined total is 28-30 points and raises to 3NT.

The opening lead: As a general rule, the best opening lead against a 3NT contract is from the longest and strongest suit. The correct card to lead when the suit has a three-card sequence headed by the king, queen, jack or ten is the top card—lead the king from K Q J x, lead the queen from Q J 10 x, lead the jack from J 10 9 x, and lead the ten from 10 9 8 x.

The play: The declarer has six top tricks (♠A K, ♡A K and ◇A K), and can develop four more tricks in the club suit by conceding a trick to the ace. *He should not cash his top tricks until he has established the club suit.* The first important play is to win the first trick in his hand with the ♡A, saving the ♡K in dummy as an entry card. Note that all of this counting of tricks and planning the play must be done *before you play to the first trick.*

At trick two declarer leads the ♣Q and a smart defender would "hold up" his ace. But declarer should keep leading clubs until the ace is driven out. When he regains the lead he has a total of ten winning tricks. Do you see the importance of winning the first trick with the ♡A? If declarer won the first trick with the ♡K and West did not play his ♣A the first time the suit was led, the contract would be set; lacking an entry card to dummy, declarer would not be able to win the rest of the club tricks.

The key play: Win the first trick with the ♡A, to save the ♡K as an entry to dummy.

CHAPTER THREE

RESPONSES AND REBIDS
AFTER NOTRUMP OPENINGS
(Including The Stayman Convention)

An opening notrump bid describes a hand more accurately than any other opening bid—it shows a balanced hand within a three-point range. When your partner opens the bidding with 1NT or 2NT, add your points to his and if the total is below 26, end the bidding in the lowest and safest part-score contract. If the total is between 26 and 32, bid a game; and if the total is 33 or more, bid a slam. If the total might be enough to bid a game or a slam, depending on whether partner has a minimum or a maximum point count, invite a game or a slam.

Of course you must also decide the denomination—whether to play the hand in notrump or in one of the suits. If you judge that the hand should be played in a notrump contract, pass or raise to the appropriate level. If you judge that a trump contract will (or may) be better, bid a five-card or longer suit or use the "Stayman Convention."

The specific requirements for the various bids are listed below, beginning with:

RESPONSES TO AN OPENING 1NT BID

When to pass or raise notrump: The usual procedure with a balanced hand is to pass or raise notrump. Also, it is often best to raise notrump if you have an unbalanced hand *with a long and strong minor suit.* An opening bid of 1NT shows 15-17 points. Remembering that the minimum requirement for bidding 3NT is 26 points in the combined hands, and for 6NT it is 33 points, the responder bids as follows:

> Pass with 0-8 points.
> Bid 2NT with 9 points (invites 3NT).
> Bid 3NT with 10-15 points.
> Bid 4NT with 16 or 17 points (invites 6NT).
> Bid 6NT with 18 or 19 points.

(**NOTE:** The accepted procedure is to bid game with ten points, even though the total might be only 25.)

Test Yourself

Your partner opens the bidding with 1NT. What do you respond with each of the following hands?

	(1)	♠ 7 3	(2)	♠ A J 10
		♡ K 10 6		♡ A Q 6
		◊ A Q 10 9 6 4		◊ K J 7 2
		♣ 8 4		♣ K 10 4

	(3)	♠ K 9 8	(4)	♠ 9 8 5
		♡ 7 5 4 3		♡ A K J
		◊ Q J 10		◊ A J 6
		♣ K 6 5		♣ K 10 9 4

Solutions

(5)   Bid 3NT with 11 points (two for the six-card suit). The combined total is 26, 27 or 28.

(6)   Bid 6NT with 18 points. The combined total is 33, 34 or 35.

(7)   Bid 2NT with nine points, to invite 3NT. The combined total is 24, 25 or 26.

(8)   Bid 4NT with 16 points, to invite 6NT. The combined total is 31, 32 or 33.

When to bid a suit: If your partner opens the bidding with 1NT, it is often better to bid a five-card or longer suit than to pass or raise notrump. But remember this: n*ever bid a suit in response to an opening notrump bid unless it is at least five cards long.* The requirements for suit responses to 1NT are listed below. For special reasons, the club suit will be ignored until later. The recommended point-count is for high cards and long suits.

*   A bid of 2◊, 2♡ or 2♠ shows a five-card or longer suit and a maximum of eight points. Since there are not enough points to

bid a game, opener should pass. To emphasize that these bids show weakness, they are sometimes called "drop-dead" bids.

* A jump bid to 3◊, 3♡ or 3♠ shows a five-card or longer suit and ten or more points. These jump responses are *forcing to game*—your side must continue bidding at least as far as game. What to bid with a five-card (or longer) suit and nine points is explained later.

* A jump bid to 4♡ or 4♠ shows a good six-card or longer suit and about 10-15 points. *Opener must pass.*

Test Yourself

Your partner opens the bidding with 1NT. What do you respond with each of the following hands?

(5)	♠ 7	(6)	♠ K Q 10 8 2	(7)	♠ Q J 9 6 5 3
	♡ K 9 8 6 3		♡ 7 6		♡ A 2
	◊ 10 5 4		◊ A 9 8		◊ Q 8 4 3
	♣ 9 7 3 2		♣ Q 5 3		♣ 5

Solutions

(5) Bid 2♡ with four points (one for the five-card suit). Partner will pass and 2♡ should be a better part-score contract than 1NT.

(6) Bid 3♠ with 12 points (one for the five-card suit). Your jump bid is forcing and partner should bid 4♠ with three or more spades, or 3NT with a doubleton spade. You will pass either bid.

(7) Bid 4♠ with 11 points (two for the six-card suit). With a six-card spade suit, 4♠ should be the best game contract.

THE STAYMAN CONVENTION

A 2♣ response to 1NT is Stayman. It is an artificial bid (it has nothing to do with the number of clubs you hold) and asks the opening bidder to bid a four-card (or five-card) major suit if he has one, or to bid 2◊ with no more than three cards in either major suit. Although game in notrump requires only nine tricks and game in a major suit requires ten, it is usually better to play game in a major when each partner has four trumps. Since a suit response to an opening notrump bid guarantees as least a five-card suit, the Stayman Convention is needed to discover a four-four major suit fit. The most common use of Stayman is when you have eight or more points (no upper limit) and four cards in one or both major suits; but it is not recommended when you have a four-card major and three cards in each of the other suits (4-3-3-3). A rare exception: you may bid 2♣ (Stayman) with fewer than eight points to seek a better part-score contract *provided you have length in diamonds, hearts and spades.* Your partner must bid 2◊, 2♡ or 2♠, and you will pass his bid.

Test Yourself

Your partner opens the bidding with 1NT. What do you respond with each of the following hands?

(8) ♠ 10 9 7 4 (9) ♠ A 7 5 2 (10) ♠ K 10 9 2
     ♡ 9 7 6 2   ♡ Q 10 9   ♡ J 10 8 5
     ◊ J 10 5 3 2   ◊ 8 7 3   ◊ 7
     ♣ —   ♣ K 10 4   ♣ A 9 7 6

Solutions

(8) Bid 2♣ and pass opener's rebid.
(9) Bid 2NT. Do not use Stayman with 4-3-3-3.
(10) Bid 2♣. If partner bids 2♡ or 2♠, raise to game. If partner bids 2◊, bid 2NT. (Using Stayman with just eight points is desirable because the hand becomes worth ten points if partner has a major-suit fit.)

(**NOTE:** The Stayman Convention has gained universal acceptance as a standard part of bidding and is used by virtually all good bridge players. It is also used when partner opens 2NT, or when he rebids notrump after opening with a 2♣ bid—explained in Chapter Seven.)

REBIDS BY THE OPENING 1NT BIDDER

Because responder knows a great deal about the opening 1NT bidder's hand; *responder is captain.* The 1NT opener's second bid, if any, is routine; he must describe his hand to partner as follows:

* If partner has raised to 2NT, he has nine points and is inviting you to bid 3NT. Pass with 15 points, bid 3NT with 17, and use your judgment to bid 3NT or pass with 16.
* If partner has raised to 4NT, he has 16-17 points and is inviting 6NT. You should pass with 15 points, bid 6NT with 17, and use your judgment to bid 6NT or pass with 16.
* If partner has responded 2♢, 2♡ or 2♠, he has a maximum of eight points and wants to play that contract. You should pass.
* If partner has jumped the bidding to 3♢, 3♡ or 3♠, his bid is forcing; you must bid again. Raise 3♡ or 3♠ to game with three trumps or more, or bid 3NT with only two trumps. If the suit is diamonds, 3NT is often a better choice even with three or more trumps.
* If partner has bid 2♣, Stayman: bid 2♡ or 2♠ with four (or five) cards in the suit; with no more than three cards in either major suit bid 2♢—another artificial bid that has nothing to do with the number of diamonds you hold. *No bid other than 2♢, 2♡ or 2♠ is possible.* With two four-card majors, bid the stronger.
* If partner jumps directly to any game, he wants to play that contract. You must pass.

Test Yourself

You open the bidding with 1NT and partner responds 2♣ (Stayman). What do you rebid with each of the following hands?

(11)	♠ J 9 3	(12)	♠ A J 4	(13)	♠ K 7 6 3
	♡ K J 10		♡ 10 8 6 3		♡ A Q 10 8
	♢ A Q		♢ A 2		♢ A J 9
	♣ A J 7 6 2		♣ A K J 4		♣ K 4

Solutions

(11) Bid 2♢. This is an artificial bid telling partner you have no four- (or five-) card major suit.

(12) Bid 2♡. Any four-card major suit is biddable.

(13) Bid 2♡. With two four-card majors, bid the stronger one first. If partner's next bid is 2NT or 3NT he must have four spades.

Otherwise, he would not have bid Stayman. So you should bid
4♠ over 2NT or 3NT.

REBIDS BY THE STAYMAN 2♣ BIDDER

Requirements for the rebids after responding 2♣ to partner's
opening 1NT bid are explained in the answers to the following quiz.
Decide what you would bid before reading the answers.

Test Yourself

How do you respond to an opening bid of 1NT? If you bid 2♣
(Stayman), what is your next bid if partner bids 2◊, if he bids 2♡, or
if he bids 2♠ (three answers are required)?

(14)   ♠ K J 9 2   (15)   ♠ J 8 7 5 3
       ♡ J 10 7   ♡ K 9 6 2
       ◊ 7 4   ◊ 6 4
       ♣ A 8 6 5   ♣ 10 3

(16)   ♠ K J 10 6 2   (17)   ♠ A 10 8 2
       ♡ 7   ♡ A Q 9 7 5
       ◊ K J 8 3   ◊ 4
       ♣ 9 5 4   ♣ 8 6 3

Solutions

(14) Bid 2♣ with nine points and a four-card spade suit. If partner
     bids 2◊ or 2♡, bid 2NT, inviting 3NT. Even after using
     Stayman, responder may not bid a new suit unless it is at least
     five cards long.
        If partner bids 2♠, bid 4♠. Add one point for the doubleton
     when you find an eight-card trump fit.
(15) Bid 2♠ with five points (one for the five-card suit). This hand is
     too weak to bid 2♣. It would work out nicely if partner
     responded to 2♣ with 2♡ or 2♠, but if he bids the artificial 2◊
     you cannot pass with a doubleton diamond and your hand is too
     weak to take any further action. Therefore give up on hearts and
     bid 2♠—the drop-dead bid.

(16) Bid 2♣ with nine points (one for the five-card suit). This hand is too good for a direct response of 2♠ (showing a maximum of eight points) and too weak for a direct response of 3♠ (showing ten or more points), so you bid 2♣. If partner bids 2◇ or 2♡, bid 2♠; this shows a five- or six-card spade suit and nine points.

   If partner bids 2♠, raise to 4♠—this hand is worth 11 points when you add two for the singleton.

(17) Bid 2♣ with 11 points (one for the five-card suit). If partner bids 2◇, jump the bidding to 3♡ to show a five-card or longer heart suit and ten or more points. The jump bid is forcing and partner must choose between 3NT and 4♡; usually he should bid 4♡ with three hearts, and 3NT with only two hearts. (Note that partner can deduce that you have a four-card spade suit; otherwise you would have bid 3♡ the first time, not Stayman.)

   If partner bids 2♡ or 2♠, raise to game in the major.

HOW TO BID WHEN YOU HAVE A REAL CLUB SUIT

When partner opens 1NT, there are two common ways to show a real club suit: jump the bidding to 3♣ right away, or bid 2♣ (Stayman) followed by 3♣ at your second turn. One way is used to show a weak hand (at most eight points), and the other to show a strong hand—ten points or more. For example:

(a) Partner	You	(b)	Partner	You
1NT	3♣		1NT	2♣
			2◇, 2♡ or 2♠	3♣

The direct jump bid to 3♣ in (a) shows a weak hand (at most eight points) and a six-card club suit; the opening bidder is expected to pass. The direct jump to 3♣ has the same meaning as a direct response of 2◇, 2♡ or 2♠ except: at the two-level it is desirable to bid a five-card suit. Since you must go to the three-level to bid clubs naturally, you should have a six-card suit (with only five clubs and a weak hand it is wiser to pass 1NT).

The 3♣ bid in (b)—bidding 2♣ and then rebidding 3♣—shows ten points or more and a five-card or longer club suit. It is a forcing bid.

(**NOTE:** In the old days the above procedure was played in reverse—sequence (a) showed the strong hand, and sequence (b) showed the weak hand. The old-fashioned method is inferior, but many players have not learned this and still bid the old way. To avoid a partnership misunderstanding, discuss these bidding sequences with your partners.)

With a long club suit and nine points, 2NT is often the best bid. If you decide to bid clubs, you will have to make an underbid or an overbid.

Test Yourself

Your partner opens the bidding with 1NT. What do you respond with each of the following hands?

(18) ♠ 4	(19) ♠ 9 6 4	(20) ♠ 4 2
♡ 10 9 5	♡ A J 3 2	♡ Q 9
◊ 8 7 2	◊ —	◊ 10 8 7 3
♣ Q 10 8 6 4 3	♣ A Q 10 8 7 5	♣ A Q 10 6 5

Solutions

(18) Bid 3♣ with four points (two for the six-card suit), to show a weak hand with a six-card club suit. Partner should pass 3♣.

(19) Bid 2♣ with 13 points (two for the six-card suit) If partner's next bid is 2♡, raise to 4♡. If his next bid is 2◊ or 2♠, bid 3♣ (partner will have to bid again because the 3♣ rebid is forcing).

(20) Bid 2NT with nine points (one for the five-card suit). Hands with nine points and a long club suit are awkward to bid; they are too good to bid 3♣ and too weak to bid 2♣ followed by 3♣. In general, with no interest in a major suit and a strong five- or six-card club suit, it is better to raise notrump than to bid clubs. The exceptions occur when you have a side four-card major, or freakish distribution such as 0-3-4-6. This strategy also applies with stronger hands. For example, change the ♡Q to the ♡K (giving you 10 points), and you should raise to 3NT, still ignoring the club suit.

RESPONSES TO AN OPENING 2NT BID

When to pass or raise notrump: If you have a balanced hand with no more than three cards in either major suit, pass or raise notrump in accordance with your point count. It is sometimes right to raise notrump with a "semi-balanced hand" (5-4-2-2 or 6-3-2-2 distribution), provided that you have no four-card or longer major suit. An opening 2NT bid shows 20-22 points. Remembering that the requirement for bidding 3NT is 26 points in the combined hands, and for bidding 6NT it is 33 points, respond as follows:

> Pass with 0-4 points.
> Bid 3NT with 5-10 points.
> Bid 4NT with 11 or 12 points (invites 6NT).
> Bid 6NT with 13 or 14 points.

When to bid a suit: If your partner opens the bidding with 2NT and you have an unbalanced hand, or in some cases a balanced hand with a four- or five-card major suit, it is usually better to bid the long major, or bid 3♣ (Stayman), than to pass or raise notrump. *But remember this: all below-game responses to an opening 2NT bid are forcing, opener must bid again.* When your partner has opened the bidding with 2NT:

* Bid 3◊, 3♡ or 3♠ to show a five-card or longer suit and five points or more; but if your long suit is diamonds it is sometimes better to raise notrump.
* Bid 3♣ (Stayman) with at least four points and four cards in one or both major suits. The opening bidder must rebid 3♡ or 3♠ with a four-card (or five-card) major suit; with no four-card major he must rebid 3◊.
* If you have a long club suit it is often right to raise notrump. But if you have a five-card or longer club suit and think a game or slam in clubs may be a better contract than notrump, bid 3♣ (Stayman) and then rebid 4♣ at your next turn.
* Bid 4♡ or 4♠ to show a good six-card or longer suit and 5-10 points. Game bids are not slam invitations. *Opener must pass.*

Test Yourself

Your partner opens the bidding with 2NT. What do you respond with each of the following hands?

(21)	♠ 7 4	(22)	♠ 7 4
	♡ Q 10 6 4 3		♡ Q 10 6 4 3
	◇ 9 5 2		◇ K 5 2
	♣ 9 8 5		♣ 9 8 5
(23)	♠ 9 3	(24)	♠ K 10 7 5
	♡ A K J 7 6		♡ 9 8 6 3
	◇ K J 9 2		◇ J 7 4 2
	♣ 8 3		♣ 6

Solutions

(21) Pass with only three points. A bid of 3♡ would be forcing—partner must bid again and you will be overboard.

(22) Bid 3♡ with six points. This time you have enough points to bid game. Partner should bid 3NT with only two hearts, or bid 4♡ with three or more.

(23) Bid 3♡ with 13 points. You know the combined point count is 33, 34 or 35, so depending on partner's rebids, you should bid a slam in hearts, diamonds or notrump before you are through.

(24) Bid 3♣ (Stayman) with four points. If partner rebids 3♡, raise to 4♡. If he rebids 3♠, raise to 4♠. If he rebids 3◇, bid 3NT. (Although the combined total may be only 24-26, you should bid with this four-point hand because if partner bids a major it is worth six points; in which case the total will be at least 26.)

IN REVIEW

If your partner opens the bidding with 1NT (15-17)

* Pass with eight points or less and a balanced hand.

* Bid 2♣ (Stayman) with eight or more points and four cards in one or both major suits unless your distribution is 4-3-3-3. Less common uses of Stayman are: bid 2♣ with a five- or six-card major suit and nine points; when you bid your major at your

next turn it invites game—partner should pass with a minimum, or bid game in notrump or the major with a maximum. Bid 2♣ and then 3♣ with at least five clubs and a hand that is either strong enough to consider bidding a slam, or is unbalanced with at least ten points. You may also bid 2♣ with fewer than eight points provided that you have *length in diamonds, hearts and spades;* partner must bid 2◇, 2♡ or 2♠ and you will pass.

* Bid 2◇, 2♡ or 2♠ with eight points or less and a five-card or longer suit.

* Bid 2NT to invite 3NT with nine points and a balanced- or semi-balanced hand if you have no interest in playing in a major suit.

* Jump the bidding directly to 3♣ with eight points or less and a six-card or longer club suit.

* Jump directly to 3◇, 3♡ or 3♠ with ten points or more and a five-card or longer suit (but with a long diamond suit it is often better to bid 3NT).

* Bid 3NT with 10-15 points; bid 4NT with 16-17 points; bid 6NT with 18-19 points. All of these bids show a balanced or semi-balanced hand with no interest in playing a major suit.

* Bid 4♡ or 4♠ with 10-15 points and a good six-card or longer suit.

If your partner opens the bidding with 2NT (20-22):

* Pass with 0-4 points.

* Bid 3♣ (Stayman) with four points or more and four cards in one or both major suits. Also, bid 3♣ and rebid 4♣ at your next turn to show a five-card or longer club suit and a good hand.

* Bid 3◇, 3♡ or 3♠ with five points or more and a five-card or longer suit (all forcing bids); it may be better to bid 3NT if your long suit is diamonds.

* Bid 3NT with 5-10 points, bid 4NT to invite 6NT with 11-12, and bid 6NT with 13-14. All of these bids show a balanced or semi-balanced hand with no interest in playing a major suit contract.

* Bid 4♡ or 4♠ with 5-10 points and a six-card or longer suit.

Rebids by the opening notrump bidder:

* If you open the bidding with 1NT and partner bids 2♣ (Stayman), or if you open the bidding with 2NT and he responds 3♣ (Stayman), bid a four- (or five-) card major suit if you have one (bid the stronger one first with both four-card majors). If you have no four- (or five-) card major, bid 2◇ over 2♣, or 3◇ over 3♣.

* If you open the bidding with 1NT and partner bids 2◇, 2♡, 2♠, or jumps the bidding to 3♣, he has a very weak hand and expects you to pass.

* If you open the bidding with 1NT or 2NT and partner bids any game or slam contract, you must pass.

* If you open the bidding with 1NT or 2NT and your partner bids 3◇, 3♡ or 3♠, his bid is forcing; raise his suit or bid 3NT.

* If you open the bidding with 1NT or 2NT and your partner raises to 4NT, pass with a minimum point count, or bid 6NT with a maximum. For example: if you have opened the bidding with 2NT showing 20-22 points, pass 4NT with only 20, bid 6NT with 22, and use your judgment with 21.

PRACTICE DEAL

Contract: 3NT
Opening lead: ♡6

North
- ♠ 10 8 3 2
- ♡ A 2
- ◇ A Q 7 5
- ♣ J 5 4

West
- ♠ 9 7 4
- ♡ K J 9 6 5
- ◇ 10 4
- ♣ 8 6 3

East
- ♠ K 6 5
- ♡ Q 10 7 3
- ◇ 9 8 2
- ♣ K Q 7

South
- ♠ A Q J
- ♡ 8 4
- ◇ K J 6 3
- ♣ A 10 9 2

West	North	East	South
—	—	—	1NT
Pass	2♣	Pass	2◊
Pass	3NT	All Pass	

The bidding: South's 1NT opening bid shows 15-17 points. North has a balanced hand with 11 points and knows that the combined total is at least 26, so he plans to bid a game. He first bids 2♣ (Stayman), intending to raise a 2♠ bid to 4♠. However, South bids 2◊ to deny more than three cards in either major, so North bids 3NT.

The opening lead: West leads his fourth-best heart. Without a three-card sequence headed by the king, queen jack or ten, the usual choice is the fourth highest card from the longest and strongest suit; in this case the ♡6.

The play: Declarer can count seven tricks (one spade, one heart, four diamonds and one club). Since he has only one heart stopper and the opponents have nine hearts between them, the contract will be set unless he can run nine tricks without giving up the lead. The two needed tricks are available with the ♠Q and ♠J if East has the ♠K, by "finessing." This is done by leading small cards toward high cards. In this case, declarer should win the first trick with his ♡A and lead a spade from dummy toward the ♠A Q J. After East plays a low spade, South should play the queen or jack—this is a finesse. As you can see the finesse does work, so declarer returns to dummy via one of the high diamonds and repeats the spade finesse. Note that declarer can win an overtrick without jeopardizing his contract. After taking the two finesses he cashes the ♠A. When the ♠K falls, dummy's fourth spade becomes good, and he still has a high diamond in dummy to get to it. If the spade finesse failed, West would win with the ♠K and run four heart tricks to set the contract. Sometimes you need a little luck.

The key play: Take the spade finesses.

CHAPTER FOUR

RESPONSES TO OPENING SUIT BIDS OF ONE

An opening bid of one in a suit shows 13-22 points and may include just about any distribution. With such a vague picture of opener's hand it is rarely possible for responder to judge the best contract without further inquiry. Therefore, the responder's duty is to begin describing his hand. Since it may take two, three, or even more rounds of bidding to decide which contract to play, some of responder's bids are *forcing* (opener is not allowed to pass), while some are *not forcing* (opener is allowed to pass). For example, if the responder changes suits, his new-suit bid is forcing. It is vital that you learn the difference between forcing bids and nonforcing bids. There is nothing more frustrating to a bridge player than when his partner passes his forcing bid.

Before studying what the various responses mean and which bid to make, you must decide whether your hand qualifies for any bid.

WHEN TO PASS

If your partner opens the bidding with 1♣, 1◇, 1♡ or 1♠, you should pass with five points or fewer. The general rule is to keep the bidding open (do not pass) with six points or more because partner could have 20, 21 or 22 points. But he seldom has more than 20, so you should not risk bidding with fewer than six points.

Do not fear passing an opening bid of 1♣ or 1◇ without trump support simply because partner may have opened with a three-card suit. For one thing, it is rarely necessary to open the bidding with a three-card minor. Further, and more important, a response with sub-minimum values will mislead partner, and that spells trouble.

Therefore, *pass* with five points or fewer; *keep the bidding open with six points or more.*

PLANNING AHEAD

There are three point-ranges for the responder:

* 6-10 points: plan to bid only once. You may change your mind and bid again if partner's second bid indicates that the combined hands may have 26 points or more, or if a pass will leave you in the wrong part-score contract.
* 11-12 points: plan to make two forward-going bids. Game is likely, but give partner a chance to stop bidding below game if he has a minimum opening bid.
* 13 points or more: you know the combined point count is at least 26 and should bid a game as soon as you decide where to play it. Do not make a bid below game that your partner is allowed to pass. If the subsequent bidding reveals that the combined hands may have 33 or more points, consider slam.

WEAK NON-JUMP RESPONSES (6-10 Points)

The two common weak responses are to raise partner's suit to the two-level, and to bid 1NT. They both show 6-10 points. (Remember to count points for short suits, as well as for high cards and long suits, when you raise partner's suit with adequate trump support.)

* Raise opener's major suit to the two-level (partner-1♡, you-2♡) with 6-10 points and at least three trumps. Since an opening bid of 1♡ or 1♠ shows at least a five-card suit, raising with three trumps is good practice.
* Raise opener's minor suit to the two-level (partner-1♣, you-2♣) with 6-10 points and four or more trumps. Partner might open the bidding with 1♣ or 1♢ on a three-card suit (although he usually has at least four), so do not raise him directly with fewer than four trumps.
* Bid 1NT (partner-1♣, 1♢, 1♡ or 1♠; you-1NT) to show 6-10 points and deny possession of a four-card or longer major suit that can be bid at the one-level.

THE ONE-OVER-ONE RESPONSE

A response in a new suit at the one-level (partner-1♣; you-1♢, 1♡ or 1♠) is called "one-over-one" and shows six points or more—*no upper limit*—and a four-card or longer suit. The reason you can make a one-over-one response with a strong hand is that *a new suit bid is forcing for one round.* Exception: if you had a chance to open the bidding and passed—you are a "passed hand"—you cannot have more than 12 points. Consequently, when your partner opens the bidding in third or fourth seat, a response in a new suit is *not forcing*; at the one-level it shows 6-12 points.

(**NOTE:** If your hand is in the 6-10 point range and qualifies for more than one of the above bids: your first choice is to raise partner's major suit. If you do not have adequate trump support to raise partner's suit, bidding a new major suit at the one-level takes priority over raising partner's minor suit, or bidding 1NT. *The first search is for an eight-card {or longer} fit in a major suit.* THIS IS VERY IMPORTANT; READ IT AGAIN.)

Test Yourself

In the following quiz, answer each question three times. What do you bid if partner opens 1♠; if he opens 1♡, if he opens 1◊?

(1)	♠ A 2	(2)	♠ 8 5
	♡ 10 6 3		♡ J 10 7 2
	◊ A J 10 9		◊ 10 6
	♣ 8 5 4 2		♣ K 9 8 4 3
(3)	♠ A J	(4)	♠ 6 5
	♡ 10 9 4 3		♡ Q 9 4 3
	◊ 7 4 2		◊ A 10 8 6 2
	♣ K 10 8 6		♣ 9 7

Solutions

(1)   If partner opens 1♠, bid 1NT. If he opens 1♡, bid 2♡. If he opens 1◊, bid 2 ◊.

(2)   If partner opens 1♠ or 1◊, pass. If he opens 1♡, raise to 2♡; this five-point hand is promoted to seven points when partner bids 1♡ (add a point for each doubleton). If you are having trouble counting the points, review Chapter One.

(3)   If partner opened 1♠, bid 1NT. If he opened 1♡, bid 2♡. If he opened 1◊, bid 1♡.

(4)   If partner opened 1♠, bid 1NT. If he opened 1♡, bid 2♡. If he opened 1◇, bid 1♡.

(**NOTE:** If partner opens the bidding with 1♣ or 1◇ and you respond 1NT or raise his minor suit, *you deny four or more cards in either major suit.*)

THE TWO-OVER-ONE RESPONSE

The point-count requirement to bid a new suit at the two-level (partner-1♠, you-2♣, 2◇ or 2♡) is 11 points or more including distribution. You should have a five-card or longer suit to bid 2♡ over a 1♠ opening bid, but it is sometimes necessary to bid a new minor suit at the two-level with just a four-card suit.

Make sure you understand that a "two-over-one" response is not a jump bid. If partner opens with 1♡, a 2♣ or 2◇ response is two-over-one, while 2♠ is a jump bid—you could have bid 1♠. The jump bid in a new suit is commonly called a "jump shift," and will be explained later in this chapter. Examples of two-over-one responses are shown in the quiz that follows, but first let us look at which suit the responder should bid first when he has two or three biddable suits.

WHICH SUIT TO BID FIRST

When your partner opens the bidding in one of a suit and you have two (or three) four-card or longer suits, you must decide which suit to bid first. Provided you have the point count required to bid the suit, bid as follows:

*   With one suit longer than any other, bid it first.
*   With two five-card suits, or two six-card suits, disregard the strength of the suits and bid the higher-ranking first.
*   With two or three four-card suits, bid up-the-line; disregard the strength of the suits and bid the one that keeps the bidding lowest first. A debatable case is which suit to bid if partner opens 1♣ and you hold four diamonds and a four-card major suit; but do not worry about it at this stage of your game, just bid 1◇. The 1◇ response *does not* deny a four-card major.

Test Yourself

Your partner opens the bidding with 1◇ and your right-hand opponent passes. What do you bid with each of the following hands?

(5) ♠ J 8 7 4 3   (6) ♠ A K 9 8   (7) ♠ 8 7 5 4 2
     ♡ A K 10 9 4   ♡ 10 7 6 3   ♡ A K Q J
     ◇ 10 2   ◇ Q J 10   ◇ 7 3
     ♣ 3   ♣ 7 2   ♣ K 6

(8) ♠ Q 6 4 3   (9) ♠ A K J 9   (10) ♠ J 7 6 3
     ♡ 7 2   ♡ 7 2   ♡ 9 8
     ◇ Q 9   ◇ Q 9   ◇ A 7 2
     ♣ K J 10 4 3   ♣ K J 10 4 3   ♣ A K Q 10

Solutions

(5) 1♠. With two five-card suits, bid the higher ranking first.

(6) 1♡. With two four-card suits, bid up-the-line.

(7) 1♠. With one suit longer than any other, bid it first.

(8) 1♠. You have only nine points and need at least 11 points to bid a new suit at the two-level, so bidding 2♣ is ruled out.

(9) 2♣. Now you have enough points to bid a new suit at the two-level and it is proper to bid your longest suit first. You intend to bid spades next.

(10) 1♠. With two four-card suits, bid up-the-line.

STRONG RESPONSES (13 Points or More)

Any *single-jump* response to an opening suit bid of one by an unpassed hand (such as opener-1♡, responder 2♠, 2NT, 3♣, 3◇ or 3♡) is *forcing to game*.

(**NOTE:** Most good players play that single-jump-raises {such as opener-1♡, responder-3♡} invite game—showing 11-12 points—but this complicates the way to bid the stronger hands. I recommend that you ignore this until you get more experience. Although considered old fashioned by many, the easiest and best way to start is *all of the jump bids by responder listed below are forcing to game.*)

However, it is often better not to jump the bidding even though you have a strong hand. If you have 13 points or more and are unsure about which game (or slam) contract to play, it is usually best to make a nonjump bid in a new suit. The new-suit bid is forcing for one round (partner cannot pass) and saves bidding space that will be needed to decide which trump suit (or notrump) to play. The possible strong jump bids, and what you need to make them, are shown below:

* **Jump-raise opener's major suit** (partner-1♠, you-3♠) to show 13-16 points and at least four trumps. Although you may raise partner's major-suit opening to the two-level with just three trumps, you need at least four to jump-raise directly. Knowing that you have at least four trumps makes it easier for partner to judge whether or not to bid a slam. With just three trumps and 13-16 points, bid a new suit first and jump-raise the major suit later.

* **Jump-raise opener's minor suit** (partner-1♣, you-3♣) to show 13-16 points and at least four trumps (usually five trumps). This bid denies a four-card or longer major suit.

* **Jump to 2NT** (partner-one of any suit, you-2NT) to show 13-15 points, a balanced hand, stoppers in all three unbid suits, and no four-card major that can be bid at the one-level.

* **Jump to 3NT** (partner-one of any suit, you-3NT) to show 16-18 points, a balanced hand, stoppers in all three unbid suits, and no four-card major that can be bid at the one-level.

* **Jump shift:** Skip exactly one level of bidding and bid a new suit (partner-1♡, you-2♠, 3♣ or 3◊) to show 17-19 points. You cannot be sure whether or not to bid a slam, so the plan is to tell partner you have 17-19 points and leave it up to him. After your second bid he will be in a good position to decide. Exception: do not make a jump-shift bid with a two-suited hand, even when you have 17-19 points. You may need the

bidding space to reach the best contract, so make a nonjump bid in one of your suits with the intention of showing your second suit and your strength later.

* With 20 points or more you probably have a slam; maybe a grand slam. Deciding which trump suit (or notrump) to play and how high to bid *is up to you*, and in most cases the best way to get started is to make a *nonjump* bid in a new suit. After partner's second bid you will be in a better position to decide the best contract.

Test Yourself

Your partner opens the bidding with 1♡ and your right-hand opponent passes. What do you bid with each of the following hands?

(11) ♠ A Q 9 8 ♡ Q 10 7 2 ◇ 6 2 ♣ A J 3	(12) ♠ 7 2 ♡ A Q 9 ◇ K 10 8 6 3 ♣ A 5 2	(13) ♠ A J 6 ♡ Q 10 8 ◇ K 2 ♣ A K 9 7 4
(14) ♠ K 10 7 ♡ A J 9 ◇ Q 4 3 ♣ K J 8 5	(15) ♠ 7 6 3 ♡ A J 9 ◇ K Q 4 ♣ K J 8 5	(16) ♠ A J 10 ♡ 9 8 ◇ K 7 3 2 ♣ A K Q 4

Solutions

(11) 3♡, with 14 points (one for the doubleton) and four-card trump support.

(12) 2◇, intending to bid 4♡ at your next turn. You have the right point-count (13-16) to bid 3♡ directly, but that would show at least four hearts.

(13) 3♣, a jump-shift bid showing 17-19 points. Your plan is to raise hearts at your next turn and leave it up to partner whether or not to bid a slam.

(14) 2NT, showing a balanced hand with 13-15 points, stoppers in all three unbid suits, and no four-card or longer major suit.

(15) 2♣, intending to reach some game contract when you decide where to play it (probably 4♡ since you know there is an eight-card fit). It is tempting to respond 2NT, but that is wrong without a spade stopper.

(16) 3NT, showing a balanced hand with 16-18 points, stoppers in all three unbid suits, and no four-card or longer spade suit.

ELEVEN- AND TWELVE-POINT HANDS

A raise of partner's opening suit bid of one to the two-level shows 6-10 points, while a jump-raise to the three-level shows 13-16 points. A 1NT response shows 6-10 points, while a jump to 2NT shows 13-15 points. Therefore, with 11-12 points you should not raise your partner or bid notrump directly. *Your first bid should be in a new suit,* even when you have good trump support or a notrump type hand. Your plan is to make two forward-going bids, but to give partner a chance to stop bidding below game if he has a minimum opening bid. Your first bid in a new-suit gives a vague picture of your hand, but it is forcing. You will reveal more about your distribution at your next turn by raising partner's suit, bidding notrump, rebidding your own long suit, or bidding a second new suit with a two-suited hand.

Test Yourself

Your partner opens the bidding with 1♠ and your right-hand opponent passes. What do you bid with each of the following hands?

(17) ♠ J 9 6 4   (18) ♠ J 3
     ♡ 7 5   ♡ A Q 8
     ◇ A K 7 6   ◇ J 10 9 5
     ♣ Q 3 2   ♣ K 10 7 2

Solutions

(17) This 11-point hand (one for the doubleton) is too strong for 2♠ and too weak for 3♠, so bid 2◇ with the intention of raising spades at your next turn. For example, if partner rebids 2NT, bid 3♠ to show 11-12 points and three- or four-card spade support; partner may pass with a minimum.

(18) This 11-point hand is too strong for a 1NT response and too weak for 2NT, so bid 2♣ with the intention of making a minimum notrump bid at your next turn. For example, if partner rebids 2♠, bid 2NT to show 11-12 points and stoppers in the unbid suits; but if he rebids 2NT, bid 3NT.

WEAK JUMP RESPONSES (PREEMPTIVE BIDS)

Suit responses in which you skip *two or three levels of bidding* are weak (preemptive bids). For example: a double-jump raise (partner-1♠, you-4♠; or partner-1♣, you-4♣) shows a weak hand in high cards (a maximum of 7 or 8 high-card points), good support for partner's suit (usually five or six trumps); and good distribution (i. e., very unbalanced such as 5-5-2-1 or 6-5-1-1). In a minor suit, a raise to the five-level (partner-1♣, you-5♣) is also preemptive.

A leaping bid in a new suit that skips two levels of bidding (partner-1♢, you-3♡, 3♠ or 4♣) is also preemptive and shows a good seven-card suit and a weak hand—usually about 4-8 high-card points. A leaping bid in a new suit that skips three levels of bidding (partner-1♢, you-4♡, 4♠ or 5♣) is also weak, but shows a better or longer suit.

These preemptive bids are desirable with hands that will win several tricks if the contract is played in the long suit, but virtually none otherwise. Since you really have no ability to take tricks on defense, the opponents figure to score well if they get into the bidding and play the hand in their long trump suit. You hope that your leaping bid will shut them out. Even if your contract is doubled and set it will be a good "sacrifice" if the opponents could have won more by bidding and making a contract their way.

The requirements for these leaping bids are similar to the requirements for opening preemptive bids, which are described in detail with illustrations in Chapter Seven, but here are two examples:

Test Yourself

Partner opens the bidding with 1♡ and your right-hand opponent passes. What do you bid with each of the following hands?

(19)	♠	2	(20)	♠	K Q 10 9 8 5 4
	♡	K 10 9 6 3		♡	6 3
	◇	J 9 8 7 4		◇	2
	♣	7 5		♣	10 7 4

(19) 4♡. Based on your good trump support and distribution, there is a good chance that partner will fulfill the contract. But even if the 4♡ contract is set, you are likely to get a good score. The opponents probably have nine or ten spades between them and can make 4♠ unless your partner has four defensive tricks; your leaping bid may discourage them from bidding.

(20) 3♠, suggesting to partner that your hand is likely to be useless unless the contract is played in spades. He should pass 3♠, or bid 4♠ if he thinks you can make it. Add another spade, to give you an eight-card suit, and you should respond 4♠.

PASSED-HAND BIDDING

If your partner opens the bidding in third or fourth seat *he already knows that your hand was too weak to open the bidding*. Many passed-hand responses (especially jump bids) have a different meaning than they would if you had not passed earlier. If your point count is in the 6-10 range, make the same bid as you would have if partner had opened the bidding in first or second seat. It is when you have 11-12 points (or maybe even 13-15 points, which is possible when you have good support for partner's suit and add extra points for short suits) that being a passed hand affects your response. If your partner opens the bidding in third or fourth seat (after you have passed):

* A bid in a new suit at the one-level (you-pass, partner-1◇, you-1♡ or 1♠) shows 6-12 points and a four-card or longer suit.

* A bid in a new suit at the two-level (you-pass, partner-1♡, you-2♣ or 2◇) shows 11-12 points and *a good five-card or longer suit*. If your partner has a minimum opening bid, he may pass your two-over-one response with as few as two trumps. So, when you are a passed hand, *do not bid a four-card suit or*

a weak five-card suit at the two level; raise partner's suit or bid notrump instead.

* A jump bid of 2NT (you-pass, partner-1◊, you-2NT) shows 11-12 points and a balanced hand; it is not forcing.

* A jump-raise of partner's major suit to the three-level (you-pass, partner-1♡, you-3♡) shows a hand with three or more trumps and 11-13 points; it is not forcing. If you have four or more trumps and your point count builds up to 14-15 (by adding two or three extra points for short suits), raise partner's major suit to game (you-pass, partner-1♠, you-4♠).

* A jump-raise of partner's minor suit to the three-level (you-pass, partner-1♣, you-3♣) shows a hand with at least four trumps to an honor (or any five trumps), at least 11 points, and no four-card or longer major suit.

* DO NOT jump in a new suit. If you were an unpassed hand, that would show 17-19 points. So do not jump the bidding unless you can raise partner's suit or bid notrump, because you may find yourself too high too fast with no trump fit.

Test Yourself

Your partner opens the bidding in third seat with 1♡ (you are a passed hand). What do you bid with each of the following hands?

(21)	♠ A Q 10	(22)	♠ 7 2
	♡ J 2		♡ K 9 8
	◊ Q J 9 3		◊ A J 6 3
	♣ J 10 8 7		♣ K 10 9 4
(23)	♠ 8	(24)	♠ A Q 8 7 2
	♡ Q 10 6 3		♡ 8 5
	◊ A Q 9 7 4		◊ K 10 3
	♣ K 10 2		♣ Q 9 4

Solutions

(21) 2NT, showing a balanced hand with 11-12 points.
(22) 3♡, showing at least three-card trump support and 11-13 points.

(23) 4♡. This 14-point hand with excellent trump support is too good to bid just 3♡; partner might pass with a minimum opening bid and you will miss a game.

(24) 1♠. Some players would jump to 2♠ to tell partner they have a maximum passed hand. But this is a mistake, and unnecessary. Partner will not pass 1♠ if he has 14 points or more.

IN REVIEW

When partner has opened the bidding with a suit bid of one:
* With five points or fewer, pass.
* With six points or more, bid.

The weak non-jump responses:
* Raise opener's major to the two-level with 6-10 points and three or more trumps.
* Raise opener's minor to the two-level with 6-10 points, at least four trumps, and no four-card or longer major suit.
* Bid 1NT with 6-10 points and no four-card or longer major suit that can be bid at the one-level.

New-suit responses are forcing, showing a wide range of points:
* Bid a new suit at the one-level with six points or more (no upper limit) and a four-card or longer suit.
* Bid a new suit at the two-level with 11 points or more (no upper limit). You may bid a four-card minor suit at the two-level (partner-1♠, you-2♣ or 2♢), but you should have at least a five-card suit for a 2♡ response to 1♠.

When you have a choice of two or three suits to bid:
* With one suit longer than any other, bid it first, but remember that you need at least 11 points to bid a new suit at the two-level.
* With two five- or six-card suits, bid the higher ranking first whether it is stronger or not.
* With two or three four-card suits, bid up the line—the cheapest first.

The strong responses are:

* Jump-raise opener's major (partner-1♡, you-3♡) with 13-16 points and at least four-card trump support.

* Jump-raise opener's minor (partner-1♢, you-3♢) with 13-16 points, at least four-card trump support, and no four-card or longer major suit.

* Jump to 2NT (opener-1♡, you-2NT) with 13-15 points, a balanced hand, stoppers in the three unbid suits, and no four-card major suit that can be bid at the one-level.

* Jump to 3NT (opener-1♢, you-3NT) with 16-18 points, a balanced hand, stoppers in the three unbid suits, and no four-card major that can be bid at the one-level.

* Jump the bidding in a new suit (partner-1♢, you-2♡, 2♠ or 3♣) with 17-19 points and a good idea of which trump suit (or notrump) to play.

Eleven- and twelve-point hands:

* Your hand is too strong to bid 1NT or to raise partner's suit to the two-level, and it is too weak to bid 2NT or to jump-raise partner's suit to the three-level. When you have 11-12 points your first bid should be in a new suit. Do not bid notrump or raise your partner's suit, even when you have trump support or a good notrump pattern, because doing so immediately would misrepresent your point count.

Weak jump responses:

* Jump-raise opener's major to the four-level (opener-1♡, you-4♡), or his minor to the four or five-level (opener-1♣, you-4♣ or 5♣) with a maximum of about eight points in high-cards, excellent trump support, and freakish distribution (5-5-2-1, 6-5-2-0, etc.)

* Jump two or three levels of bidding into a new suit (opener-1♢, you-3♡, 3♠, 4♣, 4♡, 4♠ or 5♣) with a weak hand; typically a seven-card or longer suit with about 4-8 points in high cards.

Responses to third- and fourth-seat opening bids:

* When you are a passed hand and hold 6-10 points, bid the same way as you would bid if you were not a passed hand.
* A new suit bid at the one-level shows a four-card or longer suit and 6-12 points.
* A new-suit bid at the two-level shows a *good five-card or longer suit* and 11-12 points.
* A jump to 2NT shows 11-12 points, a balanced hand and no four-card major that can be bid at the one-level.
* A jump-raise of opener's major to the three-level (opener-1♡, you-3♡) shows 11-13 points and at least three trumps to an honor.
* A jump-raise of opener's major to game (opener-1♠, you-4♠) shows 14-15 points—which is possible if you have four or five trumps and can add two or three points for short suits.
* A jump-raise of opener's minor to the three-level (opener-1♣, you-3♣) shows 11-14 points, at least four trumps, and no four-card or longer major.

PRACTICE DEAL

Contract: 4♠
Opening lead: ◇10

```
              North
              ♠ J 3 2
              ♡ 8 5
              ◇ A J 6 3
              ♣ J 7 5 4
   West                      East
   ♠ A 6 5                   ♠ 7 4
   ♡ Q 10 7 2                ♡ 9 6 3
   ◇ 10 9 8                  ◇ K Q 7 4
   ♣ K 6 3                   ♣ Q 10 8 2
              South
              ♠ K Q 10 9 8
              ♡ A K J 4
              ◇ 5 2
              ♣ A 9
```

West	North	East	South
—	—	—	1♠
Pass	2♠	Pass	4♠
All Pass			

The bidding: North's raise to 2♠ shows 6-10 points and at least three-card trump support. Since his suit has been raised, South revalues his 18-point hand by adding two points for each doubleton. With 20 points opposite at least six from partner, he bids 4♠.

The opening lead: West leads the ◊10, the top card of a three-card sequence.

The play: The recommended procedure in a trump contract is to count the *losing tricks* in one hand (usually the hand with the long trump suit), rather than counting the winning tricks in the combined hands as is done in notrump contracts. In this case declarer counts five losers in his hand (one spade, two hearts, one diamond and one club). Since he cannot afford to lose more than three tricks, his only good chance is to ruff his ♡4 and ♡J in the dummy. After winning the first trick with the ◊A, he cashes his two top hearts and ruffs the ♡4 in dummy *with a low spade.* To get back to his hand, he leads a club to his ace and ruffs the ♡J *with the ♠J.* He has won six tricks—and the ♠ K Q 10 9 8 assure him of four more.

Do you see a way for West to beat the contract? Answer: an opening lead of the ♠A followed by another spade; dummy would be left with only one trump, and declarer would not be able to ruff both of his heart losers. However, the ♠A lead is a strange choice, and few good players would even consider it.

The key play: Ruffing the third heart lead with one of dummy's low spades. It was risky, because East could overruff if he had been dealt only two hearts. But declarer had to take the chance; the ♠J is needed to ruff the fourth round of hearts.

CHAPTER FIVE

REBIDS BY THE OPENER

QUIZ

In Chapter Four you learned how to respond to an opening bid of one of a suit. This knowledge is also vital to the opening bidder. Before learning about opener's rebids, here is a quiz to make sure you know the meaning of the various responses. As dealer, you open the bidding with 1♡ and your left-hand opponent passes. What do each of the following responses tell you about your partner's hand?

(a) 1♠   (b) 1NT   (c) 2♣   (d) 2♡   (e) 2♠
(f) 2NT   (g) 3♡   (h) 3♠   (i) 3NT   (j) 4♡

DO NOT READ THE ANSWERS UNTIL
YOU HAVE ANALYZED THE MEANING OF EACH BID.

Answers

(a)   1♠ is a one-over-one response, showing six points or more and four or more spades; forcing for one round.

(b)   1NT shows 6-10 points, fewer than four spades, and denies good trump support; not forcing.

(c)   2♣ is a two-over-one response, showing 11 points or more and a four-card or longer suit; forcing for one round. 2♢ would also be a two-over-one response.

(d)   2♡ is a major-suit raise, showing 6-10 points and at least three trumps; not forcing.

(e)   2♠ is a jump-shift, showing 17-19 points. Not only is it forcing to game, it invites a slam. 3♣ and 3♢ would also be jump-shift responses.

(f)   2NT shows a balanced hand with 13-15 points, stoppers in the three unbid suits and denies a four-card major suit; forcing to game.

(g)   3♡ is a jump-raise, showing 13-16 points and at least four trumps; forcing to game.

(h)   3♠ is a preemptive bid, showing a long spade suit (usually a
      seven-card suit) and a weak hand—about 4-8 high-card points;
      not forcing. 4♣ and 4◇ would also be preemptive responses.

(i)   3NT shows a balanced hand with 16-18 points, stoppers in the
      three unbid suits, and denies a four-card major suit.

(j)   4♡ is a preemptive raise, showing excellent trump support
      (usually at least five trumps), a weak hand in high cards (at most
      eight high-card points), and good distribution (such as 5-5-2-1).

PLANNING AHEAD

An opening suit bid of one gives responder a vague picture of his
partner's hand. It is the opening bidder's second bid that gives a good
description of his *point count* and *distribution;* it is the key bid in
most auctions.

Point count: An opening suit bid of one shows 13-22 points. At his
second turn to bid, opener describes his strength more accurately by
dividing the 13-22 points into three ranges:

$$13\text{-}16 = \text{minimum range}$$
$$17\text{-}19 = \text{invitational range}$$
$$20\text{-}22 = \text{game range}$$

Distribution: An opening bid of one of a suit can be made with just
about any distribution. At his second turn to bid opener describes his
distribution more accurately by:

>   raising responder's suit with adequate trump support
>   bidding notrump with a balanced hand
>   rebidding his original suit with one long suit
>   bidding a new four-card or longer suit

The requirements for the various rebids are explained in the
analysis of the following 34 illustrations. Do not expect to learn it all
before you start playing. When you are unsure about which rebid to
make, remember your goal—to tell partner which of the three

point-count ranges you have, and to give a better description of your distribution.

AFTER A ONE-OVER-ONE RESPONSE

When the responder bids a new suit at the one-level (opener-1♣, responder-1◇,1♡ or 1♠), it is the least informative bid he can make. The strength of his hand is unlimited, so it is almost impossible at this stage for opener to decide how high to bid. For example, if opener has 13 points and his partner can have six points or more (no upper limit), opener cannot tell whether the contract should be played in a part-score, a game or a slam. Therefore, more exchange of information is needed. The opener must bid again and describes his hand as follows:

Raise partner's suit: You open the bidding with 1♣, partner responds 1♠, and you hold:

(1)	♠ K 10 6 3	(2)	♠ Q 9 7 6	(3)	♠ Q J 10 2
	♡ 7 2		♡ A K 10 3		♡ 8 5
	◇ A K 5		◇ 2		◇ A K
	♣ Q J 9 2		♣ A Q J 8		♣ A K J 9 3

(1) Bid 2♠ with 14 points (one for the doubleton). The 2♠ bid shows 13-16 points and adequate trump support. You may raise partner's suit to the two-level with just three trumps, but do not do so if you have a reasonable alternative bid because partner is likely to have a four-card suit.

(2) Bid 3♠ with 18 points (two for the singleton). The jump-raise is invitational and shows 17-19 points with four trumps.

(3) Bid 4♠ with 21 points (one for the five-card suit and two for the two doubletons). The jump-raise to game shows 20-22 points and four trumps.

Rebid notrump: You open the bidding with 1◇, partner responds 1♡, and you hold:

(4)	♠ J 10 2	(5)	♠ A 10
	♡ 8 3		♡ K 8 3
	◊ A Q 9 7 6		◊ A K J 7 4
	♣ A Q 4		♣ K 6 5

(4) Bid 1NT with 14 points (one for the five-card suit). This bid shows 13-14 points (occasionally 12), and a balanced hand.

(5) Bid 2NT with 19 points (one for the five-card suit), showing 18-19 points, a balanced hand, and stoppers in the two unbid suits.

The point ranges for the 1NT and 2NT rebids are different from rebids in a suit because you would open a balanced 15-17 point hand with 1NT, and a balanced 20-22 point hand with 2NT. So a 1NT rebid shows a balanced hand too weak to open with 1NT (13-14 points, occasionally 12), while a jump to 2NT shows a balanced hand too strong to open with 1NT and too weak to open with 2NT (18-19 points). *Also note that a jump to 2NT promises stoppers in all unbid suits, while the 1NT rebid does not.*

Rebid your original suit: You open the bidding with 1♡, partner responds 1♠, and you hold:

(6)	♠ 9 2	(7)	♠ 7	(8)	♠ K 6
	♡ K 10 7 6 4 3		♡ A K J 9 8 5		♡ A Q J 10 9 7 2
	◊ A Q		◊ A Q 3 2		◊ A K 10
	♣ K 5 4		♣ K 10		♣ 3

(6) Bid 2♡ with 14 points and a six-card suit. Rebidding your suit at the two-level shows 13-16 points and a six-card suit. On rare occasions it may be necessary to rebid a good five-card suit because no other reasonable bid is available, *but tend to avoid rebidding five-card suits.*

(7) Bid 3♡ with 19 points. The jump rebid of your suit shows 17-19 points and a good six-card suit (or maybe a seven-card suit).

(8) Bid 4♡ with 20 points (three for the seven-card suit). The jump rebid to game shows 20-22 points and an *independently strong six-card or longer suit—at least K Q J 10 x x.*

Bid a new suit: You open the bidding with 1♡, partner responds 1♠, and you hold:

(9)	♠ 8 3	(10)	♠ 5	(11)	♠ K 5
	♡ A K 10 7 4		♡ A Q 10 3 2		♡ A K J 3 2
	◇ 6 5		◇ A K 8 7 6		◇ 8 4
	♣ K Q J 3		♣ K 9		♣ A K Q 6

(9)   Bid 2♣ with 14 points. A rebid in a suit that ranks lower than two of your first suit shows 13-19 points and a four-card or longer suit. *The new-suit bid does not distinguish between 13-16 and 17-19 points.* Therefore, although this rebid is not forcing, responder should not pass unless he has a very weak hand with more clubs than hearts (in which case 2♣ is probably the best contract). A bid of 2♡ by responder would show a weak hand with equal length in the two suits, or more hearts. Choosing to go back to partner's first suit is called "taking a preference." (**NOTE:** With five-four distribution, you should bid the five-card suit first and the four-card suit second; do not rebid the five-card suit and ignore the four-card suit.)

(10) Bid 2◇ with 18 points. As stated above, a bid of a new-suit shows 13-19 points and four cards or more in that suit. Partner may pass 2◇, but if you get a third chance, make another bid to show that you have 17-19 points as opposed to 13-16. For example, if partner's second bid is 2♡, a rebid of 3◇ would show your five-five distribution and 17-19 points; with 13-16 points you would pass 2♡.

(11) Bid 3♣ with 21 points. You certainly want to reach game with this strong hand, but where? You need more information from partner to help you decide. A jump bid in a new suit, called a "jump-shift," shows 20-22 points and is forcing to game. If partner's next bids is 3NT, he promises a diamond stopper and you should pass. If he bids 3◇, bid 3NT; if he rebids his spade suit, bid 4♠; if he bids 3♡ or 4♣, bid game in that suit.

(**NOTE:** A jump-shift by the opening bidder shows 20-22 points and is forcing to game. Do not confuse it with a jump-shift by the responder, which shows 17-19 points and is a slam invitation.)

The Reverse Bid: If the opening bidder has a strong hand and wants to make sure his partner does not pass, there are two ways to force him to bid again. The jump-shift we have already discussed is forcing to game, and a "reverse bid" is forcing for one round. A reverse bid is a nonjump bid at the two-level in a new suit *that ranks higher than the suit you bid first.* For example, if you open with 1◇ and partner responds 1♠, 2♡ would be a reverse (because it is higher than 2◇), but 2♣ would not. A reverse shows a two-suited hand with 17 points or more and it is *forcing for one round.* It is only when partner's response was at the one-level that the reverse bid shows 17 points or more. (If the response was at the two-level, the opener may reverse with a weaker hand; as low as 15 points.)

In the next two deals, partner responds 1♠ to your opening 1◇ bid:

	(12)		(13)	
	♠	K 2	♠	A 2
	♡	A Q 8 5	♡	A Q 7 4
	◇	A K J 10 2	◇	A 10 9 5 3
	♣	7 3	♣	5 2

(12) Bid 2♡. This is a reverse, showing 17 points or more, and it is forcing for one round. A reverse bid is usually made with a two-suited hand (5-4, 6-4 or 6-5 distribution), with greater length in the first suit. Although it is sometimes desirable to reverse with two four-card suits, *responder should assume that the opening bidder has greater length in his first bid suit when he reverses the bidding (at least a five-card suit). Never reverse with five-five distribution.*

(13) Bid 1NT with 15 points. You *must* bid again over 1♠ and you *must not* bid 2♡ because that would be a reverse. It is unattractive to bid 1NT with two small clubs, but it is better than rebidding this mediocre five-card diamond suit. If partner responded 2♣, a 2♡ rebid with 15 points is all right.

(**NOTE:** The reverse can be a complicated topic and there is more to it than I have told you. I was tempted to leave it out of the book, but decided even a beginner should know something about a reverse bid. So read on and do not worry if you do not fully understand the reverse bid. You should eventually learn more about it.)

AFTER A 1NT RESPONSE (Showing 6-10 Points)

The opening bidder is allowed to pass his partner's 1NT response with a minimum opening bid (13-16 points), but he should not pass if he thinks there might be a better part-score available. For example, in the following three deals, you open the bidding with 1♠, partner responds 1NT, and you hold:

(14) ♠ A Q 8 6 5	(15) ♠ K J 10 7 3	(16) ♠ K J 9 8 7 2
♡ K 10 3	♡ A 9 8	♡ 7
◊ 7 2	◊ 6	◊ A 9 4
♣ K J 3	♣ A J 5 4	♣ A J 2

(14) Pass with 14 points and a balanced hand. When you know the combined hands cannot have as many as 26 points, stop in the lowest and safest part-score contract. Rebidding 2♠ with just a five-card suit would be a poor bid; partner is very unlikely to have more than two spades.

　　The point-count requirement to raise a 1NT response to 2NT is 17-19, and to raise to 3NT it is 20-22.

(15) Bid 2♣ with 14 points, to seek a better part-score contract than 1NT. A new-suit bid that ranks below two of your first suit is not forcing (it is not a reverse), *but it does show 13-19 points.* Partner should bid again if he thinks there is a better part-score than 2♣, or a reasonable chance to bid and make a game.

(16) Bid 2♠ with 15 points. It is desirable to rebid a six-card suit. You do not have enough points to bid game, but it is wrong to pass 1NT because 2♠ figures to be a much better part-score contract. Partner should pass 2♠.

AFTER A TWO-OVER-ONE RESPONSE

When partner responds in a new suit at the two-level (you-1♡, responder-2♣ or 2◇), he shows 11 points or more and usually a five-card or longer suit (with some awkward hands he may bid a four-card suit). Although you know that responder has at least 11 points, you should bid conservatively with a minimum opening bid. Remember that your partner is just as anxious as you to get to game. He heard you open the bidding; he will not pass your next bid if it is below game.

(**NOTE**: Whenever responder makes a two-over-one response, he will not pass his partner's next bid if it is below game. This is the best way to play, although the old-fashioned way allowed the responder to pass if the opener rebid his suit at the two-level.)

In the following three examples you open the bidding with 1♡, your partner responds 2◇, and you hold:

(17) ♠ A Q 5	(18) ♠ 6 5	(19) ♠ 2
♡ K Q 10 7 3	♡ A J 9 7 2	♡ A Q J 4 3
◇ 7 4	◇ K J 2	◇ A 10
♣ K 10 2	♣ A 10 8	♣ A K 8 6 5

(17) Bid 2NT with a balanced hand and stoppers in the unbid suits

(18) Bid 3◇. When partner bids a new suit at the two-level he usually has a five-card or longer suit, so it is all right to raise him with three trumps. If he has bid a four-card suit, he probably has another contract in mind which he will reveal by his next bid.

(19) Bid 3♣. There is an excellent chance that you can make a slam, but where? You need to exchange more information before you decide which trump suit to play and whether or not to bid a slam. The 3♣ bid is forcing after partner's two-over-one response, so there is no need to jump the bidding and waste bidding space.

AFTER YOUR MAJOR SUIT
HAS BEEN RAISED TO THE TWO-LEVEL

After partner has raised your major suit opening, you should revalue your hand by adding points for short suits. Pass with 13-16 points, make a bid that invites game with 17-19 points, or bid game with 20-22 points. For example, suppose your partner raises your 1♡ opening bid to 2♡, showing 6-10 points and at least three trumps, and you hold:

(20)	♠ 7 4	(21)	♠ A 10 3	(22)	♠ K J 9
	♡ A Q 8 7 6		♡ K Q 10 7 6 2		♡ A K J 4 3
	◇ 8 5 3		◇ K J 8		◇ 7
	♣ A Q 10		♣ 5		♣ A Q 10 2

(20) Pass with 14 points, the minimum range. Partner's 2♡ bid shows 6-10 points, so there is no game.

(21) Bid 3♡ with 17 points, the invitational range. Partner should pass 3♡ with a minimum (six, seven or maybe eight points), or bid 4♡ with a maximum (nine, ten, or a good eight).

(22) Bid 4♡ with 21 points, the game range.

AFTER YOUR MINOR SUIT
HAS BEEN RAISED TO THE TWO-LEVEL

The point-count requirement to bid game in a major suit or notrump is 26, while 29 points are needed for a minor-suit game. This means you should be reluctant to bid game in a minor suit (which requires 11 tricks) until the possibility of playing game in a major suit (ten tricks) or notrump (nine tricks) is ruled out. When partner raises your minor suit directly he denies holding more than three cards in either major suit, so the hope for game in a major is remote; *but you should explore the possibility of playing game in notrump before resorting to game in a minor.* Here is how to do it!

If partner raises your minor-suit opening bid to the two-level (showing at least four trumps, 6-10 points, and no four-card or longer major suit): with 13-16 points, always pass. With 17-19 points and the three unbid suits stopped, bid 2NT; with 20-22 points and the three unbid suits stopped, bid 3NT. The way to bid when you have 17 points or more and one or two of the unbid suits stopped, is to bid a suit in which you have a stopper. The new suit is not necessarily four-cards long, so you are not attempting to make it the trump suit, *but it is a forcing bid* and asks responder to show his stoppers. If he has one unbid suit stopped, he bids that suit; if he has both unbid suits stopped, he bids notrump. Here are three examples of what to do when your partner raises your 1◇ opening bid to 2◇:

(23)	♠ J 9 8 7	(24)	♠ A 9 6 3	(25)	♠ 3 2
	♡ Q 10 6		♡ K 10		♡ K J 2
	♡ A Q 8 3		◇ K J 10 8 2		◇ A K Q 10 8 4
	♣ A J		♣ A Q		♣ A 6

(23) Pass. When partner raises your suit to the two-level, do not bid again with fewer than 17 points.

(24) Bid 2NT, to show 17-19 points and stoppers in all three unbid suits. Your partner should pass or bid 3◇ with a minimum. He will make some other bid, most commonly 3NT, with a maximum. (Add a queen to this hand and you should bid 3NT yourself.)

(25) Bid 2♡, showing 17 points or more and at least one stopper in hearts. Partner must bid again. If he has stoppers in spades and clubs he bids 2NT or 3NT; you will raise 2NT to 3NT. If he bids 2♠ to show a spade stopper, you will bid 3NT. If he bids 3♣ or 3◇ it means he has no spade stopper, in which case the hand should be played in diamonds; probably just 3◇.

AFTER YOUR SUIT HAS BEEN
JUMP-RAISED TO THE THREE-LEVEL

A jump-raise to the three-level shows 13-16 points and at least four-card trump support. When a major suit has been raised the contract should be played in the major suit. But do not bid game in a minor suit as long as there is hope to play game in notrump. In example #26 below, you open the bidding 1♡ and partner raises to 3♡;

in examples #27 and #28, you open the bidding with 1♣ and partner raises to 3♣:

(26) ♠ A K 10 (27) ♠ A K 10 (28) ♠ K 10
     ♡ A Q J 3 2   ♡ 7 4   ♡ A J 9 5
     ◊ 9 8 5   ◊ 9 8 5   ◊ K 2
     ♣ 7 4   ♣ A Q J 3 2   ♣ Q 10 8 7 3

(26) Bid 4♡. Partner's jump-raise to 3♡ shows 13-16 points and at least four hearts, so 4♡ is the logical game contract.

(27) Bid 3♠. This hand is the same as #26 except the hearts and clubs are reversed and partner has raised a minor suit (not a major). In an effort to get to 3NT, you should bid 3♠. The 3♠ bid is not an attempt to make spades the trump suit; its only purpose is to show a stopper. If partner has stoppers in diamonds and hearts he should bid 3NT. Otherwise he should bid something else and you will play a club contract.

(28) Bid 3NT. You have stoppers in all three unbid suits, so you can bid game in notrump yourself. Note that partner denied a four-card or longer major suit when he raised clubs, so bidding hearts in the hope of reaching a 4♡ contract is a waste of time (and gives the opponents information about your hand for no good reason).

AFTER A 2NT RESPONSE

In the next three deals you open the bidding with 1♠ and partner responds 2NT (showing a balanced hand with 13-15 points and stoppers in all three unbid suits), and you hold:

(29) ♠ A Q 8 5 3 (30) ♠ A 9 8 5 2 (31) ♠ K J 10 7 5 2
     ♡ K 10 2   ♡ K J 9 6   ♡ 8
     ◊ 7 4   ◊ A J 3   ◊ A K 4
     ♣ A 9 8   ♣ 7   ♣ Q 9 4

(29) Bid 3NT, with your balanced 5-3-3-2 distribution.

(30) Bid 3♡, showing four or more hearts. The decision whether to bid game in hearts, spades or notrump is now up to your partner.

(31) Bid 4♠, although a bid of 3♠ is okay since it would be forcing. The six-card suit makes spades the most attractive game contract—partner's 2NT bid shows a balanced hand, so he must have either two or three spades.

AFTER A JUMP-SHIFT RESPONSE

Responder's jump bid in a new suit, called a jump-shift, shows 17-19 points. It is not only forcing to game, but suggests slam possibilities. In the following three deals you open the bidding with 1♠, partner responds 3◊, and you hold:

(32)	♠ A J 9 6 3	(33)	♠ K Q 9 7 4	(34)	♠ A Q 9 8 6 3
	♡ K 10 2		♡ 9 5		♡ 7
	◊ 7 4		◊ K 10 3 2		◊ A 5
	♣ K Q 9		♣ A 6		♣ A Q 5 4

(32) Bid 3NT to show a minimum opening bid and a balanced hand with stoppers in the two unbid suits.

(33) Bid 4◊, with good trump support for partner's suit. Although you have a minimum opening, slam prospects are bright.

(34) Bid 3♠, with your good six-card suit. You have 18 points and partner has at least 17, so you should bid a small slam (or maybe a grand slam) before you are through. Partner's next bid will help you decide which slam to bid.

IN REVIEW

After partner has responded in a new suit at the one-level (showing six points or more):

* With 13-16 points: raise partner's suit to the two-level with four trumps (or occasionally raise a major suit with three); bid 1NT to show a balanced hand that is too weak to open with 1NT (12-14 points); rebid a six-card or longer suit at the two-level (rarely a good five-card suit); or bid a new four-card

or longer suit at the one-level, or at the two-level if it ranks lower than your first suit.

* With 17-19 points: jump-raise partner's suit to the three-level with four trumps; rebid a good six-card or longer suit at the three-level; or bid any new four-card or longer suit. A jump bid to 2NT shows a balanced or semi-balanced hand with stoppers in the unbid suits and 18-19 points (a hand too strong to open the bidding with 1NT).

* With 20-22 points: bid game if you know where to play it, or make a forcing bid—jump in a new suit or make a reverse bid.

After partner has responded 1NT (showing 6-10 points):

* With 13-16 points: pass 1NT with a balanced (or semi-balanced) hand; rebid any six-card or longer suit (rarely a strong five-card suit), or bid a new four-card or longer suit that is lower in rank than your first suit.

* With 17-19 points: raise 1NT to 2NT with a balanced (or semi-balanced) hand; jump to three of your original six-card or longer suit; or bid any new four-card or longer suit.

* With 20-22 points, bid game or make a forcing bid. Raise 1NT to 3NT with a balanced (or semi-balanced) hand, or bid game in your original suit with a very strong six-card or longer suit. If you are unsure about which game to bid, jump the bidding in a new suit, or reverse the bidding to force partner to bid again.

After partner has bid a new suit at the two-level (showing 11 points or more):

* With 13-16 points: raise partner's suit to the three-level with three or more trumps; bid 2NT with a balanced hand and stoppers in the unbid suits; rebid a good five-card or longer suit (but avoid rebidding a five-card suit if another reasonable bid is available); or, bid a new four-card or longer suit.

* With 17-19 points, you know the combined hands have enough points to bid at least a game. Any nonjump rebid is forcing and in many cases it is wrong to jump the bidding right away—just make the nonjump bid that best describes your distribution.

However, with the right hand you may: jump-raise partner's suit with four good trumps and 17-19 points; jump the bidding in your original suit with a strong six-card or longer suit and 17-19 points; or bid 3NT to show a balanced hand with stoppers in the unbid suits and 18-19 points (a hand too strong to open the bidding with 1NT).

* With 20-22 points, there is a good chance you can make a slam. Partner will not pass your next bid, so it is not necessary to jump the bidding right away. If you want to save bidding space to exchange more information, make any nonjump bid.

After partner has raised your suit to the two-level (showing 6-10 points):
* With 13-16 points, pass.
* With 17-19 points, make a game try. Bid three of the agreed suit with good trumps; bid 2NT with a balanced (or semi-balanced) hand and the unbid suits stopped; or bid a new suit (usually showing a stopper after a minor-suit raise). *The new-suit bid is forcing.*
* With 20-22 points: bid game in the agreed suit; bid 3NT with a balanced hand and stoppers in the unbid suits; or bid a new suit (forcing) if you are undecided about which game to play.

After partner has jumped the bidding:
* When partner has raised your suit to the three-level (showing 13-16 points and at least four trumps): if your point-count is in the 13-16 range, bid game in the agreed suit if it is a major. If the agreed suit is a minor, bid 3NT with stoppers in the unbid suits, or bid a new suit below 3NT to show a stopper in the suit you bid. If it turns out that you do not have stoppers in all of the suits, in which case bidding 3NT would be wrong, return to the agreed minor. With 17 points or more, make a "slam try" (see Slam Bidding, Chapter Eight).
* If partner has responded 2NT (showing a balanced hand with 13-15 points and stoppers in the unbid suits): with 13-16 points, bid 3NT with a balanced or semi-balanced hand, rebid your own six-card or longer suit, or bid any new four-card or

longer suit. With 17 points or more, make a slam try (see Slam
Bidding, Chapter Eight).

* If partner has jumped the bidding in a new suit (a jump-shift,
  showing 17-19 points), he is inviting you to bid a slam. The
  usual procedure is to make a second bid below game to further
  describe your hand. Raise partner's suit with adequate trump
  support, bid notrump with a balanced hand and stoppers in the
  unbid suits, rebid your own six-card or longer suit, or bid any
  new four-card or longer suit. After partner's next bid you will
  be in a better position to decide whether to stop in game or bid
  a slam. Do not forget that partner has 17-19 points; as few as
  14 or 15 points might produce a slam.

PRACTICE DEAL

Contract: 4♡   North
Opening lead: ♠Q   ♠ 5 4 3
                                  ♡ Q 10 2
                                  ◊ A K 9 8
                                  ♣ Q 7 2

    West   East
    ♠ Q J 10   ♠ K 8 6 2
    ♡ A 6   ♡ 9 7
    ◊ 6 5 3   ◊ Q J 10 7 4
    ♣ A 9 8 5 4   ♣ 10 3

               South
               ♠ A 9 7
               ♡ K J 8 5 4 3
               ◊ 2
               ♣ K J 6

West	North	East	South
—	—	—	1♡
Pass	2◊	Pass	2♡
Pass	3♡	Pass	4♡
All Pass			

The bidding: North's 2◊ response to the 1♡ opening bid shows a four-card or longer suit and 11 points or more. South correctly rebids his six-card heart suit. North's raise to 3♡ shows 11-12 points and invites game; with 13 points he would raise to 4♡. South accepts the invitation to game by bidding 4♡.

The opening lead: West leads the ♠Q. Once again, the top card from a three-card sequence is the desirable choice.

The play: This deal depends on the timing in drawing trumps. Upon seeing dummy, declarer counts the losing tricks in his own hand and he has four (two spades, one heart and one club). The ♡A and ♣A are inevitable losers, so he must limit his spade losers to one to make his contract. Can you see the winning line of play? Answer: win the first trick with the ♠A, cash the two top diamonds and discard one of your spade losers. Then lead a trump to drive out the ace. The opponents can take two more tricks if they choose—one spade and the ♣A—but the contract is safe if you draw the missing trumps as soon as you regain the lead.

Note that if declarer played a trump before discarding a spade loser, he would be set; the opponents can win two spade tricks when West gets the lead with the ♡A. Also note, it was important to draw the trumps before cashing the club winners—else East would be able to ruff the third club lead.

The key plays: Discard a losing spade on a high diamond before leading a trump, and then draw all of the missing trumps before cashing your club winners.

CHAPTER SIX

REBIDS BY THE RESPONDER

QUIZ

Responder's rebid depends on what he knows about opener's hand. Here is a little quiz for you before reading this chapter. In a noncompetitive auction (the opponents never bid), if the opening bid is 1◇ and responder bids 1♠, what do each of the following rebids by opener mean?

(a) 1NT   (b) 2♣   (c) 2◇   (d) 2♡   (e) 2♠
(f) 2NT   (g) 3♣   (h) 3◇   (i) 3♠   (j) 4♠

DO NOT READ THE ANSWERS UNTIL
YOU HAVE ANALYZED THE MEANING OF EACH BID.

Answers

(a) 1NT shows a balanced hand with 12-14 points; a hand too weak to open 1NT.

(b) 2♣ shows 13-19 points and a four-card or longer club suit. Note that the new suit bid does not distinguish between 13-16 and 17-19 points.

(c) 2◇ shows 13-16 points and a six-card or longer suit (rarely a good five-card suit).

(d) 2♡ (a reverse) shows 17 points or more and a two-suited hand usually with greater length in the first bid suit (5-4, 6-4 or 6-5); forcing for one round.

(e) 2♠ shows 13-16 points and usually four trumps (occasionally three trumps).

(f) 2NT shows a balanced hand with 18-19 points (a hand too strong to open 1NT and too weak to open 2NT) and stoppers in the unbid suits.

(g) 3♣ (a jump-shift) shows 20-22 points and usually a four-card or longer club suit; forcing to game.

(h) 3◇ shows 17-19 points and a good six-card or longer suit.

(i)   3♠ shows 17-19 points and four trumps.

(j)   4♠ shows 20-22 points and four trumps.

(If you get any wrong answers, review the ones you missed in Chapter Five before reading further.)

PLANNING AHEAD

If the opener's rebid was not in a new suit, responder knows whether he has 13-16, 17-19 or 20-22 points and considers the possibilities of the combined hands. If responder knows which contract to play he bids it, or passes if that leaves him in the best contract. If responder does not have enough information to figure out which contract to play, he makes a rebid to further describe his hand. The rebid chart for responder:

> 6-10 points = the minimum range
> 11-12 points = the invitational range
> 13 or more points = the game range

Test yourself on these 15 illustrations as you go along.

AFTER OPENER HAS RAISED
YOUR SUIT TO THE TWO-LEVEL

After opener has raised your suit to the two-level, pass with 6-10 points, invite game with 11-12 points, and bid game with 13 or more points. For example:

(1)	Partner	You	♠ A 7 4
	1♣	1♡	♡ K 10 8 5 2
	2♡	?	♢ 9 8 6
			♣ 6 3

Pass. You have nine points (one for the five-card suit, and one for the doubleton after partner raises your suit) and partner has shown 13-16. The combined total is 22-25—not enough for game. You need at least 11 points to bid again (with 11-12 points bid 3♡ to invite game; with 13-16 points bid 4♡). If partner had jumped to 3♡, showing 17-19 points, the total would be 26-28 and you would bid 4♡.

AFTER OPENER HAS REBID 1NT

After opener has rebid 1NT and you are in the 6-10 point range, you know there is no game. However, it is often right to bid again to seek a better part-score contract. Here are four examples:

(2)	Partner	You		♠ 7 6 4
	1♣	1♡		♡ K 9 6 5 2
	1NT	?		◊ K 8
				♣ Q 5 2

Pass. Partner has a balanced hand with 12-14 points and you have a balanced hand with nine points. The total is 21, 22 or 23, so there is no game and 1NT should be the best part-score contract. When you have a balanced hand like this one you should raise to 2NT with 11-12 points, and raise to 3NT with 13-17.

(3)	Partner	You		♠ K 10 7 4 3 2
	1◊	1♠		♡ 8 2
	1NT	?		◊ 9 6
				♣ K 8 5

Bid 2♠, showing 6-10 points and a six-card suit. Partner has advertised a balanced hand, so he normally has two or three spades, and 2♠ should be a better part-score contract than 1NT. Partner must pass 2♠.

You learned in Chapter Four that if responder did not pass earlier, a jump bid is forcing to game. If at his second turn to bid responder jumps the bidding it is still forcing to game. Consequently, hands with 11-12 point sometimes pose rebidding problems. One solution, played by many experienced players, is to play that certain jump bids show 11-12 points (inviting game). This is confusing to an inexperienced player. I suggest you ignore this until you get more experience and play that *all jump bids by responder are forcing to game (unless he passed originally)*. Some consider this old fashioned, but your partner will understand your bids.

Suppose you change the spade holding in this deal so that you hold ♠A K 10 7 4 3, which gives you 12 points. If you bid 2♠ it shows 6-10 points and partner will pass! If you jump to 3♠ it shows 13 points or more and partner will bid game! What do you do with 11-12 points when there is no way to invite game? You must make an underbid or an overbid; in this case bid 2♠ or 3♠. I suggest 3♠. Remember, bidding is an estimation of probabilities, not an exact science. You will at times have a close decision and may choose the wrong bid; we all do. So smile, and on to the next deal.

(4)	Partner	You	♠ K 9 8 6 4
	1♣	1♠	♡ 7
	1NT	?	◇ 10 3 2
			♣ A 10 5 2

Bid 2♣, showing 6-10 points and four or more clubs. Partner may have three clubs, but he usually has four or five, so 2♣ should be a better part-score contract than 1NT. Partner should pass, or maybe bid 2♠ with three trumps, but all other bids should be ruled out. With this same distribution and 13 points or more you should jump to 3♣. With this same distribution and 11-12 points you would have to choose between the underbid of 2♣ and the overbid of 3♣.

(5)	Partner	You	♠ K 10 6 4 3
	1◇	1♠	♡ Q J 10 8 5
	1NT	?	◇ 9 2
			♣ 7

Bid 2♡, showing 6-10 points and a two-suited hand—at least five spades and four hearts. You learned in Chapter Five that a new suit bid by responder is forcing (unless he is a passed hand). If the responder bids a new suit at his second turn to bid, it is still forcing *unless the opener has rebid 1NT*. In this case opener should pass 2♡ or make a preference bid of 2♠; he may also raise to 3♡ with four trumps and a maximum point count. Once again you would have a problem with 11-12 points—with 5-5 in the majors you would have to choose between an underbid of 2♡ and an overbid of 3♡.

AFTER OPENER HAS
REBID HIS SUIT AT THE TWO-LEVEL

After opener has rebid his suit at the two-level and you have 6-10 points, you should usually pass, but you may rebid a good six-card suit. With 11-12 points, invite game by raising partner's suit to the three-level or bidding 2NT. You need a reasonably good hand to rebid in a new suit (rarely fewer than 11 points), but *the new-suit bid is forcing for one round*. With 13 points or more, bid game or make a forcing bid—bid a new suit or jump the bidding.

(6)	Partner	You		♠ A J 10
	1♢	1♡		♡ Q 9 8 4
	2♢	?		♢ 5 2
				♣ A 10 7 3

Bid 2NT to invite game with 11 points and stoppers in the unbid suits. With 6-10 points you should pass 2♢. With 13 points or more you would bid 3NT.

AFTER OPENER HAS SHOWN
AN INVITATIONAL-RANGE OPENING BID

If the opener makes an invitational-range opening bid showing 17-19 points (by making a jump-raise of your suit, a jump bid in his original suit, or raising a 1NT response to 2NT), it usually pays to bid game with about eight points.

(7)	Partner	You		♠ 9 8 5
	1♡	1NT		♡ 7 4
	3♡	?		♢ A 10 9 3
				♣ K Q 6 2

Bid 4♡ with nine points. The point total is 26-28 and partner must have a good six-card suit to rebid 3♡. Change your ◊A to the ◊Q, so you have just seven points, and you would pass 3♡.

AFTER OPENER HAS REBID A NEW SUIT

After opener's rebid was in a new suit and the bidding is still below two of his first suit (partner-1♡, you-1NT, partner-2♣ or 2◊, but not 2♠), his bid shows a four-card or longer suit and 13-19 points. The new-suit bid does not distinguish between 13-16 and 17-19 points, and it is not forcing.

(8)	Partner	You	♠ J 10 9 6
	1♣	1♡	♡ A 7 4 3
	1♠	?	◊ 8 6 5
			♣ K 2

Bid 2♠, to show a hand with 8-10 points (or maybe seven points) and at least four trumps. Partner should pass 2♠ with 13-16 points, or bid on to game with 17-19.

(9)	Partner	You	♠ A 9 7 6 3
	1♡	1♠	♡ J 2
	2◊	?	◊ J 5
			♣ Q 10 9 8

Bid 2♡, a "preference," which shows 6-10 points and most likely two hearts—with three trumps you probably would have raised to 2♡ the first time. Bidding 2♡ is better than passing because you know partner has at least five hearts and he may have only four diamonds; further, you may have a game if partner has 18-19 points. If partner bids again over 2♡ he has 17-19 points; you should bid 3NT. Rebidding your anemic spade suit is a poor choice; you know the combined hands have a seven-card heart fit and partner is likely to have a singleton or a void in spades. You most definitely should not bid 2NT; that bid would show 11-12 points.

(10)	Partner	You	♠ 7 4
	1♠	1NT	♡ K Q J 9 5
	2◊	?	◊ J 2
			♣ 10 6 4 3

Bid 2♡. You could not bid 2♡ directly over 1♠ because a two-over-one response shows 11 points or more. By bidding 1NT first and following with 2♡, you show 6-10 points and a very good five-card or any six-card heart suit. This 2♡ bid tells partner that you do not have good support for either of his suits, but that you do have a very good suit of your own.

AFTER OPENER HAS
JUMPED THE BIDDING IN A NEW SUIT

After opener has jumped the bidding in a new suit—showing 20-22 points—his jump-shift is forcing to game.

(11)	Partner	You	♠ K 7 6 4
	1♡	1♠	♡ 9 2
	3♣	?	◊ K 10 9 5
			♣ 8 3 2

Bid 3NT with a stopper in diamonds. If your hand were any weaker you would have passed 1♡, but once your partner jumps in a new suit *you are not allowed to pass below game.*

AFTER OPENER HAS MADE A REVERSE BID

If opener's rebid was in a new suit at the two-level that ranks higher than his first suit (partner-1◊, you-1♠, partner-2♡), he has made a reverse bid. The reverse shows a two-suited hand and is forcing for one round; if your response was at the one-level, it shows 17 points or more; if your response was at the two-level, it shows 15 points or more. Opener's distribution may be 5-4, 6-4 or 6-5, with greater length in his first bid suit (he may also reverse with 4-4 distribution, but never with 5-5 or 3-4). Although the opening bidder may occasionally reverse with 4-4, *responder should assume that he has at least five cards in his first-bid suit.* Here is one example:

(12)	Partner	You	♠ 7 4 3
	1◊	1NT	♡ K 8 5
	2♡	?	◊ K 3 2
			♣ 10 6 5 3

Bid 3◊. You are not allowed to pass partner's reverse bid. Without stoppers in spades and clubs you cannot bid 2NT, and it is generally wrong to raise partner's second suit *directly* with just three trumps (he most likely has four hearts and five or six diamonds), so the preference bid of 3◊ is best.

AFTER A TWO-OVER-ONE RESPONSE

If your first response was a nonjump bid in a new suit at the two-level, you showed 11 points or more. You should not pass your partner's rebid (unless he bids a game), but if you have just 11-12 points make no further aggressive bids. The rebids that show 11-12 points are all nonjump bids: rebid your first suit, raise partner's suit, or bid notrump; these bids are not forcing. You may also bid a new suit with 11 points or more (no upper limit), *a forcing bid.* With 13 points or more, bid game directly if you know where to play it; if not, bid a new suit or jump the bidding to force your partner to bid again.

(13)	Partner	You	♠ A K 10 7
	1◊	2♣	♡ 5 2
	2◊	?	◊ 6 3
			♣ A 10 9 8 4

Bid 2♠, a forcing bid showing 11 points or more. Note that it was correct to bid the five-card suit first, even though it is a minor and the four-card suit is a major.

(14)	Partner	You	♠ 7 4 3
	1♡	2♣	♡ 10 9 2
	2◊	?	◊ K 5
			♣ A K 9 8 7

Bid 2♡. This is not forcing, but your partner knows you have 11-12 points. If partner has a weak opening bid and passes 2♡, you probably cannot make a game.

(15)	Partner	You	♠ A K 9 8 7
	1♡	1♠	♡ 10 9 2
	2◊	?	◊ K 5
			♣ 7 4 3

Bid 3♡. This is the same hand as #14, except the spades and clubs have been reversed. Your 1♠ bid showed six points or more. If you now bid just 2♡, partner will think you have 6-10 points and a doubleton heart. Although 3♡ is a slight overbid—it is forcing to game and shows 13 plus points—it is clearly a better bid than anything else. *The last two hands show that every bid you make depends on what you told your partner in your previous bid.*

IN REVIEW

If opener raises your suit to the two-level (opener-1◊, you-1♡, opener-2♡, you-?):
* Pass with 6-10- points.
* Invite game with 11-12 (bid 3♡, 2NT or a new suit).
* Bid game or a new suit with 13 or more points.

If opener's rebid is 1NT (opener-1♣, you-1♠, opener-1NT, you-?):
* Pass with 6-10 points and a balanced hand.
* A 2♣ bid shows 6-10 points and at least four clubs.
* A 2◊ or 2♡ bid shows 6-10 points and at least a four-card suit—*these new-suit bids are not forcing after the 1NT rebid.*
* A 2♠ bid shows 6-10 points and at least six spades.
* A 2NT bid shows a balanced hand with 11-12 points. All jump bids are forcing to game.

If opener rebids his suit at the two-level (opener-1◊, you-1♠, opener-2◊, you-?):
* Pass with 6-10 points, or rebid a six-card or longer suit.

* A 2NT bid shows 11-12 points and stoppers in the unbid suits.
* A raise to 3◇ shows 11-12 points and usually three diamonds, or at least a doubleton.
* Any new-suit bid is forcing for one round, and any jump bid is forcing to game.

If opener shows an invitational-range hand—17-19 points (opener-1♡; you-1♠; opener-2NT, 3♡ or 3♠; you ?):

* These jump bids are not forcing, but you should usually bid again with eight points or more.

If opener's rebid is a new suit at the one-level (opener-1♣, you-1♡, opener-1♠, you-?):

* Pass shows 6-7 points and probably three or four spades.
* A rebid of 1NT shows 6-10 points.
* A preference to 2♣ shows 6-10 points and at least four clubs.
* A new-suit bid of 2◇ is forcing; it usually shows 11 points or more; but you may have less with extraordinary distribution such as 6-5.
* A 2♡ bid shows 6-10 points and at least six hearts.
* A raise to 2♠ shows 8-10 points and at least four spades. All jump bids are forcing to game.

If opener jumps the bidding in a new suit (opener-1♡, you-1♠, opener-3♣ or 3◇, you-?):

* His jump shift shows 20-22 points and is forcing to game. Make the rebid that best describes your hand.

If opener makes a reverse bid after you have responded at the one-level (opener-1◇, you-1♠, opener-2♡, you-?):

* His bid shows a two-suited hand with 17 points or more, and is forcing for one round. Make the bid to best describe your hand.

If opener's rebid is a new suit at the two-level that ranks lower than his first suit (opener-1♡, you-1♠, opener-2◇, you-?):

* Pass shows 6-10 points and longer diamonds than hearts.

* A 2♡ bid shows 6-10 points and probably just two hearts.
* A 2♠ bid shows 6-10 points and at least six spades.
* A 2NT bid shows 11-12 points and a stopper in clubs.
* A raise to 3◇ shows 11-12 points and at least four diamonds.
* All jump bids are forcing to game.

If your first response was a nonjump bid in a new suit at the two-level (opener-1♡, you-2♣ or 2◇), it shows 11 points or more.
* You should not pass your partner's next bid (unless he bids a game).
* You may bid 2NT, raise partner's suit, or rebid your first suit with 11-12 points (nonforcing bids).
* A new suit shows 11 or more points and is forcing.
* Any jump bid shows 13 or more points and is forcing to game.

If you have already jumped the bidding (opener-1♡; you-2♠, 2NT, 3♡, etc.), you have created a forcing auction.
* Neither you nor your partner may pass below game.

PRACTICE DEAL

Contract: 3NT
Opening lead: ♠4

North
♠ A 7
♡ J 9 8 7
◇ 8 6 5 4
♣ Q 5 4

West
♠ Q J 6 4 3
♡ 5 2
◇ 9 3 2
♣ K 7 3

East
♠ 10 9 8 5
♡ 10 6 4 3
◇ A 7
♣ A 6 2

South
♠ K 2
♡ A K Q
◇ K Q J 10
♣ J 10 9 8

West	North	East	South
—	—	—	1◇
Pass	1♡	Pass	2NT
Pass	3NT	All Pass	

The bidding: South's jump to 2NT showed 18-19 points, so North was entitled to bid 3NT with just seven.

The opening lead: When the opening leader's longest suit is not headed by a *three-card* sequence, the fourth-best card is the customary choice against a notrump contract.

The play: You have six top tricks (two spades and four hearts), and can win three more in diamonds after the ◇A has been knocked out. *But you must be careful to cash your tricks in the right order.* Win the first trick in your hand with the ♠A (you will need the ♠K as an entry to dummy to win a trick with the ♡J). Next cash the three top hearts, then keep leading diamonds until the ace is driven out. When you regain the lead you have nine tricks, but this would not be true if you cashed your tricks in any other order.

The key plays: Winning the first trick with the ♠K and cashing the three top hearts before leading any diamonds.

CHAPTER SEVEN

OPENING SUIT BIDS AT THE TWO-LEVEL AND HIGHER

This chapter includes:

* Preemptive opening bids (opening bids in a suit at the three-level and higher).
* Weak two-bids (opening bids of 2◊, 2♡ and 2♠).
* The strong artificial 2♣ opening bid.

PREEMPTIVE OPENING BIDS

Opening suit bids at the three-level (3♣, 3◊, 3♡ or 3♠) and at the four-level (4♣, 4◊, 4♡ or 4♠), as well as a minor suit at the five-level (5♣ or 5◊) are preemptive. An opening preemptive bid shows a weak hand with a long suit. You might have as many as nine or ten *high-card* points, but most of them should be in your long suit. At the three-level your suit should be seven cards long (rarely a good six-cards), and at the four-level you need a good seven- or an eight-card suit. The ideal hand is one that will win several tricks if your long suit is trump, but *at most* one trick if the opponents play the hand in their trump suit. For example:

(1) ♠ K Q J 10 9 7 5
     ♡ 6 2
     ◊ 9 5
     ♣ 8 3

This is a perfect hand for a preemptive bid. After the ♠A is driven out, it will provide six winners if spades are trump, while it is unlikely to win any tricks if another suit is trump.

The main purpose of a preemptive bid is to make life more difficult for your opponents by depriving them of bidding space. They may decide not to enter the bidding at such a high level and miss a game; and, if they do bid, they are more likely to reach the wrong contract. In addition, an opening preemptive bid describes the nature of a hand reasonably well, so partner can make an intelligent decision whether to pass, or to bid on to a game or slam if he has a good hand. It may also lead to a good "sacrifice" (explained in Chapter Ten).

How to value your hand for a preemptive bid: The point-count system is the best way to estimate the value of most hands, but it is not accurate when it comes to highly distributional hands. So when contemplating a preemptive bid, *do not count points* (except to make sure that you do not have too many high-card points for a preemptive bid). Instead, *count tricks.* For example, in hand (1) above you can count six winning tricks if spades are trump.

It is sometimes right to "overbid" your hand by two, three or more tricks, even though the opponents may double and set you. Just how daring you should be depends on how much it will cost per undertrick if your are doubled and set, as compared with how much it will cost if the opponents bid and make a game or a slam. Since it will cost more if you get doubled and are set when you are *vulnerable,* it stands to reason you should take more chances when you are *not vulnerable.* The opponents' vulnerability is also important; the bonuses they get for games and slams are higher when vulnerable. To figure out when your hand qualifies for a preemptive bid, and if it does how high to bid, you must know how vulnerability affects the score. Keep in mind that bold tactics are a winning style when it comes to preemptive bids, because it is usually the opponents who suffer, not your side.

THE THREE "STAGES" OF VULNERABILITY

Unfavorable vulnerability—your side is vulnerable and the opponents are not. Estimate the number of tricks you think your hand can win if your long suit is trump and overbid by two tricks. For example, if you estimate that your hand is worth seven tricks, contract for nine tricks—bid three of your long suit.

Equal vulnerability—both sides are vulnerable or both sides are not vulnerable. Estimate the number of tricks your hand can win and overbid by three tricks. For example, if you estimate that your hand is worth seven tricks, bid four of your long suit.

Favorable vulnerability—the opponents are vulnerable and your side is not. Overbid by three, four or even five tricks. This is the time that bidding to a high level with a trashy suit is desirable. The amount you lose if your contract is doubled and set, as compared to the amount you lose if your opponents bid and make a game or slam, is usually a bargain.

Preemptive opening bids in fourth seat: The information above applies to opening preemptive bids in first, second or third seat. Since you break even if a hand is passed out, *never make a preemptive bid in fourth seat (after the other three players have passed) unless you expect to make your contract.* A preemptive opening bid in fourth seat shows a good hand—at the three-level a good seven-card suit and about 10-12 high-card points—and the requirements are not altered by the vulnerability.

Test Yourself

As dealer, what would you bid, if anything, with each of the following hands? Answer three times: first answer at favorable; second answer at equal; and third answer at unfavorable vulnerability.

(2)	♠ A 4	(3)	♠ J 5
	♡ 9 5 2		♡ K 10 9 8 5 4 3
	◇ Q J 10 9 7 3 2		◇ 7 3
	♣ 7		♣ 6 2
(4)	♠ —	(5)	♠ 7 4
	♡ 5 4 2		♡ A Q J 9 8 7 3
	◇ J 8		◇ A 8 2
	♣ A K Q 10 9 7 6 3		♣ 4

Solutions

(2) The trick-taking value of this hand is six (five diamonds and one spade), so it qualifies for 3◇ with favorable or equal vulnerability (a three-trick overbid). Later in this chapter you

will read about "weak two-bids," and this hand should be opened with 2◇ if the vulnerability is unfavorable.

(3)   It is relatively difficult to estimate the number of winners available with a broken suit (like the heart suit shown here). How many heart winners would you count? You would be a pessimist if you thought you would definitely lose three heart tricks to the ace, queen and jack. The probability is that you will lose two. Value this heart suit as worth five tricks and bid 3♡ at favorable vulnerability only (an overbid of four tricks).

(4)   You have eight club tricks, so bid 5♣ at favorable or equal vulnerability (overbid by three tricks), or 4♣ at unfavorable—overbid by two tricks.

(5)   Bid 1♡ regardless of the vulnerability. This hand is too strong for a preemptive opening bid in first, second or third seat (11 high-card points including two aces). However, in fourth seat you should open 3♡ regardless of the vulnerability.

RESPONSES TO PREEMPTIVE OPENING BIDS

How to value your hand when responding to a preemptive bid: When your partner opens with a preempt, you know how many tricks he thinks he can win if his suit is trump. To find out how many tricks the combined hands can win, add the number of tricks you think your hand can win to the number partner said he could win. Here is a typical hand for an opening 3♡ bid to help you visualize which cards in responder's hand would be useful at a heart contract.

(6)   ♠ 6 5
         ♡ A Q J 10 9 8 3
         ◇ 10 9
         ♣ 8 2

*   The only cards outside the heart suit that will be useful are "quick tricks," those that may win a trick the first or second time the suit is led—A K = 2 tricks, A Q = 1 1/2 tricks, A or K Q = 1 trick, K x = 1/2 trick. Note that stray queens and jacks are worthless.

* A king or queen in opener's long suit should be counted as a full trick.
* With good trump support (usually at least three), count tricks for singletons and voids. With the hand above, declarer could win a trick by ruffing if dummy had a singleton club, diamond or spade.

Responses to major-suit preempts: When partner opens with a preemptive bid in a major suit, it is usually best to pass or raise his suit; it is almost never right to bid 3NT or a new suit.

Test Yourself

Both sides are vulnerable and your partner opens 3♡, indicating that his hand is worth six tricks if hearts are trump. Give two answers for each of the following hands: first, how many tricks do you estimate you will contribute in a heart contract; second, what would you bid?

(7)	♠ A K 9 8	(8)	♠ K Q J 9
	♡ 2		♡ 7 5
	◇ A K 6 3		◇ K Q J 3
	♣ 10 7 5 4		♣ Q J 5
(9)	♠ 7	(10)	♠ A K 7 3
	♡ K 7 2		♡ K 4 2
	◇ A K 8 6 3		◇ 8
	♣ 10 9 6 5		♣ A K 10 7 5

Solutions

(7) You have four tricks (the ♠A K and ◇A K) to add to the six partner said he can win, so bid 4♡. Your partner usually has a seven-card suit; it is all right to raise him with a singleton. Compare with #6 to see that the needed ten tricks are available.

(8) This hand demonstrates why it is wrong to value your hand by its point count opposite a preemptive bid. Although it has 15 high-card points while #7 has only 14, it is not nearly as good

because it has only two quick tricks—the ♡K Q and ◇K Q. Your two winners plus the six partner promised equals eight. Pass 3♡ and expect the contract to be set (although if partner has hand #6 and the heart finesse succeeds, he can win nine tricks).

(9)   You have four tricks: two for the ◇A K, one for the ♡K, and one for the singleton spade. Bid 4♡ for two reasons: (1) You expect to make it. If partner has hand #6, he has ten tricks (seven hearts, two diamonds, and a spade ruff in your hand). (2) The opponents, who have nine or ten spades between them, almost surely can make four spades (or more) if they bid it; partner cannot win more than one trick defensively and you can win at most two with your ◇A K. Your 4♡ bid may discourage the opponents from bidding. But if they do bid 4♠, bid 5♡ as a "sacrifice"; if doubled, the predictable minus score of 200 for going down one is much better than the minus score you would get if the opponents were allowed to play and make 4♠.

(10) This time you have six tricks: one for the ♡K, two for the ♠A K, two for the ♣A K and one for the singleton diamond. Partner's bid showed six winners and you have six. So bid a slam if partner has an ace. To find out how many aces partner has, bid 4NT (the "Blackwood Convention," see Chapter Eight). If partner has no aces he will bid 5♣ and you will sign off in 5♡. If he has one ace he will bid 5◇ and you will bid 6♡. If he bids 5♡ to show two aces you should bid 7♡, (but it is wrong to make a preemptive bid with two aces). Note that if partner has hand #6 you can make 6♡, losing only one diamond trick.

Responses to minor-suit preempts: You have learned that when partner opens the bidding with three of a major and you have a good hand, it is usually best to raise the major suit, even with a singleton. But a minor-suit game requires 11 tricks. Therefore, when seeking the best game contract, bidding 3NT or a new suit is sometimes better than raising a minor-suit preempt. You need a strong hand to bid 3NT, plus a fit in partner's suit (at least x x x or K x) and stoppers in the unbid suits.

A new-suit bid at the game-level shows a self-sufficient suit (such as A K Q J x x, A K J x x x x, or better) and a strong desire to play that contract; partner should pass, or be ready to accept your tirade if he bids and it is wrong. A new-suit bid below game shows a strong hand with a good five-card or longer suit and is *forcing* (unless responder is a passed hand). These requirements to respond in a new suit are the same after a major-suit preempt.

Here is a typical hand for a 3◊ opening. After you have answered the following quiz, compare responder's hand with this one to see how many tricks you can take.

(11)   ♠ 9 4
       ♡ 8 7
       ◊ K Q J 10 9 6 2
       ♣ 10 3

Test Yourself

Nobody is vulnerable, partner opens with 3◊. Plan your response.

(12) ♠ A K   (13) ♠ A K 7
     ♡ Q 10 9 2   ♡ A 9 5 4
     ◊ A 4 3   ◊ 8 3
     ♣ K Q 8 6   ♣ A K 5 2

(14) ♠ 10 8 3   (15) ♠ A K 10 8 6 3
     ♡ A Q J 9 6 3   ♡ A K Q 5 2
     ◊ 5   ◊ —
     ♣ Q 7 4   ♣ 9 7

Solutions

(12) Bid 3NT. This hand meets all of the requirements: a good hand, stoppers in the unbid suits, and a fit for partner. If partner has hand #11, you will make 3NT (seven diamond tricks and two aces), but a 5◊ contract would fail.

(13) Bid 5◊. Partner has indicated that he can win six tricks and you have five. If your partner has hand #11 and you give him this

dummy, he will make 5◇—his only losers are one heart trick and the ◇A. Note that without a diamond fit, bidding 3NT is not recommended. To explain why, suppose you are playing 3NT and hand #11 is your dummy. When you lead a diamond, a good defender will hold up his ace (refuse to win the trick) until the second time you lead the suit. Since you have only two diamonds and there are no entry cards in dummy, you will never be able to win more than one diamond trick.

(14) Pass. A bid in a new suit is forcing, so if you bid 3♡ partner will probably bid something at the four-level when you are already overboard at the three-level. Count your tricks: partner says he can win six if the hand is played in diamonds and you have one and one-half tricks (♡ A Q); the best you can hope for is that the heart finesse will work and partner can win eight tricks for down one. However, if you bid 3♡ and partner has hand #11 he will bid 4◇ and be set at least two tricks, and he may be doubled.

(15) This is a rare hand type with which you should bid a new suit. You want to reach game in one of the majors, so bid 3♠ (forcing). If partner does not raise spades, bid 4♡ at your next turn. Partner should then take a choice by bidding 4♠ with equal or greater length in spades, or passing 4♡ with greater length in hearts.

The preceding examples illustrate how to respond to preempts when you have a good hand. Your goal is to arrive in a good game or slam contract. But it is often right to raise your partner's suit with a weak hand *provided you have three or more cards in his suit.* These raises are designed to make it even more difficult for the opponents to bid accurately, or to take a sacrifice—bid to a contract which if doubled and set will be less expensive than allowing the opponents to play and make their contract. You will read about sacrifice bids when you get to Chapter Ten.

REBIDS AFTER A PREEMPTIVE OPENING BID

A rule to remember: When opening with a preemptive bid, *bid as high as you dare the first time and then shut up!* Do not bid again unless your partner enters the bidding; for example, if he bids a new suit below game you must bid again. Responder has a good picture of opener's hand, while the opener knows nothing about responder's hand. Logically, responder should be in complete charge of the subsequent bidding; he is the captain.

WEAK TWO-BIDS

The old-fashioned way to handle very strong hands was to open the bidding with two of any long suit. Opening bids of 2♣, 2◇, 2♡ and 2♠ were all strong, natural and forcing. But it has been proven that there is no need to waste four bids to show a strong hand, so a vast majority of good players now use opening bids of 2◇, 2♡ and 2♠ as "weak two-bids," and 2♣ as the only strong two-bid. This is what I recommend that you do, as outlined in the following pages.

Opening bids of 2◇, 2♡ and 2♠ show a hand with a good six-card suit and 5-10 *high-card* points (a hand too weak to open the bidding with a one-bid). It is inadvisable to make a weak two-bid in first- or second-seat with a side four-card major.

You might say that a weak two-bid is a "mini-preempt" hoping to confuse the opponents' bidding. As with preemptive bids at the three-level and higher, how daring you should be is governed by the vulnerability.

Test Yourself

As dealer, what do you open, if anything, with each of the following hands? Give more than one answer if vulnerability influences your decision.

(16) ♠ 8 7
♡ K 9 5
◇ A Q J 10 6 3
♣ 4 2

(17) ♠ K 10 7 6 4 3
♡ 8
◇ Q 9 6 3
♣ 7 2

(18) ♠ 7
♡ A J 9 8 7 5 3
◇ J 4 3
♣ 10 2

(19) ♠ 7 6
♡ A K 9 6 5 2
◇ A J 4
♣ 10 3

Solutions

(16) Bid 2◊ regardless of the vulnerability with this very good
      six-card suit and ten high-card points; a "maximum" weak
      two-bid.

(17) Bid 2♠ at favorable vulnerability—the opponents are vulnerable
      and your side is not. You have a poor six-card suit and only five
      high-card points, so you should pass with any other
      vulnerability.

(18) Bid 3♡ with favorable vulnerability, but bid only 2♡ with equal
      or unfavorable vulnerability. It is seldom right to make a weak
      two-bid with a seven-card suit, but this hand does not measure
      up to bidding 3♡ unless the vulnerability is favorable.

(19) Bid 1♡, regardless of the vulnerability. This hand is too strong
      for a weak two-bid in first, second or third seat. But in
      fourth-seat only (after the other three players have passed), an
      opening suit bid of two shows a reasonably good hand; good
      enough to expect a plus score. Hands #16, #17 and #18 should
      be passed in fourth seat, but it is all right to open #19 with 2♡.

RESPONSES TO WEAK TWO-BIDS

The possibilities are: raise partner's suit, bid a new suit, bid a game
directly, bid 2NT, or pass:

* Raise your partner's suit to the three-level with good trump
  support (three or more trumps) and poor defensive strength.
  This is not a constructive bid; in fact, you fully expect your
  partner to be set by one or more tricks. The opponents probably
  can make a game, and the purpose of your raise is to deprive
  them of bidding space, or even maybe to block them out of the
  bidding entirely. With especially good trump support and
  distribution you should raise to game (the higher you bid, the
  harder it will be for the opponents to get into the bidding), and
  consider a sacrifice bid if the opponents bid a game or a slam.
  Raising partner's suit does not invite him to bid again, in fact
  he is barred from bidding again when you raise his suit.

* Bid a new strong six-card suit (rarely a strong five-card suit).
  A nonforcing bid, but partner may raise your suit with three

trumps or a doubleton honor, or rebid his very strong six-card suit without support for you.

    (**NOTE:** A popular variation is to play that a new-suit response to a weak two-bid is forcing. I prefer the nonforcing style, but you should discuss this with your regular partners.)

* Bid game directly if you know where to play it.

* Bid 2NT when you have a strong hand but are unsure whether or not to bid a game, or which game to bid. The 2NT response is an artificial bid which says nothing about your distribution—you could have a balanced hand, or some extraordinary distribution such as 6-5-1-1. In fact it is not a "telling bid," it is an "asking bid," asking the opening bidder to further describe his hand. After opener's rebid (explained in the following pages), you will be in a better position to decide the best contract.

* Pass when your hand does not qualify for any of the above bids. Let the weak two-bid take its effect on the opponents.

Test Yourself

With neither side vulnerable your partner opens the bidding 2♡ and your right-hand opponent passes. What do you bid, if anything, with each of the following hands?

(20) ♠ 7 2   (21) ♠ K 7 6 5 3 2   (22) ♠ A K J 9 5 2
    ♡ K 10 5   ♡ K 5 3 2   ♡ 7 4
    ◇ A Q 8 3   ◇ 8 5   ◇ 10 3
    ♣ 9 6 5 4   ♣ 6   ♣ 9 8 4

(23) ♠ A Q 7 6   (24) ♠ A Q 9 8 5 2   (25) ♠ K 10 9 6
    ♡ A 9 6   ♡ 7 3   ♡ 3
    ◇ 5 2   ◇ A K J   ◇ A K 5 2
    ♣ K J 8 3   ♣ K Q   ♣ K 8 7 2

Solutions

(20) Bid 3♡. With equal vulnerability partner is presumably overbidding by three tricks—he can win five tricks if hearts are

trump. Since your hand will probably produce two or three tricks, the 3♡ contract figures to be set by one or two tricks. Yet with three trumps, 3♡ is a good bid. The opponents have eight, nine or ten spades between them and your only possible defensive tricks are the ace and queen of diamonds. Unless partner can win at least two tricks (unlikely), the opponents can make 4♠ if they bid it. You do not want them to bid and hope your 3♡ bid will shut them out. If the opponents double 3♡ and set the contract by one or two tricks, the minus score will be smaller than the one you would get if they bid and make 4♠.

(21) Bid 4♡. With such good trump support and distribution, you should raise to game. This time you have virtually no defensive strength and the opponents can almost surely make a game, or maybe even a slam. You are hoping to shut the opponents out of the bidding, and the higher you bid the more likely you are to succeed. Partner figures to be set a trick or two in 4♡ (although he may have the magic hand and make it), but even if the opponents double and set the contract you will lose less than if they were to bid and make a game.

(22) Bid 2♠ with this good six-card suit. A new-suit bid is not forcing.

(23) Before deciding what you should bid, let us talk about point count. A weak two-bid shows 5-10 *high-card* points, and this may seem strange to you because in all other areas of bidding we have counted points for long cards as well. But counting just high-card points is the popular way to value a hand for weak two-bids. Do not forget, when your partner opens the bidding with a weak two-bid he has a six-card suit which is worth two points; so his actual point count is 7-12, not 5-10.

Now consider that partner would revalue his hand and add extra points for short suits if you raised his suit. Since you have good trump support (♡A 9 6), you should give your partner those two extra points for short suits (he has only seven cards outside his six-card suit, so he must have a void, a singleton, or two doubletons). Now partner has a hand that is actually worth 9-14, not 5-10. You have 14 and 26 is required to bid game. If partner has a maximum (12-14), you should bid 4♡; if he has a minimum (9-11), you want to play 3♡.

The way to find out whether partner has a minimum or a maximum weak two-bid is to bid 2NT. He is still thinking of valuing his hand by high-card points: if he has a minimum (5-7 high-card points), he will rebid his suit at the three-level; if he has a maximum (8-10 high-card points), he will bid a new suit or 3NT. Therefore, you should bid 2NT with this hand: if partner bids 3♡, pass; if he bids anything else, bid 4♡.

(24) Bid 2NT. You certainly want to reach game with this powerful hand, and partner might pass if you bid 2♠. After partner's next bid you will bid 3♠ to show your long spade suit, and that bid is forcing. Opener's third bid will help you place the contract in the best game.

(25) Pass. This is a "misfit." Without support for your partner's suit, or a good suit of your own, you need a much stronger hand than this to bid anything.

REBIDS BY THE WEAK TWO-BIDDER

When partner raises your suit (you-2♠, partner-3♠, you-?), you are barred from bidding again.

When partner bids a new suit (you-2♡; partner-2♠, 3♣ or 3◊; you-?), his bid is not forcing but he has a very good suit. In most cases you should pass, but you ought to raise his suit with three trumps or a doubleton honor (such as K x) and a maximum weak-two bid. It is acceptable to rebid a *very strong* six-card suit—such as K Q J 10 x x.

What's left? The forcing 2NT response (you-2♠, partner-2NT, you-?). When partner responds 2NT, rebid three of your long suit with a minimum (5-7 high-card points), and rebid in a new suit containing a "feature"—ace or king—with a maximum (8-10 high-card points). If you have a maximum and a very good suit (such as A K Q x x x, or A K J 10 x x), rebid 3NT.

Test Yourself

With both sides vulnerable, your partner answers your 2♡ opening bid with 2NT. What is your rebid?

(26) ♠ 8 4	(27) ♠ 4	(28) ♠ 8 3
♡ Q J 8 7 5 3	♡ K Q 10 8 5 2	♡ A K Q 10 9 5
◇ A 6 4	◇ 9 6 4	◇ 7 5 2
♣ 10 5	♣ A 7 6	♣ 6 4

(26) Rebid 3♡ with seven high-card points, to show a minimum weak two.

(27) Rebid 3♣ with nine high-card points, to show a maximum weak two bid and a "feature" (ace or king) in the bid suit.

(28) Rebid 3NT to show a *very strong* six-card suit.

THE STRONG, ARTIFICIAL 2♣ OPENING BID

An opening suit bid of one shows 13-22 points. When your hand is too strong to begin with a suit bid of one, open the bidding with 2♣. The 2♣ opening is artificial—it has nothing to do with how many clubs you hold—and shows one of two types of hands:

* A balanced hand with 23 or more points.

* An unbalanced hand with 23 or more points, but you may shade it down to 21 or 22 points with one long and strong major suit, or a very good two-suited hand.

RESPONSES TO OPENING 2♣ BIDS

The negative response: If responder has a poor hand, seven *high-card* points or less, he makes the "negative response" by bidding 2◇. This is another artificial bid—it has nothing to do with the number of diamonds responder holds. (If the responder's right-hand opponent bids over 2♣, pass becomes the negative response.)

The positive response: With eight *high-card* points or more, or seven *high-card* points consisting of an ace and a king, responder makes a "positive response" by bidding 2♡, 2♠, 3♣ or 3◇ to show length in that suit, or by bidding 2NT to show a balanced hand.

Test Yourself

Partner opens the bidding with 2♣ and your right-hand opponent passes. What is your response with each of the following hands?

(29) ♠ 7 6 2   (30) ♠ K J 2   (31) ♠ K J 9 8 4 3
      ♡ 6 3   ♡ 9 7 6 4 3   ♡ 7
      ◊ 9 8 5 4   ◊ 4   ◊ Q 6
      ♣ J 8 7 3   ♣ J 8 7 3   ♣ 8 5 3 2

(32) ♠ A 10 6 4 3 (33) ♠ 7   (34) ♠ K 9 7
      ♡ 6 5   ♡ J 10 2   ♡ 10 6 5 4
      ◊ 9 8 2   ◊ A K J 9 4   ◊ Q 8
      ♣ K 7 4   ♣ J 8 5 2   ♣ A 10 5 2

Solutions

(29) Bid 2◊ with one high-card point; the negative response.

(30) Bid 2◊ with five high-card points.

(31) Bid 2◊ with six high-card points. After partner's rebid you will show your long spade suit.

(32) Bid 2♠ with seven high-card points. You normally need at least eight high-card points to make a positive response, but seven is enough when you have an ace and a king.

(33) Bid 3◊ with 10 high-card points. To show a positive response in diamonds you must jump the bidding because 2◊ is the negative response.

(34) Bid 2NT with nine high-card points and a balanced hand.

REBIDS BY THE OPENING 2♣ BIDDER

It is opener's second bid that begins to describe his distribution. With a balanced hand he rebids 2NT with 23-24 points, 3NT with 25-27 points, and 4NT with 28-30 points. Otherwise he bids 2♡, 2♠, 3♣ or 3◊ to show length in the bid suit (these new-suit bids are forcing).

Test Yourself

You open the bidding with 2♣ and partner responds 2◊—an artificial bid showing 0-7 high-card points. What do you rebid with each of the following hands?

(35) ♠ A 10 5   (36) ♠ A Q   (37) ♠ A Q
     ♡ A K Q   ♡ A K 9   ♡ A K Q J
     ◇ A Q J   ◇ A Q J 6   ◇ K Q 2
     ♣ K 7 4 3   ♣ K Q 10 4   ♣ A K J 10

(38) ♠ K 8   (39) ♠ A Q 9 8 7 (40) ♠ 7
     ♡ A K Q 9 7 5   ♡ A K Q 9 4   ♡ A K Q J
     ◇ A Q 6   ◇ A J   ◇ A K J 9 8 5
     ♣ K 2   ♣ 3   ♣ A J

Solutions

(35) Bid 2NT, showing a balanced hand with 23-24 points. *This bid is not forcing,* but partner should bid again with three points or more, or maybe with less if he has a long major suit. If responder does bid again he should bid the same way he would if partner had opened the bidding with 2NT (including Stayman), except he knows his partner has 23-24 points, rather than 20-22. (If partner's response had been 2♡ or 2♠, you would still rebid 2NT; if it was 3♣ or 3◇, you would rebid 3NT.)

(36) Bid 3NT, showing a balanced hand with 25-27 points.

(37) Bid 4NT, showing a balanced hand with 28-30 points. Partner should bid a slam with five points or more, or maybe with four.

(38) Bid 2♡ with 23 points, a forcing bid. *If opener rebids his suit (in this case bids 3♡ at his next turn), responder may pass with a completely worthless hand. If, however, the opening bidder makes any other bid, responder is not allowed to pass below game, not even with zero points.*

(39) Bid 2♠ with 22 points. Consistent with other areas of bidding, bid the higher ranking of two five-card suits first. Your plan is to bid hearts next.

(40) Bid 3◇ with 25 points. Partner's 2◇ bid was artificial, so your 3◇ bid is the same as bidding a new suit. However, if the hand is played in diamonds, your partner will be declarer.

IN REVIEW

Opening preemptive bids: An opening suit bid in a major suit at the three- or four-level, or in a minor suit at the three- four- or five-level, is preemptive, showing a hand with a very long suit (usually seven or eight cards) and a limited number of high cards—a maximum of ten *high-card* points.

* The opening bidder should value his hand by estimating how many tricks he thinks he will win if his long suit is trump, not by counting points.

* Vulnerability determines how high you should bid. Estimate how many tricks you think you can win and if your side is vulnerable and the opponents are not, overbid by two tricks; with equal vulnerability, overbid by three tricks; and if your side is not vulnerable and the opponents are, overbid by three, four, or perhaps even five tricks.

Responses to opening preemptive bids: Value your hand by counting tricks, not points. In the side suits count quick tricks: A K = two tricks; A Q = one and one-half tricks; A or KQ = one trick; and K x = one-half trick. In partner's long suit, count one trick for the king or queen. If you have trump support for partner's suit, count tricks for singletons or voids.

* If partner opens with three of a major suit (3♡ or 3♠), add your tricks to the number of tricks partner should have for his preemptive bid and pass or raise his suit; it is rarely right to bid 3NT or a new suit.

* If partner opens with three of a minor suit (3♣ or 3♢) and you have a strong hand, it is all right to bid 3NT with a fit in partner's suit (at least K x or x x x) and stoppers in the other three suits. A bid in a new suit below game shows a long and strong suit and a good hand; it is forcing unless you are a passed hand.

Rebids by the opening preemptive bidder: You are barred from bidding again if your partner does not enter the bidding. Even if he has bid you should be reluctant to bid again unless his bid was forcing.

Weak two-bids: Opening bids of 2◇, 2♡ and 2♠ are weak two-bids. The requirements are a long suit (usually six cards), and 5-10 high-card points.

Responses to weak two-bids: Raise your partner's suit with poor defensive strength and three or more trumps. Bid a good six-card or longer suit (rarely a very strong five-card suit). Bid game directly if you know where to play it. Bid 2NT with a strong hand to inquire whether partner has a minimum or a maximum weak two-bid.

Rebids by the weak-two bidder: If partner raises your suit, always pass. If partner bids a new suit his bid is not forcing, but you may raise his suit with three or more trumps, or with a doubleton honor, and you may rebid a very strong six-card suit. If partner bids 2NT you are forced to bid again: to show a minimum (5-7 high-card points), rebid three of your suit; to show a maximum (8-10 high-card points), bid a new suit containing a "feature" (ace or king), or rebid 3NT to show an excellent suit—such as A K Q x x x.

The 2♣ opening bid: An opening bid of 2♣ is artificial (it has nothing to do with the number of clubs). It shows a very strong hand—23 or more points—but may be shaded down to 21-22 with a good six-card major suit, or with two long and strong five-card suits (especially if they are major suits).

Responses to 2♣ opening bids: The "negative response" is 2◇, showing 0-7 *high-card* points. Any other bid is natural and a "positive response," showing eight or more *high-card* points, or seven points with an ace and a king.

Rebids by the 2♣ bidder: With a balanced hand: rebid 2NT with 23-24 points, 3NT with 25-27 points, and 4NT with 28-30 points. Otherwise rebid a long suit.

PRACTICE DEAL

Contract: 4♠

Opening lead: ◊J

North
♠ 8 4 3
♡ K 7 2
◊ 9 6 5
♣ Q 6 4 3

West
♠ Q 10 5
♡ J 9 6 4
◊ J 10 7
♣ K 8 7

East
♠ J 9
♡ 10 3
◊ K Q 8 2
♣ J 10 9 5 2

South
♠ A K 7 6 2
♡ A Q 8 5
◊ A 4 3
♣ A

West	North	East	South
—	—	—	2♣
Pass	2◊	Pass	2♠
Pass	3♠	Pass	4♠
All Pass			

The bidding: South opens 2♣, and, after his partner's negative 2◊ response, he rebids 2♠. North is forced to bid again regardless of his point count and raises to 3♠. South bids game.

The opening lead: West leads the ◊J because leading the top of a two-card sequence is less likely to jeopardize a trick than leading any of the other suits (although, in this case leading a different suit would do no damage).

The play: This is another hand about trump management. Declarer must lose two diamonds and one spade (if he loses two spade tricks, the contract is hopeless, so he must rely on a 3-2 spade break). If hearts do not divide 3-3, the fourth heart in his hand will be lost unless he ruffs it in dummy. The best line of play to avoid losing a heart trick is to win the first trick with the ◇A and cash the ♠A and ♠K. The spades divide 3-2, so the contract is safe. Declarer cashes the three top hearts to learn that suit does not divide three-three, so he leads the fourth heart and ruffs it with dummy's last spade. He still has to lose the two diamonds and one spade, but that is all. Note that if declarer did not cash the two high spades before leading three rounds of hearts he would lose two trump tricks and be set—East would ruff the third heart trick and West would still have a trick with his ♠Q.

The key plays: Cashing the ♠A and ♠K before running the heart suit, and ruffing the fourth heart in dummy.

CHAPTER EIGHT

SLAM BIDDING

THE REQUIREMENTS TO BID SLAMS

To bid a small slam in a suit, the requirements are:
* A good trump suit.
* 33 points or more (including distributional points) in the combined hands.
* The opponents cannot win the first two tricks.

The scoring table makes it desirable to bid a small slam if you think you have better than an even chance to make it.

To bid a grand slam in a suit: You need 37 or more points and first-round control of every suit, but when many of your points are being counted for distribution it is dangerous to bid seven unless you have figured out in advance that 13 tricks are available.

To bid 6NT or 7NT: The bidding target for 6NT is 33 high-card points, and for 7NT it is 37, but you may bid a slam in notrump with fewer high cards if you have a long, strong suit and good controls (aces and kings) in the side suits. However, if the combined hands have eight cards or more in one suit, it is usually better to play in a trump contract.

SLAM BIDDING PROCEDURES
There are five basic approaches to slam bidding:
* Bid a slam directly.
* Keep the bidding low to save bidding space, *but be sure your bids are forcing.*
* Use the Blackwood Convention, or the Gerber Convention.
* Make a quantitative raise of a notrump bid.
* Make a control-showing bid (a cue-bid).
These bids are all explained in the following pages:

BID A SLAM DIRECTLY

Bid a slam directly if the combined hands meet all of the requirements. For example:

(1)   ♠ A 10 9 8 6   You   Partner
         ♡ A Q 4   1♠   3♠
         ◇ A K 5 2   ?
         ♣ 7

This hand meets all three requirements to bid 6♠ directly. Partner has at least four spades, so spades will make a good trump suit. You have 20 points (17 in high cards, one for the five-card suit, and two for the singleton) and partner's 3♠ bid showed 13-16; the total point count is between 33 and 36. You have three aces and a singleton club, so the opponents cannot win the first two tricks.

(2)   Partner   You   ♠ K J 10
         1NT   ?   ♡ A Q 7
                                 ◇ K 8 4 3
                                 ♣ K Q 2

Bid 6NT directly with this balanced hand. Partner has 15-17 points and you have 18. The combined total is 33, 34 or 35. Note that you do not have to worry about losing the first two tricks—the opponents have at most seven points between them; they cannot have two aces.

KEEP THE BIDDING LOW

Keep the bidding as low as possible when you do not know which trump suit to play. For example:

(3)   Partner   You   ♠ K Q 3
         1◇   ?   ♡ A Q 9 7 6
                                 ◇ 7
                                 ♣ A K Q 10

You have 21 points and intend to bid a slam before you are through. It is you who must decide which trump suit (or notrump) to play and whether to bid six or seven, so bid just 1♡ to evoke a natural second bid from partner and save bidding space. In the subsequent bidding, it may be necessary to make other bids below slam to learn more about partner's hand. Just make sure that you never make a bid below slam that your partner is allowed to pass—new-suit bids (unless partner has rebid 1NT) and jump bids below game are forcing, but bids at the game-level are not.

THE BLACKWOOD CONVENTION

Blackwood is a convention used to find out how many aces and kings your partner holds. A bid of 4NT asks about aces and partner responds in "steps" beginning with the lowest possible bid, as follows:

5♣ shows	no aces, or all four aces
5♢ shows	one ace
5♡ shows	two aces
5♠ shows	three ace

When to Use Blackwood: The right time to bid 4NT to ask for aces is when your hand meets the following four requirements:

* You do not have two quick losers in an unbid suit. Holdings such as Q J x or x x should rule out Blackwood.
* Your hand does not contain a void. Partner's response will tell you how many aces he has, not which aces. If he holds the ace in your void suit it may be worthless.
* You know the intended trump suit and are reasonably sure the combined hands have at least 33 points. You will then be prepared to bid a slam if no more than one ace is missing, or to play at the five-level if two aces are missing.
* Partner's last bid was not a natural bid of 1NT, 2NT or 3NT, and your own last bid was not 2♣ Stayman. In these situations 4NT is used as the "quantitative raise," it is not Blackwood.

The following hand is perfect for Blackwood:

(4)	Partner	You	♠ K 9 8 6 5
	1♠	?	♡ A K Q 8 7 2
			◇ 3
			♣ 7

Bid 4NT. If partner bids 5◇ to shows one ace, sign off in 5♠. If he bids 5♡ to show two aces, bid 6♠. If he bids 5♠ to show three aces, bid 7♠. If he bids 5♣ to show no aces, sue Mr. Blackwood.

How to ask for kings: If you have bid 4NT and found out how many aces your partner has and follow with a bid of 5NT, then, *and only then,* the 5NT bid asks for kings. The 5NT Blackwood bid is rare; *it should be used only when your side has all four aces and you are interested in bidding a grand slam.*

The responses to 5NT are also in bidding steps:

6♣ shows	no kings
6◇ shows	one king
6♡ shows	two kings
6♠ shows	three kings
6NT shows	four kings

Here is an illustration:

(5)	♠ A 9 8 3	Partner	You	♠ K Q 10 7 2
	♡ A 10	1♣	1♠	♡ K Q 3
	◇ A 6 5	4♠	4NT	◇ K 4
	♣ A K 7 2	5♣	5NT	♣ Q 9 5 2
		6◇	?	

Bid 7NT. Partner's 5♣ bid showed all four aces. Now, you can see that 13 tricks are available if partner has the ♣K. Hence your 5NT bid. His 6◇ bid showed that he has the missing king; you bid 7NT (not 7♠) because it is a safer contract and you will get a 150-point bonus for partner having all four aces. If partner did not have the ♣K he would have bid 6♣ and you would have settled for a small slam.

THE QUANTITATIVE RAISE

A 4NT bid is not always Blackwood. As explained in Chapter Three, if your partner's last bid was 1NT, 2NT or 3NT, a raise to 4NT invites 6NT. Partner should pass 4NT with a minimum point count, or bid 6NT with a maximum. The only other time 4NT is a quantitative raise is when your own last bid was 2♣ (Stayman); be sure to get it straight. Here are two examples of the quantitative raise:

(6)	Partner	You	♠ K Q 10
	1NT	?	♡ A J 7
			♦ A Q 8 3
			♣ 6 5 2

Bid 4NT with 16 points. Your partner's opening 1NT bid showed 15-17 points, and your 4NT response shows a balanced hand with 16-17 points. Your partner should pass 4NT with only 15 points, bid 6NT with 17 points, and use his skillful judgment with 16 points.

(7)	Partner	You	♠ A J 8 5
	1NT	2♣	♡ K Q 6 4
	2♦	?	♦ 7 2
			♣ A Q J

Bid 4NT with 17 points. Your plan was to bid a slam in a major suit if partner answered your Stayman bid with 2♡ or 2♠. But when he responds 2♦ to deny a four-card major suit, you bid 4NT as a quantitative raise—inviting partner to pass with a minimum notrump opening, or to bid 6NT with a maximum. If you had one more point, you should bid 6NT yourself.

THE GERBER CONVENTION

Gerber is a way to find out how many aces your partner has, as is Blackwood, but 4♣ is the asking bid. Gerber is used in most auctions where a 4NT bid would serve as a quantitative raise, not Blackwood. More specifically, the only time a 4♣ bid is used to ask for aces is when your partner's last bid was 1NT or 2NT, or your own last bid was a 2♣ Stayman bid. *Note that 4♣ is never Gerber unless it is a jump bid.* If partner's last bid was 3NT, a bid of 4♣ is not Gerber.

You may be thinking that it is better to use Gerber all of the time, instead of Blackwood, because it keeps the bidding lower. This is not true—4♣ is too important as a natural bid to show clubs, or as a cue-bid, to give it up entirely to ask for aces. Therefore, it is only used to cover most of the situations when a 4NT bid does not ask for aces.

The responses to a 4♣ Gerber bid are in bidding steps beginning with the lowest possible bid, as they are in Blackwood.

4◇ shows	no aces, or all four aces
4♡ shows	one ace
4♠ shows	two aces
4N shows	three aces

Here is one example:

(8)   Partner   You   ♠ K Q J 10 7 4
         1NT   ?   ♡ 7
                                               ◇ K Q J 3
                                               ♣ K 2

Bid 4♣, Gerber. If partner responds 4♠ to show two aces, pass; if he responds 4NT to show three aces, bid 6♠; if he responds 4◇ to show four aces you have 13 top tricks, so bid 7NT. Note that the opponents cannot have more than two aces because only 8, 9 or 10 high-card points are missing (you have 15 and partner has 15-17).

CONTROL-SHOWING BIDS (CUE-BIDS)

If you or your partner has raised a major suit at the three-level or higher, a new suit bid is a slam try showing first-round control—*an ace or a void.* If you or your partner has raised the other's minor suit at the three-level or higher, a new suit bid *at the four-level or higher* is a slam try showing first-round control. Remember that after a minor suit has been raised, a new-suit bid *below 3NT* is not a slam try—it shows a stopper. The following three examples show when control-showing bids should be used in preference to Blackwood.

(9)   ♠ A Q 10 9 6 2   You   Partner
   ♡ 9 4   1♠   3♠
   ◇ K 8   ?
   ♣ A K 3

Bid 4♣. Partner's raise showed at least four trumps, so you have ten spades between you. The combined point count is 33-36—you have 20 points (16 in high cards, two for the six-card suit, and two for the two doubletons) and partner's bid showed 13-16 points. But that does not entitle you to bid a slam because you might lose the first two tricks. Bidding 4NT (Blackwood) is wrong because of your heart holding; if you bid 4NT and partner shows one ace by bidding 5◇, he might have the ◇A and you could lose the first two heart tricks. The right bid is 4♣, showing first-round control of clubs, interest in bidding a slam, and asking partner to cue-bid his first-round controls.

(10)   ♠ A K Q 7 6 5   You   Partner
   ♡ —   2♣   2♡
   ◇ K 6   2♠   3♠
   ♣ A K Q 8 2   ?

Make a control-showing bid of 4♣. If partner bids 4◇ to show that ace, bid 7♠. But if he bids 4♡ to show the ♡A, or 4♠ to deny holding either ace, you should bid just 6♠. Once again it is wrong to use Blackwood. If you bid 4NT and partner responds 5◇ to show one ace, you will not know whether he has the ♡A or ◇A. *Do not use Blackwood when you have a void—you are interested in which ace partner has, not how many.*

(11)   ♠ K Q 9 8 4 3   You   Partner
   ♡ K Q 2   1♠   3♠
   ◇ A 10 4   ?
   ♣ 7

Bid 4◇. This time you do not have two quick losers in an unbid suit and you do not have a void, but you still should not use Blackwood because you are not sure the combined hands have 33 points; your 18 added to partner's 13-16 totals 31-34. You may, however, make a control-showing bid below game to try for slam. If partner follows your 4◊ bid with 4♡ to show that ace, bid 4♠. You have already made a slam try and now you are putting the brakes on. Partner is invited to bid again with a maximum 3♠ bid (15-16 quality points), or to pass 4♠ with a minimum.

Now suppose partner bids 4♠ over your 4◊ bid. That bid denies the ♡A and discourages slam, so you should pass 4♠. But if he bids 5♣—goes beyond game—he not only shows the ♣A, but also a maximum 3♠ bid (15-16 quality points); you should bid 6♠.

Note that if you add two points to this hand so you have 20 points (maybe change the diamonds to ◊A Q 4), the combined total would be 33-36 and it would be appropriate to bid 4NT (Blackwood) over partner's 3♠ bid. *To use Blackwood you must bid beyond game, and that is something you should not do unless you are reasonably sure the combined hands have 33 points or more.*

Now let's move to the other side of the table. The next three examples show how you should bid if your partner makes the 4◊ cue-bid as shown in #11:

	Partner	You
	1♠	3♠
	4◊	?

(12) ♠ A 10 6 5	(13) ♠ A 10 6 5	(14) ♠ A 10 6 5
♡ A 6	♡ 4 2	♡ 4 2
◊ Q 8 3	◊ Q 8 3	◊ K 8 3
♣ Q 10 4 2	♣ A Q 10 6	♣ A K 10 6

(12) Bid 4♡ to show that ace. You have a minimum three-spade bid—13 points—but cue-bidding the ♡A does not promise extra values because you are not bidding beyond game. If partner's next bid is 4♠, you should pass.

(13) Bid 4♠, which denies possession of the ♡A, and discourages partner from bidding a slam (it does *not* necessarily show the

♠A). It would be wrong to cue-bid 5♣—to make the first bid beyond game—because you have a minimum 3♠ bid (13 points). When your partner makes a control-showing bid, the best way to discourage him from bidding a slam is to return to the agreed suit—in this case bid 4♠.

(14) Bid 5♣. Replacing the minor-suit queens shown in #13 with minor-suit kings improves this hand dramatically. With 15 quality points (a maximum 3♠ bid with three and one-half quick tricks), you should bid 5♣ to show that ace and encourage partner to bid a slam.

Note that if partner has hand #11, a slam can be made with #14 but not with hands 12 or 13.

Show second-round control: When you bid a suit in which you or your partner have already made a control-showing bid, it shows second-round control—*the king or a singleton.* These bids are especially useful when investigating a grand slam. Here are two examples:

(15)	Partner	You		
	1♡	3♡	♠	A K J 2
	4♣	4♠	♡	K J 9 8
	5◊	?	◊	Q 10 3
			♣	7 6

Why is partner bidding 5◊ when he already knows the opponents cannot win the first two tricks? Answer, he is trying for a grand slam and wants to hear about your second-round controls. So you bid 5♠, to show second-round control of spades. If you held the ♣K, you would bid 6♣; if you held the ◊K, you would bid 6◊; with no second-round controls, you would bid 5♡.

(16)	♠ A K 10 7 6 4	Partner	You	♠ J 9 8 2
	♡ K 2	1♠	3♠	♡ A J 6
	◊ A Q 9 8 3	4◊	4♡	◊ K 7
	♣ —	5♣	?	♣ Q J 10 2

Bid 5◇, to show second-round control. This time partner's hand is shown so you can see that he can visualize a grand slam if you have two key cards, the ♡A and the ◇K; and he has bid well to find out. He can assume no spade losers—your 3♠ bid promised at least four spades and it is very unlikely that he will lose a spade trick. If you did not bid 4♡ to show the ♡A, and follow his 5♣ bid with 5◇ to show the ◇K, he would bid just 6♠. As it is, he of course bids 7♠.

IN REVIEW

The three requirements to bid a small slam in a suit are: You have found a good trump suit; the combined hands have 33 points or more; and the opponents will not be able to win the first two tricks.

The point-count requirement to bid a grand slam in a suit is 37 points or more. However, since many points are being counted for distribution, it is dangerous to bid seven unless you have figured out in advance how you are going to win all 13 tricks.

The bidding target for six notrump is 33 high-card points, and for seven notrump it is 37 high-card points. You may bid a slam in notrump with fewer high-card points if you have a long, strong suit and good controls (aces and kings) in the side suits.

There are five ways to approach slam bidding:
* Bid a slam directly if the hands meet all of the requirements.
* Keep the bidding as low as possible when you do not know the intended trump suit.
* Use the Blackwood Convention, or the Gerber Convention, to find out how many aces and kings your partner has.
* Raise partner's notrump bid to 4NT. This is the quantitative raise, inviting partner to bid 6NT with a maximum point count, or pass 4NT with a minimum.
* Make a control-showing bid—a cue-bid—if you and your partner both know the intended trump suit. This informs partner that you are interested in bidding a slam and begins an exchange of information to make sure the combined hands have

the point-count needed to bid a slam, and enough controls so the opponents will not be able to beat the contract before you get the lead.

PRACTICE DEAL

Contract: 6♡
Opening lead: ◊2

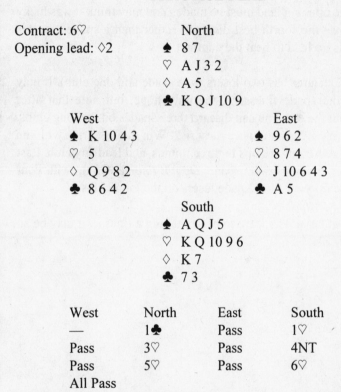

North
♠ 8 7
♡ A J 3 2
◊ A 5
♣ K Q J 10 9

West
♠ K 10 4 3
♡ 5
◊ Q 9 8 2
♣ 8 6 4 2

East
♠ 9 6 2
♡ 8 7 4
◊ J 10 6 4 3
♣ A 5

South
♠ A Q J 5
♡ K Q 10 9 6
◊ K 7
♣ 7 3

West	North	East	South
—	1♣	Pass	1♡
Pass	3♡	Pass	4NT
Pass	5♡	Pass	6♡
All Pass			

The bidding: North's jump-raise to 3♡ shows 17-19 points and at least four hearts. South started with 16 points, but after his suit is raised he adds two points for the two doubletons—and that gives him 18. South knows the combined total is 35, 36 or 37, enough to bid a slam, but to make sure he does not lose the first two tricks he bids 4NT to ask for aces (since North bid clubs, South is willing to use Blackwood with two little clubs). When his partner bids 5♡ to show two aces, he bids the slam.

The opening lead: There is no good lead here. A singleton trump is usually a poor lead because it could jeopardize a trump trick for partner (who might have Q x x), and leading a club (dummy's bid suit) should be ruled out. Leading a spade from the king or a diamond from the queen are questionable choices, but they are the two unbid suits and the opening lead must be made. You may think it was lucky that we chose the fourth best diamond rather than a spade, but this time there is no lead to beat the contract.

The play: Declarer has two losers (one spade and one club). It may seem that the spade finesse is the only hope, but note that after knocking out the ♣A you can discard three spades on the long clubs. The spade finesse is an unnecessary risk. Win the first trick with the ◇K, draw the missing trumps in three rounds, and lead any club. East will take his ♣A and lead a spade. *Do not finesse.* Go up with your ♠A and discard your three spade losers on the long clubs.

As a general rule: Think twice before taking a finesse; it may be an unnecessary risk.

CHAPTER NINE

OVERCALLS AND TAKEOUT DOUBLES

So far we have covered how to bid when *your* side opens the bidding. Now we will discuss how to bid when *their* side opens. The two common ways to enter the bidding are the "overcall" and the "takeout double." The requirements are quite liberal and it pays to get into the bidding early and often for several reasons: you may bid and make a contract your way; you may have a good sacrifice (bid to a contract which if doubled and set will cut your losses); you may push the opponents too high and set them; or, if outbid, your overcall may indicate a good opening lead to your partner.

OVERCALLS IN A SUIT

The requirements for making an overcall vary with the level of bidding and the vulnerability, as illustrated below. If you wish to challenge yourself as you go along, decide what you would bid, if anything, with each hand before reading the analysis.

Overcalls at the one-level: An overcall at the one-level (opponent-1♣; you-1♢, 1♡ or 1♠) is appropriate with from 9-17 points and a five-card or longer suit. With a bad five-card suit you need a better hand—13-17 points. For example, suppose your right-hand opponent opens with 1♢ and you hold:

(1)	♠ 7 4	(2)	♠ 7 4
	♡ K 10 5 4 2		♡ J 6 5 3 2
	♢ 8 6 3		♢ Q 6 3
	♣ A Q 9		♣ A Q 9
(3)	♠ 7 4	(4)	♠ 7 4
	♡ K J 10 5 2		♡ A Q 9 8 5
	♢ 8 6 3		♢ A 6 3
	♣ Q 9 2		♣ A Q 9

(1) Overcall 1♡ with this ten-point hand if not vulnerable, but pass if vulnerable. You need a more substantial suit, or more high cards, to overcall vulnerable.

(2) Pass this ten-point hand, regardless of the vulnerability. Do not overcall with a weak suit and a minimum point count. You are a favorite to be outbid and do not want to encourage your partner to lead a heart. It would be all right to bid 1♡ with this bad five-card suit if you had a better hand. For example, change the diamond holding to ◊A Q x so you have 14 points, and you would overcall 1♡.

(3) Pass, regardless of the vulnerability. It is true that you have an adequate suit and would like to encourage a heart lead, but if you overcall with fewer than nine points you mislead your partner; he will assume that you have a better hand and may bid too much, or double a contract that cannot be set.

(4) Overcall 1♡ with 17 points. This the maximum point-count for an overcall. With a long suit and 18 points or more you should make a takeout double, which is explained later.

Overcalls at the two-level: You need a better "trick-producing" hand to make a nonjump overcall in a suit at the two-level (opponent-1♠, you-2♣, 2◊ or 2♡). The requirements are 11-17 points and usually a six-card or longer suit, but a good five-card suit is adequate with extra strength, or good distribution (something other than 5-3-3-2). Here are four examples. Suppose the bidding is opened with 1♠ by your right-hand opponent and you hold:

(5)	♠ K 3	(6)	♠ K 2
	♡ A Q J 9 8 5		♡ Q 7 6 5 4 3
	◊ 7 5		◊ 7 3
	♣ 10 6 2		♣ A J 10
(7)	♠ 7 4	(8)	♠ J 4 3
	♡ A K J 10 5		♡ K J 7 6 5
	◊ A 6		◊ A Q J
	♣ 9 8 3 2		♣ 9 2

(5) Overcall 2♡ with this excellent six-card heart suit at any vulnerability.

(6) Overcall 2♡ if not vulnerable, but pass if vulnerable with this shaky six-card heart suit.

(7) Overcall 2♡ with this excellent five-card heart suit any time.

(8) Although you have 12 high-card points, you should pass, regardless of the vulnerability. If the opening bid were 1♣, it would be right to overcall 1♡. But to overcall at the two-level you need a better five-card suit, more high cards, or better distribution than 5-3-3-2. Change the heart suit to K J 10 9 8 (good "body cards"), and a 2♡ overcall would be a reasonable risk, especially if not vulnerable.

Overcalls at the three-level and higher: Logically, you need a better hand to chance an overcall at the higher levels of bidding, especially when you are vulnerable. The challenge of whether or not to overcall at the three- or four-level usually comes after an opening preemptive bid. The purpose of the preemptive bid is to deprive your side of bidding space and make it harder to bid accurately. My advice is: do not be timid; aggressive bidders seem to come out on top. (For example, if your right-hand opponent opens the bidding with 3♣, regardless of the vulnerability overcall 3♡ with #5 and #7. But if the opening bid were 3♠, discreetly pass with both hands.)

A time not to overcall: When your right-hand opponent opens the bidding in your long suit, it is usually right to pass, even when you have a strong hand. For example:

(9)	♠ A J 10 9 6	(10)	♠ 7 4
	♡ 4		♡ A Q 5
	◇ A 10 8		◇ 10 8
	♣ A Q 7 2		♣ A Q J 10 9 2

(9) Over an opening bid of 1♣, 1◇ or 1♡, bid 1♠ with this 16-point hand. But *over an opening bid of 1♠, pass.* There is no good bid to describe this hand over a 1♠ opening and the most likely

chance for a profit is to defeat the opponent's contract. You are pretty sure to beat 1♠ if the bidding ends there, and the opponents may get into trouble if they bid further. As the auction progresses, you may decide to make a bid, or double, at a later turn.

(10) Over an opening bid of 1◊, 1♡ or 1♠ bid 2♣. *Over an opening bid of 1♣, pass.* You may be thinking that opener has a short club suit and that you should overcall 2♣! You cannot because an overcall in the opponent's suit is not a natural bid; it is a "cue-bid," showing a very strong hand and it is forcing to game (an illustration is coming up). The way to show that you have a good hand with length in the enemy suit is to pass first and bid their suit at your next turn if the bidding does not get too high. For example:

Opponent	Partner	Opponent	You
—	—	1♣	Pass
1♠	Pass	2♠	?

On this auction you would bid 3♣ over 2♠.

RESPONSES TO OVERCALLS

The four categories of responses to an overcall are: raise partner's suit; bid notrump; bid your own suit; or cue-bid the opponent's suit (i.e., opponent-1♠, partner-2♡, opponent-pass, you-2♠). Here is an example of each. Suppose the bidding goes:

Opponent	Partner	Opponent	You
1◊	1♡	Pass	?

and you hold:

	(11)	♠ A J 8 5	(12)	♠ A 10 5 4
		♡ K 7 4		♡ Q 2
		◊ 10 2		◊ Q J 8
		♣ 10 9 7 6		♣ 9 8 7 3

(13)   ♠ A Q J 10 6   (14)   ♠ K Q J 4
       ♡ 9 6   ♡ 8 3
       ◇ 7 4 2   ◇ A 5
       ♣ K J 8   ♣ A Q 10 6 2

(11)   Bid 2♡ with eight points. When your partner overcalls at the one-level and you have three-card or longer support for his suit, raise to the two-level with 7-11 points, jump-raise to the three-level with 12-14 points, or jump-raise to game (major suit only) with 15 points or more. If partner makes a nonjump overcall at the two-level and you have three or more trumps, raise him to the three-level with 7-11 points, or jump-raise to the four-level with 12-14 points.

(12)   Bid 1NT with nine points. When your partner overcalls in a suit at the one-level, a 1NT response shows 8-11 points; a jump to 2NT shows 12-14; and a jump to 3NT shows 15 points or more. If partner makes a nonjump overcall at the two-level, a 2NT response shows about 9-11 points, and 3NT shows 12 or more. *In all cases, you must have at least one stopper in the enemy suit to bid notrump.*

(13)   Bid 1♠ with 12 points. A response in a new suit shows a good *five-card or longer* suit and 8-13 points, and it is *not forcing*. A jump bid in a new suit shows about 13-15 points and an independently strong suit—such as K Q J 10 x x—but even the jump bid is *not* forcing.

(14)   Bid 2◇ with 17 points. Your hand is strong enough to bid game, but you need more information from partner to decide where to play it. *A cue-bid of the enemy suit is the only way to force your partner to bid again.*

     (**NOTE:** Be sure not to confuse responses to overcalls with responses to opening suit bids of one: when partner opens the bidding with a suit bid of one, responses in a new suit and jump bids are forcing; but when he overcalls, they are not. So if partner overcalls and you want to force him to bid again, you must cue-bid the opponent's suit.)

WEAK JUMP OVERCALLS

If your hand is too strong to overcall (18 points or more), you should make a takeout double with the intention of bidding your long suit at your next turn. Since you do not need two ways to bid a strong hand with a long suit, *a jump overcall in a new suit over an opponent's opening suit bid of one shows a weak hand.* For example, if your right-hand opponent opens 1♡, a jump to 2♠, 3♣ or 3♢ is a "weak-jump overcall." This is contrary to the idea that single-jump bids are strong and it is confusing to some social players even though they have played for many years; but the weak-jump overcall is used by virtually all good players because it gets marvelous results. While a weak-jump overcall describes your hand accurately for partner's benefit, it has a devastating effect on the opponents' bidding—they often fail to reach their best contract.

The requirements: A jump overcall shows a weak hand (generally fewer than nine high-card points) and a long suit. Typically, the suit is six cards long at the two-level, and seven cards long at the three-level. Note that the requirements for weak-jump overcalls are similar to those for weak two-bids and preemptive bids (described in Chapter Seven).

If you skip more than one level of bidding it is also a weak bid. For example, if your right-hand opponent bids 1♡, overcalls of 2♠, 3♠ and 4♠ all show weak hands. However, you may make a jump overcall to game (opponent-1♢, you-4♡ or 4♠) with a strong hand if you are willing to give up on slam. The best strategy is to bid as high as you dare. You run the risk of being doubled and set, but the higher you bid, the harder it will be for the opponents to reach their best contract. The vulnerability governs how daring you should be. Follow the guidelines for preemptive opening bids as described in Chapter Seven: estimate the value of your hand and overbid by two tricks if your side is vulnerable and the opponents are not; by three tricks with equal vulnerability; and by three, four or five tricks if your side is not vulnerable and the opponents are.

Here are four examples. Both sides are vulnerable and your right-hand opponent opens the bidding with 1♡.

(15)	♠ Q J 10 9 7 2	(16)	♠ 10 5
	♡ 3		♡ 7 2
	◇ A 8 5		◇ K Q J 10 8 5 3
	♣ 7 6 4		♣ Q 9

(17)	♠ K Q J 10 8 5 3	(18)	♠ K J 8 7 5 4
	♡ 7 2		♡ 9
	◇ 10 5		◇ 10 6 3
	♣ Q 9		♣ 9 8 2

(15) Bid 2♠ with five tricks. Overbid by three.

(16) Bid 3◇ with six tricks. Overbid by three.

(17) Bid 3♠ with six tricks. Overbid by three.

(18) Pass with only four tricks, but 2♠ would be a good bid at favorable vulnerability.

Weak jump overcalls apply when the enemy has opened the bidding with a suit bid of one. If the bidding is opened with a higher bid in a suit, or any notrump bid, jump overcalls are strong—showing 18-21 points and a very good six-card or longer suit.

NOTRUMP OVERCALLS

The 1NT overcall: The requirements to overcall 1NT are 15-18 points and a balanced hand *with at least one stopper in the enemy suit.* Respond to a 1NT overcall the same way you would to an opening 1NT bid, except a cue-bid of the opponent's suit (opponent-1◇, partner-1NT, opponent-pass, you-2◇) is forcing to game and asks partner to bid a four-card major suit.

If you have a balanced hand that is too strong to overcall 1NT (19 points or more), double first, with the intention of bidding notrump at your next turn. For example:

Your right-hand opponent opens the bidding 1♡, and you hold:

(19)	♠ A Q 10	(20)	♠ A J 10
	♡ K 8 7		♡ K J 9
	◇ 9 5 4		◇ A K Q 2
	♣ A K J 2		♣ Q J 3

(19) Bid 1NT with 17 points and a stopper in the heart suit. If the opening bid had been 1◊, you would not bid 1NT without a diamond stopper. You would double instead. (All about doubles coming up next.)

(20) Double with 21 points, intending to bid notrump at your next turn. This hand qualifies for an opening bid of 2NT, but *do not make the mistake of overcalling 2NT;* your partner will expect an entirely different hand.

The unusual 2NT overcall: The jump overcall to 2NT has a special meaning: it shows a hand with at least five cards in each of the two low-ranking unbid suits; *it does not show a strong balanced hand with a desire to play notrump.* For example, over an opponent's 1♡ or 1♠ opening bid, 2NT shows at least five clubs and five diamonds; over a 1◊ opening bid, it shows at least five clubs and five hearts; and over a 1♣ opening bid, it shows at least five diamonds and five hearts. The unusual notrump overcall does not promise a good hand, and how daring you should be depends on the vulnerability. With favorable vulnerability you may overcall 2NT with as few as six or seven high-card points, but you should always have two decent five-card or longer suits. Your 2NT overcall asks partner to bid one of your suits, and he may have to bid a three-card, or even a two-card suit.

Your right-hand opponent opens with 1♡, and you hold:

(21)	♠ 7 2	(22)	♠ 6 4
	♡ 3		♡ 8
	◊ A Q J 9 6		◊ K 10 8 5 2
	♣ K J 10 8 5		♣ K J 7 4 3

(21) With two good five-card minor suits, bid 2NT regardless of the vulnerability. This asks your partner to bid his longer minor suit.

(22) With two poor five-card minor suits, bid 2NT at favorable vulnerability only; you need better suits to bid 2NT with other vulnerabilities.

(**NOTE:** This brief explanation of the unusual two-notrump overcall is to make you aware of its existence. You will probably be better off if you ignore the bid until you learn more about it.)

The natural 2NT overcall: A 2NT overcall of a weak two-bid *is not unusual.* It shows a balanced hand with 16-19 points and at least one stopper in the enemy suit. Partner should respond in the same way as he would to an opening 2NT bid, while remembering that the 2NT overcall shows 16-19 points, not 20-22.

The 3NT overcall: You should know by now that if your opponent has opened the bidding with one of a suit and you have a balanced hand too strong to overcall 1NT (19 points or more), you should double first, intending to bid notrump at your next turn. Therefore, a *jump overcall* to 3NT has a special meaning—it shows a strong hand with a long solid suit and at least one stopper in the opponent's suit.

It is when the bidding is already at the three-level (for example, your right-hand opponent opens the bidding with 3♡) that it may be necessary to bid 3NT with questionable values. Over an opponent's opening suit bid at the three-bid, an overcall of 3NT is recommended with 17 points or more and at least one stopper in the enemy suit. The two following two examples illustrate what you should do over opening bids of both 1♡ and 3♡:

	(23)	♠ J 10 3	(24)	♠ K 10 4
		♡ K 2		♡ A J 10
		◇ A K Q J 10 8 4		◇ A Q 9
		♣ A		♣ K Q 7 4

(23) Bid 3NT over an opening bid of 1♡ or 3♡. Over the 1♡ opening, the jump to 3NT shows this kind of hand—a long running suit and a stopper in hearts. But over the 3♡ opening, 3NT is the best bid with a hand like this, or like the one in #24—a strong balanced hand with at least 17 points. If the opening bid had been 2♡, you should still overcall 3NT.

(24) Over an opening bid of 1♡, double, intending to bid notrump next. With a balanced hand containing 19 or more high-card

points the first step is always to double. Over the 3♡ opening, bid 3NT and hope for the best. If the opening bid had been 2♡, you should overcall 2NT.

TAKEOUT DOUBLES

The takeout double asks your partner to bid, and the most common takeout double is over your right-hand opponent's opening suit bid of one. So that is where we will begin. The first and most important thing to consider is your distribution; the point-count requirements to double vary with your distribution.

* The ideal distribution for a takeout double is four cards in each of the three unbid suits (4-4-4-1 or 5-4-4-0 distribution, with the short suit being the one bid by your opponent); no matter which suit partner bids, you will have four trumps for him. With ideal distribution you may double with as few as ten or 11 points.

* With 4-4-3-2 distribution (the doubleton in the enemy suit), the minimum requirement to double is about 12-13 points. As the distribution becomes less attractive, you need more high cards.

* Doubling with fewer than three cards in all of the unbid suits should be ruled out unless you have a strong hand—18 points or more. This is because your short suit is the one partner is most likely to bid and you are not supposed to bid again with fewer than 18 points. If you double and partner bids your short suit you are left with a choice of evils—to mislead your partner by bidding again without the values to do so, or to pass and leave him to play a miserable contract with a shortage of trumps.

Other considerations when contemplating a takeout double are the level of bidding and the vulnerability. For example, a takeout double of a 1♣ bid, which forces your partner to bid at the one-level, may be made with scantier values than a double of a 1♠ bid, which forces him to bid at the two-level. Also, the takeout doubler may take more chances at favorable vulnerability; if something goes wrong and you get doubled in your eventual contract, the penalty is not as costly.

In the following examples, your right-hand opponent opens 1◇:

(25) ♠ K 10 7 3   (26) ♠ 9 3   (27) ♠ A 10 8
     ♡ A Q 4 3   ♡ K 10 7 2   ♡ A Q J 9 8 3
     ◇ 6   ◇ A Q 4   ◇ A Q 7
     ♣ Q 9 8 2   ♣ K J 8 5   ♣ 4

(25) Double with 11 points and ideal shape—four cards in all three
     unbid suits. *If the opening bid had been in any suit but
     diamonds, you should most emphatically pass.*

(26) Pass with 13 points. If you double and partner responds 1♠ you
     are stuck—your hand is too weak to bid again and spades will
     probably make a horrendous trump suit. If the opening bid were
     1♠, double would be all right.

(27) Double with 19 points. This hand is too strong for a simple
     overcall of 1♡—which would show a maximum of 17 points.
     Your partner will probably respond 1♠ or 2♣, and you will
     follow with 2♡ to show 18-21 points and a good five-card or
     longer suit.

RESPONSES TO TAKEOUT DOUBLES

When your partner makes a takeout double he wants you to bid one
of the unbid suits, especially a major suit. Depending on whether your
point count is 0-9, 10-12, or 13 or more, bid as follows:

* With 0-9 points, if your right-hand opponent passes, make a
  nonjump bid in a suit. You may also respond 1NT with 6-9
  points and at least one stopper in the enemy suit. If your right-
  hand opponent bids over partner's double, make a nonjump bid
  in a suit with 6-9 points, but pass with 0-5.
* With 10-12 points, jump the bidding in your best suit or
  notrump. Jump bids are *not* forcing.
* With 13 points or more, bid game directly if you know where
  to play it; if you do not know which game to bid, cue-bid the
  enemy suit. As when responding to partner's overcall, *the cue-
  bid is the only way to force partner to bid again.*

If the bidding goes as follows, what do you do with these hands?

Opponent	Partner	Opponent	You
1◇	Double	Pass	?

(28) ♠ 7 4
     ♡ 9 8 5 3 2
     ◇ 8 7 2
     ♣ 10 6 3

(29) ♠ K J 7 2
     ♡ 6
     ◇ 8 5 3
     ♣ Q 10 6 4 3

(30) ♠ K J 10 8
     ♡ 7 4 2
     ◇ 9 3
     ♣ A Q 6 5

(31) ♠ A Q 9 4
     ♡ K 10 8 5
     ◇ 6 4 3
     ♣ A 10

(28) Bid 1♡ with no high-card points. If your right-hand opponent bids over partner's double, you should pass; you need at least six points to bid anything.

(29) Bid 1♠ with seven points. Your priority is to bid a four-card major ahead of a five-card minor. Note that if your right-hand opponent bids over partner's double, this hand is strong enough for a "free bid." For example, after a 2♡ bid on your right, you should bid 2♠ to show a four-card or longer spade suit and 6-9 points.

(30) Bid 2♠ with ten points. *With 10-12 points you must jump the bidding.* If your partner bids again you will probably reach game, but *your jump bid is not forcing.*

(31) Bid 2◇ with 13 points. This hand is strong enough to bid game, probably in 4♡ or 4♠ if partner has a four-card fit, but you do not know which game to bid! The cue-bid shows a strong hand and asks partner to bid a four-card major. If partner bids 2♡ or 2♠ over your 2◇ bid, raise to game. If he bids 2NT, which shows a stopper in diamonds and denies four cards in either major, raise to 3NT.

Here are four more illustrations with the same auction:

Opponent	Partner	Opponent	You
1◇	Double	Pass	?

(32) ♠ 8 6 2
♥ A J 9
♦ Q 10 9
♣ 7 4 3 2

(33) ♠ 9 2
♥ A J 7
♦ K 10 8 5
♣ Q J 9 3

(34) ♠ A 8
♥ 9 4
♦ Q J 10 9 8
♣ J 10 3 2

(35) ♠ A 8
♥ 9 4
♦ Q 10 8 6 5
♣ J 10 3 2

(32) Bid 1NT, showing 6-9 points, at least one stopper in the opponent's suit, and no four-card or longer major.

(33) Bid 2NT, showing 10-12 points, at least one stopper in the opponent's suit, and no four-card or longer major.

(34) Pass, to convert partner's takeout double into a penalty double. Based on your exceptional holding in the opponent's suit, the expectation is that a contract of 1♦ doubled will reward you with a bigger profit than bidding and making a contract your way. You must have a powerful five-card or longer holding in the opponent's suit to pass your partner's takeout double—one that surely will win at least three trump tricks.

(35) Bid 1NT. This diamond suit is too weak to pass 1♦ doubled.

REBIDS BY THE DOUBLER

When responder answers a takeout double by making a nonjump bid in a suit, he may have no points. Therefore, the doubler should not bid again unless he has at least 18 points with one exception—if his partner has responded in a suit at the one-level, he may raise to the two-level with 16-18 points and at least four trumps. When the doubler does have a hand good enough to bid again, his choices are to raise his partner's suit with *at least four trumps*, bid a good *five-card or longer* suit, bid notrump with at least one stopper in the enemy suit, or cue-bid the opponent's suit. The point-count requirements for these bids are described in the analysis of the following hands.

Suppose you hold the following, and the bidding goes:

Opponent	Partner	Opponent	You
—	—	1◇	Double
Pass	1♠	Pass	?

(36)	♠ A J 7 4	(37)	♠ A Q 10 7
	♡ K J 3		♡ K 10 9
	◇ 5 2		◇ 7 2
	♣ K 10 8 6		♣ A Q 5 3

(38)	♠ A Q 10	(39)	♠ A Q 5
	♡ A Q 9 8 5		♡ A K J 2
	◇ 7		◇ A Q 10
	♣ K Q J 2		♣ 9 8 4

(36) Pass with 13 points. Partner showed 0-9 points and may have just a four-card spade suit; he may be set in 1♠. You should also pass if partner jumps to 2♠, showing 10-12 points.

(37) Bid 2♠ with 16 points (one for the doubleton). A raise of responder's suit shows at least four trumps: at the two-level it shows 16-18 points; a jump to 3♠ shows 19-21 points, and a jump to 4♠ shows 22 points or more. If partner had responded 2♣, you would pass; when partner's suit response is at the two-level, a nonjump raise to the three-level shows 18-20 points.

(38) Bid 2♡ with 19 points. This is the way to bid with a hand that is too strong for an overcall—double first, and then bid your suit to show a good five-card or longer suit and 18-21 points. Note: here it is wrong to raise partner's spades with only three trumps.

(39) Bid 1NT with 20 points. When your hand is too strong to overcall 1NT (19 points or more), double first and bid notrump later. If you had 21-23 points, you should double first and then jump to 2NT. If the opening bid had been 1♣, the best rebid would be a cue-bid of 2♣; do not bid notrump without a stopper in the opponent's suit.

THE DIRECT CUE-BID

A direct cue-bid of the opening bidder's suit (opener-1♡, you-2♡) asks your partner to bid one of the unbid suits, as does the takeout double, but the cue-bid is *forcing to game.* For example:

(40)	Opponent	You	♠ A K 10 8 5
	1◇	?	♡ A K J
			◇ 7
			♣ K Q J 9

Bid 2◇ with 22 points, to ask your partner to bid one of the unbid suits and then to continue bidding until you reach some game contract. For example: if partner responds 2♡, bid 2♠; there is no need to jump the bidding, partner is not allowed to pass below game.

DOUBLES: TAKEOUT OR PENALTY?

You now know that a double of right-hand opponent's opening suit bid of one is for takeout. But there are auctions where the meaning of a double is not clear—one partner doubles for takeout and the other partner thinks it is for penalty, and vice versa. Here are some guidelines to help you to tell the difference:

Takeout doubles: Provided your partner has not entered the auction, a double of any *natural* bid in a suit below game (any suit bid below 4♡) is takeout. The next four examples are takeout doubles:

(41)	Opponent	Partner	Opponent	You	♠ 7
	—	—	—	1♣	♡ K J 10 6
	1♠	Pass	Pass	?	◇ A Q 10
					♣ A K 7 4 3

Double with 17 high-card points and good support for the unbid suits. Even the opening bidder can make a takeout double. Since your partner has never bid, and you are doubling a suit bid below game, your double is for takeout.

(42)   Opponent   Partner   Opponent   You   ♠ K J 10 8
        4◇   Pass   Pass   ?   ♡ A K 9 4
                                                     ◇ 3
                                                     ♣ A Q 7 2

Double with 17 points and ideal distribution. The 4◇ bid is below
game, and your partner has never bid, so the double is takeout. You
must have a stronger hand to double at higher levels, but this very
good hand with four-card support for all three unbid suits is perfect.

(43)   Opponent   Partner   Opponent   You   ♠ 7 5
        1♣   Pass   1♠   ?   ♡ A Q 10 6
                                                     ◇ K J 10 9 3
                                                     ♣ A 2

Double with 15 points. When your opponents have bid two suits,
double shows length in the two unbid suits (in this case hearts and
diamonds) and asks partner to take a choice. Since partner has only
two suits to choose between, double is a doubtful action with fewer
than four cards in each of the unbid suits, unless you have a very
strong hand.

(44)   Opponent   Partner   Opponent   You   ♠ 5
        1♠   Pass   1NT   ?   ♡ A Q 10 6
                                                     ◇ K J 10 9
                                                     ♣ A 8 3 2

Double with 14 point and ideal distribution. A double of a 1NT
response to an opening suit bid of one is takeout, asking partner to bid
one of the three unbid suits; it has the same meaning as a double of
your right-hand opponent's opening bid of one in a suit.

Penalty doubles: The most important thing to remember is that a
double of an enemy bid after your partner has been in the auction
(done anything but pass) is *not* a takeout double. Even when your
partner has not bid, *a double of any notrump bid is for penalty* (except

when it is a response to an opening suit bid of one, as shown in #44). A double of any game contract is for penalty, with rare exceptions that you should ignore for the time being. Penalty doubles of overcalls, games, slams, and lead-directing doubles are covered in Chapter Ten, but here is one example of a penalty double of a 1NT opening bid.

(45)   Opponent   Partner   Opponent   You   ♠ K Q J 10
                            1NT   ?   ♡ A 7
                                                ◇ K 8 4
                                                ♣ A 9 5 2

Double with 17 high-card points and a good opening lead—the ♠K. This is a penalty double, but your partner may bid if he has a worthless hand *and* a long suit.

IN REVIEW

Overcalls: The first bid by your side after the opponents open the bidding is an overcall.

* An overcall at the one-level (opponent-1♡, you-1♠) shows 9-17 points and a five-card or longer suit, but you should pass with fewer than 13 points if your five-card suit is very weak. A nonjump overcall at the two-level (opponent-1♠, you-2♣) shows 11-17 points and a good five-card or longer suit; but overcalls at the two-level with just a five-card suit are questionable unless you have a very good suit, or extra high cards. More chance-taking is in order at favorable vulnerability, and at the lower levels of bidding. When your hand is too strong to overcall (18 points or more), *the first step is to double,* with the intention of bidding your suit (or notrump) at your next turn.

* A jump overcall in a suit, skipping one or two levels of bidding (opponent-1♡, you-2♠, or 3♠), shows a weak hand (a hand too weak to make a nonjump overcall) with a long suit—usually six cards long at the two-level, or seven at the three-level. A jump overcall to game (opponent-1♡, you-4♠) shows a very

good seven-card or longer suit, but since you are bidding game, not necessarily a weak hand.

* A 1NT overcall shows a balanced hand with 15-18 points and at least one stopper in the opponent's suit. With a balanced hand that is too strong to overcall 1NT, (19 points or more), double first, with the intention of bidding notrump next.

* A 2NT overcall of an opening suit bid of one has an artificial meaning; it is the "unusual 2NT overcall" showing a hand with at least five cards in each of the two lower ranking unbid suits. A 2NT overcall of a weak two-bid shows a strong balanced hand (16-19 points) and at least one stopper in the opponent's suit; it is not unusual.

* A jump overcall of 3NT (opponent-1♠, you-3NT) shows a hand with a long solid suit and a stopper in the opponent's suit. A 3NT overcall of an opponent's preemptive bid (opponent-3♡, you-3NT) shows a balanced hand with at least 17 points and a stopper in the opponent's suit.

* A direct cue-bid in an opponent's suit (opponent-1♠, you-2♠), asks partner to bid a suit, as does a takeout double, and is *forcing to game*.

Responses to overcalls: Assuming that partner has made a nonjump overcall at the one- or two-level:

* With three or more trumps, raise partner's suit with 7-11 points, jump-raise with 12-14 points, and raise a major suit to game or cue-bid the opponent's suit with 15 or more points. With a balanced hand and at least one stopper in the opponent's suit: if partner's overcall was at the one-level, bid 1NT with 8-11 points, jump to 2NT with 12-14, jump to 3NT with 15 or more. If partner's overcall was at the two-level, bid 2NT with 9-11, and jump to 3NT with 12 or more.

* Bid a new suit with 8-13 points and a good five-card or longer suit. A jump in a new suit shows 13-15 points and a long, strong suit—such as K Q J 10 x x. These bids are *not* forcing.

* Bid game directly with 15 points or more if you know which game to bid. If you do not know which game to bid, cue-bid

the enemy suit; the cue-bid is the only way to force partner to bid again.

Takeout doubles: With rare exceptions, a double of any natural suit bid below game (below 4♡), is for takeout unless your partner has been in the auction. The point-count requirement for takeout doubles varies, depending on your distribution, the level of bidding, and the vulnerability.

Responses to takeout doubles: Responder should bid one of the unbid suits, with emphasis on unbid majors.
* A nonjump response in a suit shows 0-9 points. If your right-hand opponent bids over partner's double, bid your suit with 6-9 points, but pass with 0-5 points.
* A 1NT response shows 6-9 points and at least one stopper in the opponent's suit. Never bid 1NT with five points or fewer.
* Any jump response, skipping one level of bidding, shows 10-12 points; it is an invitational bid, it is not forcing.
* With 13 points or more bid game if you know where to play it. If not, cue-bid the opponent's suit; the cue-bid is the only way to force the doubler to bid again.

Rebids by the doubler: When partner has responded by making a nonjump bid in a suit:
* Raise partner's suit with at least four trumps: raise to the two-level with 16-18 points; jump-raise to the three-level with 19-21 points; and jump-raise a major suit to game, or cue-bid the enemy suit, with 22 points or more. If partner has responded by bidding a suit at the two-level and you have four trumps, raise to three with 18-20 points, and jump-raise or cue-bid with 21 or more.
* Bid a new five-card or longer suit with 18-21 points. Jump the bidding in a new suit with 19-21 points and a very strong six-card or longer suit. With more, bid game directly, or cue-bid the enemy suit.

* Bid notrump with a balanced hand and at least one stopper in the opponent's suit. A rebid of 1NT shows 19-20 points, and a jump rebid of 2NT shows 21-23. A nonjump rebid of 2NT shows 19-21, and a jump rebid of 3NT shows more.

PRACTICE DEAL

Contract: 4♠
Opening lead: ◇6

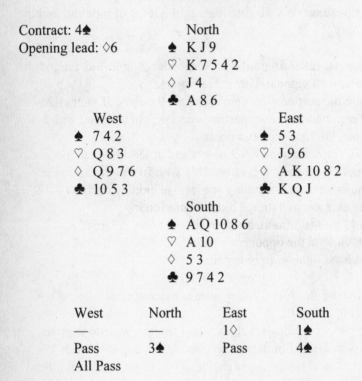

North
♠ K J 9
♡ K 7 5 4 2
◇ J 4
♣ A 8 6

West
♠ 7 4 2
♡ Q 8 3
◇ Q 9 7 6
♣ 10 5 3

East
♠ 5 3
♡ J 9 6
◇ A K 10 8 2
♣ K Q J

South
♠ A Q 10 8 6
♡ A 10
◇ 5 3
♣ 9 7 4 2

West	North	East	South
—	—	1◇	1♠
Pass	3♠	Pass	4♠
All Pass			

The bidding: South has 11 points and a good five-card suit, so he overcalls the 1◇ opening bid with 1♠. North's jump-raise to 3♠ is invitational, showing 12-14 points and at least three trumps. South has 13 points when he revalues his hand by adding two points for the two doubletons. So, although a close decision, he bids game.

The opening lead: West leads a diamond because his partner bid the suit, and the correct card to lead from Q x x x is fourth best.

The play: Declarer has five losers in his hand (two diamonds and three clubs). East wins the first two tricks with high diamonds and then leads the ♣K. Declarer must hold his club losers to one, and the only hope is to discard two clubs on dummy's long heart suit. This requires good luck (very good luck): the six missing hearts must divide 3-3, and, since the only entry to dummy is in the trump suit, spades must divide 3-2. After winning the third trick with the ♣A, declarer cashes two rounds of trumps and sees that suit divides 3-2; *he must not cash the third trump as that would leave him without an entry to dummy.* He then cashes the ♡A and the ♡K and ruffs the third heart in his hand. Since hearts divide 3-3, the two remaining hearts in dummy are now good. So he leads a spade, which draws the last trump and puts the lead in dummy, and discards two club losers on the hearts. If declarer played this way, he justified his aggressive 4♠ bid.

The key plays: Draw no more than two rounds of spades, saving the third round as an entry to dummy, and then ruff the third round of hearts in your hand.

CHAPTER TEN

COMPETITIVE BIDDING

This chapter includes the following:
* Responses after an opponent overcalls, including penalty doubles.
* Responses after an opponent makes a takeout double, including redoubles.
* Penalty doubles of games and slams.
* Lead-directing doubles of artificial bids.
* Sacrifice bids.

RESPONSES AFTER AN OPPONENT OVERCALLS

If your partner opens the bidding and your right-hand opponent overcalls (partner-1♦, opponent-1♠, you-?), you may be deprived of making the bid you would have made if there were no overcall, and even if the same bid is available it sometimes has a different meaning. Your partner will get another chance to bid if you pass, so the rule that responder must not pass with six points or more is abandoned; when no convenient bid is available it is best to pass with as many as nine or ten points. When you do decide that your hand qualifies for a bid after an overcall—a "free bid"—you may raise partner's suit, bid a new suit or bid notrump; you may also double the overcall.

Raise partner's suit: The requirements for a single raise of partner's suit (partner-1♦, opponent-1♠, you-2♦) are the same as when there is no overcall—6-10 points and at least three trumps in a major suit, or at least four trumps in a minor. The requirements to jump-raise partner's suit in noncompetitive auctions are 13-16 points and at least four trumps, but after an overcall (partner-1♥, opponent-2♦, you-3♥), it is sometimes necessary to jump-raise with 11-12 points (as well as with 13-16), or jump-raise a major suit with three trumps; but the jump-raise is still forcing. A double jump-raise (partner-1♠, opponent-2♣, you-4♠) is preemptive; it has the same meaning as when there is no overcall.

Bid a new suit at the one-level: In a noncompetitive auction a response in a new suit at the one-level shows six points or more and a four-card or longer suit. To respond in a new suit at the one-level after an intervening overcall (partner-1♣, opponent-1◇, you-1♠), you need a four-card or longer suit and at least eight points, or seven points with a good suit. Your new-suit bid is forcing.

(1)	Opponent	Partner	Opponent	You		♠ Q 7 3 2
	—	1◇	1♡	?		♡ 9 8 5
						◇ J 6 3
						♣ K 5 4

Pass with only six points. Partner will get another chance to bid, so it is not obligatory to respond with six points as it would be if your right-hand opponent passed.

(2)	Opponent	Partner	Opponent	You		♠ A Q 8 6 3
	—	1◇	1♡	?		♡ 9 4 2
						◇ 8 5
						♣ 10 7 4

Bid 1♠ with seven points and a good five-card suit (a forcing bid).

Bid a new suit at the two-level: To bid a new suit at the two-level after an overcall (partner-1♠, opponent-2♣, you-2♡), the requirements are nine points or more (as opposed to the 11 points or more required if your right-hand opponent passes); but don't do it with nine or ten points unless you have a good five-card or longer suit. For example:

(3)	Opponent	Partner	Opponent	You		♠ 8 3 2
	—	1♡	1♠	?		♡ 6 5
						◇ 7 4
						♣ A K 10 9 4 2

Bid 2♣ (forcing). This nine-point hand with a good six-card suit just barely qualifies for a free bid at the two-level over an enemy overcall. If your right-hand opponent passes, you should bid 1NT because then you would need at least 11 points to bid a new suit at the two-level. If the overcall is 2◊, you should pass; add a king somewhere and a 3♣ bid would be all right.

(4)   Opponent Partner   Opponent You   ♠ K 10 3
       —   1◊   1♡   ?   ♡ 7 6 4
                                                ◊ 9 5 2
                                                ♣ A Q 9 8

    Pass with nine points and no convenient bid. You should not bid 2♣ with just a four-card suit and only nine points. Introducing a four-card suit at the two-level is usually frowned upon, but you may do so in a minor if you have 11 points or more.

1NT responses: In a noncompetitive auction, a 1NT response shows 6-10 points. A 1NT response over an opponent's overcall (partner-1◊, opponent-1♠, you-1NT) shows 8-10 (or maybe 11) points and a stopper in the opponent's suit. For example:

(5)   Opponent Partner   Opponent You   ♠ K 10 2
       —   1◊   1♠   ?   ♡ 7 6 3
                                                ◊ 10 4 3
                                                ♣ Q J 9 8

    Pass with only six points. Without the 1♠ overcall, bid 1NT.

(6)   Opponent Partner   Opponent You   ♠ K 10 2
       —   1◊   1♠   ?   ♡ 7 6 3
                                                ◊ 10 4 3
                                                ♣ A J 9 8

    Bid 1NT with eight points and a stopper in the opponent's suit. If we change the overcall from 1♠ to 1♡, you should pass; do not bid 1NT without a stopper in the opponent's suit.

2NT responses: A 2NT response to an opening suit bid of one in a noncompetitive auction shows a balanced hand with 13-15 points and stoppers in the three unbid suits. The requirements to jump to 2NT after a one-level overcall (partner-1♣, opponent-1♠, you-2NT) are a little more flexible—a balanced hand with 12-15 (or maybe with 11) points and at least one stopper in the opponent's suit; it is not necessary to have stoppers in all the unbid suits, but the jump bid is still forcing.

After a two-level overcall, a nonjump bid of 2NT (partner-1♠, opponent-2◇, you-2NT) shows 11-12 points and a stopper in the opponent's suit (nonforcing); with 13-15 points jump to 3NT.

(7)	Opponent	Partner	Opponent	You	♠ Q J 7
	—	1♡	1♠	?	♡ A 9 5
					◇ 9 8 4 3
					♣ A Q 10

Bid 2NT with 13 points and a stopper in the opponent's suit; this jump bid is forcing to game. If we change the overcall from 1♠ to 2♣, you should bid 3NT (a nonjump bid of 2NT would show 11-12 points). After a 2◇ overcall you cannot bid notrump without a stopper, so jump to 3♡.

Doubles of overcalls: If you double your right-hand opponent's overcall (partner-1♡, opponent-2♣, you-double) it is a penalty double; see "Note" below. The requirements to double an overcall at the one- or two-level are length and strength in the opponent's suit (A Q 9 2, Q 10 8 7, etc.), shortness in your partner's suit—a singleton is ideal—and a reasonably good hand, at least one and one-half quick tricks. Partner is expected to pass the double, but might bid if his hand is very unsuitable for defense.

(**NOTE:** There is a very good modern convention, "Negative Doubles," where doubles of most overcalls are for takeout. You cannot learn everything at once and I did not put it in this book. But it is something you should learn when you get a little experience.)

To double an overcall of 1NT (partner-1♠, opponent-1NT, you-double) you need about 9-10 *high-card* points. Logically, if you and your partner have most of the high cards, you should be able to win more than half of the tricks.

It is true that the opponents will occasionally make a doubled contract due to some fluky distribution or poor defense, but if you never double a contract you cannot beat, you are too conservative. When your hand qualifies as described above, take a chance and double an overcall. Doubling an overcall is sometimes very rewarding, but here is something to take into account. If your opponents make a doubled contract of 2◇ it becomes the equivalent of 4◇, not enough for game and not an expensive loss. If your opponents make a double contract of 2♡ it becomes the equivalent of 4♡, enough for game and costly. Therefore, do not double a part-score of 2♡ or higher unless you are reasonably certain you can beat it.

(8)	Opponent	Partner	Opponent	You	♠ K J 10 8
	—	1♡	1♠	?	♡ 7
					◇ K 9 5
					♣ A 8 6 4 3

Double. A penalty double of an overcall at the one-level is rare, but this hand meets all of the requirements: length and strength in the opponent's suit, shortness in partner's suit, and plenty of high cards—two quick tricks.

(9)	Opponent	Partner	Opponent	You	♠ K 9 3
	—	1♡	2◇	?	♡ 6 3
					◇ A Q 8 5
					♣ 10 9 7 2

Double. But if partner's opening bid had been 1♠, raising to 2♠ with three trumps would be better than doubling 2◇.

(10) Opponent Partner Opponent You   ♠ K 2
      —   1♣   4♠   ?   ♡ 10 6 3
                                              ◊ A 9 8 7 4 3
                                              ♣ 5 2

Double. You do not need length in the enemy trump suit to double a game contract. You have two defensive tricks (♠K and ◊A) and partner opened the bidding, so you are a big favorite to beat the 4♠ contract, maybe by two or three tricks.

RESPONSES AFTER AN OPPONENT MAKES A TAKEOUT DOUBLE

When your right-hand opponent doubles your partner's opening suit bid of one, the usual procedure is:

* With 0-5 points, pass.
* With six or more points, but a maximum of nine *high-card* points, bid something.
* With ten or more *high card* points, redouble. Partner should usually pass and let the next bid come to you, but he may bid with a distributional hand (such as 5-5-2-1), or make a penalty double if his right-hand opponent bids. At your next turn, you will describe the nature of your hand by raising partner's suit, bidding a new suit, bidding notrump, or doubling an enemy bid.

In the following six illustrations partner opens the bidding with 1♡, your right-hand opponent doubles, and you hold:

(11) ♠ 7 3   (12) ♠ 7 3   (13) ♠ Q 10 7
      ♡ Q 8 5   ♡ K 10 8 5   ♡ 8 2
      ◊ A J 10 4   ◊ A J 10 4   ◊ A 6 5 3
      ♣ 9 8 6 2   ♣ 9 8 6   ♣ Q 9 6 4

(14) ♠ J 7   (15) ♠ J 7   (16) ♠ K 10 2
      ♡ 6 3   ♡ 6 3   ♡ Q 6
      ◊ 9 8 5   ◊ 9 5   ◊ A Q 10 8 5 3
      ♣ K Q 10 9 4 2   ♣ K Q 10 9 8 4 2   ♣ J 7

(11) Bid 2♡, showing three or more trumps and 6-10 points—at most nine high-card points. This is the same bid you should make if there is no double.

(12) Bid 3♡. The jump-raise over a takeout double is not a strong bid. It shows 6-10 points (at most nine high-card points) and an *especially good trump support—at least four trumps if a major suit, and at least five if a minor.* If your right-hand opponent passes, you should bid just 2♡.

(13) Bid 1NT showing 6-9 high-card points; the same bid you should make if your right-hand opponent passes.

(14) Bid 2♣. Over the double, a new suit bid at the two-level shows a six-card suit (perhaps a good five-card suit) with six points or more, but a maximum of nine high-card points. If your right-hand opponent passes, the correct bid is 1NT because a 2♣ bid would show 11 points or more.

(15) Bid 3♣, showing six points or more but a maximum of nine high-card points, and a very good six- or seven-card suit. *Since you must redouble with ten high-card points, any bid below game, even a jump bid in a new suit, shows a maximum of nine high-card points.* If your right-hand opponent passes, the correct bid is 1NT.

(16) Redouble. With ten high-card points or more, the first step is to redouble. Presumably your opponents will bid something and you will get another chance; if they foolishly let your partner play 1♡ redoubled, he will make his contract and score a game.

PENALTY DOUBLES OF GAMES AND SLAMS

If your opponents bid a game or a slam voluntarily, they usually have the required number of points to bid it, so it rarely pays to double. The exception occurs when the early bidding has made it obvious that you and your partner have good hands between you and that the opponents have made a preemptive bid or a sacrifice bid. In these cases you should definitely double them or bid again. The purpose of a penalty double is to increase the amount that you win for beating the contract. Remember, however, that the extra amount you win for beating a doubled contract by one trick is trivial (50 or 100 points, depending on the vulnerability). So when your opponents bid a game or slam *voluntarily,* and you think you have enough tricks to beat them, do not double if it may reveal something about your hand which will help declarer in the play, or if you think the opponents may run to a better contract.

The following four illustrations show cases where it is tempting to double, but you should not.

(17)	Opponent	Partner	Opponent	You	♠ A J 5
	—	—	1NT	Pass	♡ K J 2
	2NT	Pass	3NT	?	◇ K 10 9 6
					♣ K 8 7

Pass. There is no indication that declarer will get bad breaks and you have no safe lead. You have 15 high-card points and the bidding indicates that the opponents have the other 25; leaving partner with zero. You probably cannot beat 3NT even if you pass. If you double and tell declarer you have all the missing high cards, you may remove any chance to beat the contract and increase the amount you will lose.

(18)	Opponent	Partner	Opponent	You	♠ Q J 3 2
	—	—	1♠	Pass	♡ A 7 4
	2♠	Pass	4♠	?	◇ A 6 4
					♣ 8 5 3

Pass. Double would expose your trump holding and show declarer how to play the trump suit. For example, if declarer has ♠A 10 x x x and dummy ♠K 9 x, he will first cash the ♠A and lead toward dummy's ♠K 9. If you play low from ♠Q J x, he will finesse the ♠9. If you play the jack or queen, he will win with the king. In either case you will get only one trump trick and declarer will probably make his contract. Of course declarer may play this way even if you do not double. But then he would fail if your partner had ♠Q J x x, so he is much more likely to go wrong if you pass. (If your spades were ♠Q J 10 x it would not help declarer to know you have length in his trump suit; you should double.)

(19)	Opponent	Partner	Opponent	You	♠ A 10 9
	—	—	1♡	Pass	♡ 6 2
	3♡	Pass	6♡	?	◇ A 8 7 5
					♣ 8 6 4 3

Pass. A good declarer would surely have a void; otherwise he would bid 4NT to make sure he is not off two aces before he bid a slam. Even if declarer has bid incorrectly and you beat the slam by one trick, the double gains only 50 or 100 points, depending on the vulnerability; while it will lose a lot more if declarer has a void and makes his contract, especially if he redoubles.

(20)	Opponent	Partner	Opponent	You	♠ Q J 10 9
	—	—	1♠	Pass	♡ 9 7 6
	2NT	Pass	3♠	Pass	◇ 8 4 3
	4♠	Pass	6♠	?	♣ J 5 2

Pass. You surely can beat 6♠, but if you double and warn the opponents that you have a trump stack, they may run to 6NT and make it. Do not double the only contract you can beat.

LEAD-DIRECTING DOUBLES OF ARTIFICIAL BIDS

You were told in Chapter Nine, "Provided your partner has not done anything but pass, a double of any NATURAL bid in a suit below game is for takeout." The reason for emphasizing the word "natural" is to distinguish it from an artificial bid.

A double of any artificial bid is not for takeout. It is lead directing, showing high cards in the suit doubled and asking partner to lead it. Some experienced partnerships use several artificial bids, but the only ones most players know anything about are Stayman and Blackwood. The double of a Stayman 2♣ bid shows length and strength in clubs and asks partner to lead a club. A suit response to 4NT (Blackwood) reveals how many aces are held, it has nothing to do with length in the bid suit; so a double of a suit response to Blackwood shows high cards (not necessarily length) in the bid suit and asks partner to lead it. Here is an example of each:

(21)   Opponent   Partner   Opponent   You   ♠ 7 6
       1NT   Pass   2♣   ?   ♡ Q J 3
                                                ◇ 10 5 2
                                                ♣ A K J 9 8

Double. The opponents will wind up playing a contract other than
clubs, but a club lead should offer the best defense. You need at least
a strong five-card club suit to double Stayman 2♣ If you double with
a questionable club holding the opponents may decide to play 2♣
doubled (or redoubled) if they have good clubs, and they will
probably make their contract unless your clubs are very strong.

(22)   Opponent   Partner   Opponent   You   ♠ 7 2
       1♠   Pass   2♣   Pass   ♡ K Q 10
       3♠   Pass   4♠   Pass   ◇ J 7 4 3
       4NT   Pass   5♡   ?   ♣ 9 8 6 5

Double. It is obvious that the opponents are going to play this hand
in some number of spades. The 5♡ bid is artificial, showing two aces.
Double asks your partner to lead a heart, which should offer your best
chance to beat the contract.

SACRIFICE BIDS

If the opponents bid a game or a slam that you judge they can
make, you can sometimes cut your losses by bidding to a higher
contract that you cannot make; if you get doubled and are set, it will
cost less than if the opponents are allowed to play and make their
contract. Judging whether or not the opponents can make their
contract, and how much it will cost if you make a sacrifice bid and get
doubled, is the key in deciding whether to pass or take the sacrifice;
and the vulnerability is very important. Similar to the advice given
about preemptive bids, the most advantageous time to sacrifice is with
favorable vulnerability; with equal vulnerability you should take the
middle road, and at unfavorable it rarely pays to sacrifice. In the
following two examples the vulnerability is favorable—the opponents
are vulnerable and your side is not:

(23)	Opponent	Partner	Opponent	You	♠ 8 5 4
	—	—	1♠	2◇	♡ A 2
	3♠	4◇	4♠	?	◇ K Q J 9 7 3
					♣ 10 4

The question is whether to pass or bid 5◇ as a sacrifice. First you must decide whether or not you can beat the 4♠ contract (do not sacrifice if you have a reasonable chance to beat the contract; beware the "phantom sacrifice"). You have only one defensive trick (the ♡A) and partner's 4◇ bid does not promise any defensive strength—he may be able to win a trick or two, but it is unthinkable that he can win more than two tricks. It is pretty clear that the opponents will make their contract if you pass.

Next you must decide how expensive it will be if you bid 5◇ and get doubled. The following would be the thought process of an expert: "The opponents have implied that they have nine spades or more between them—five on my right and four on my left—so it is predictable that partner has just one spade, or perhaps none. Partner bid 4◇, so he should have at least one high card that can win a trick. Suppose I give him the ◇A, a singleton spade and adequate trump support; in which case two spades can be ruffed in dummy, leaving me with four losers (one spade, one heart and two clubs). If I bid 5◇ and get doubled I will be set two tricks for a loss of 300, rather than the 620 I would lose if the opponents were allowed to play and make 4♠." This analysis makes bidding 5◇ with favorable vulnerability a bargain. Another possibility: if you bid 5◇, the opponents may bid 5♠ instead of doubling, and you might beat that contract.

Bidding 5◇ would be a reasonable decision if the vulnerability were equal, but you should pass 4♠ with unfavorable vulnerability—down two doubled when vulnerable costs 500, while the nonvulnerable game is worth only 420.

(24)	Opponent	Partner	Opponent	You	♠ K 9 7 6
	—	3♠	Double	?	♡ 2
					◇ Q J 10 8 5 4
					♣ 8 3

In Chapter Seven you learned that a preemptive bid is made with a hand that is unlikely to win more than one defensive trick. Therefore, when your partner makes a preemptive bid and you have a poor defensive hand, you should consider a sacrifice any time you have three cards or more in his suit. With this hand you have no defensive tricks and your partner has at most one, so you know that the opponents can make a small slam, or maybe a grand slam. You have excellent trump support and exciting distribution, so partner figures to win eight or nine tricks if he is allowed to play a spade contract. It would be a good result if you are doubled in some number of spades, or if the opponents stop bidding below slam.

Given all that, what should you do over 3♠ doubled to discourage the opponents from bidding a slam? The possibilities are: pass, bid 4♠, 5♠ or 6♠. If you are playing against inexperienced opponents it could work out well if you pass or bid just 4♠, hoping they double 4♠ or stop bidding in a game contract—probably 4♡ or 5♡. These are not good choices; it would be better to bid 5♠, to jam the opponents' bidding and take away Blackwood so they cannot determine how many aces they have. It would be an excellent result if the opponents double 5♠—you would probably be set three tricks for a loss of 500 points (on a good day you may be set only two tricks for minus 300). But if the opponents bid 6♡, you should bid 6♠; and if they bid 7♡, it is probably right to take out insurance and bid 7♠. A vulnerable grand slam in hearts is worth 2210 (1500 slam bonus, 500 game bonus, 210 trick score), and a small slam is worth 1430—750 slam bonus, 500 game bonus, 180 trick score. If you get doubled in a spade contract, down three costs 500, down four 800. It is no fun to lose 800 points, but you must agree that it is better than the huge amount you lose if the opponents are allowed to play and make a vulnerable slam.

IN REVIEW

Responses after an opponent overcalls:

* The requirements to raise partner's suit to the two-level after an overcall (partner-1♡, opponent-2♣, you-2♡) are the same as when there has been no overcall. However, the requirements

for the jump-raise (partner-1♠, opponent-2◊, you-3♠) are changed—12-16 points (occasionally 11) and just three cards in the major. Without the overcall, remember, you needed 13-16 points and at least four trumps to jump-raise a major.

* A new-suit bid at the one-level (partner-1♣, opponent-1♡, you-1♠) is forcing, showing a four-card or longer suit and eight points or more (or seven points with a good suit). A new-suit bid at the two-level (partner-1♠, opponent-2♣, you-2♡) is forcing, showing nine points or more—with only nine or ten points you must have a good five-card or longer suit.

* A 1NT response (partner-1♣, opponent-1♠, you-1NT) shows 8-10 (or maybe 11) points and a stopper in the opponent's suit. A jump to 2NT (partner-1◊, opponent-1♠, you-2NT) shows 12-15 (or maybe 11) points and a stopper in the opponent's suit. A nonjump bid of 2NT (partner-1♠, opponent-2◊, you-2NT) shows 11-12 points and a stopper in the opponent's suit; with 13-15 points jump to 3NT.

* A penalty double of an overcall at the one- or two-level (partner-1♡, opponent-1♠ or 2♣, you-double), shows a good four-card or longer holding in the opponent's suit, shortness in partner's suit (a singleton is ideal), and a relatively good hand in high cards—at least one and one-half quick tricks.

Responses after an opponent makes a takeout double: If your partner opens the bidding with a suit bid of one and your right-hand opponent doubles, pass with 0-5 points, and redouble with ten or more high-card points. *This means that any bid you make below game shows a minimum of six points, and a maximum of nine high-card points.* The choices are:

* Raise a major suit to the two-level (partner-1♠, opponent-double, you-2♠) with at least three trumps, or raise a minor suit to the two-level (partner-1◊, opponent-double, you-2◊) with at least four trumps.

* Jump-raise in a major (partner-1♡, opponent-double, you-3♡) with at least four trumps; or jump-raise a minor (partner-1♣, opponent-double, you-3♣), with at least five trumps.

* A 1NT response (partner-1♠, opponent-double, you-1NT) shows a balanced or semi-balanced hand without sufficient trumps to raise partner's suit.
* A new-suit bid at the one-level (partner-1♣, opponent-double, you-1♡) shows a four-card or longer suit.
* A new-suit bid at the two-level (partner-1♠, opponent-double, you-2♣) shows a six-card suit or a good five-card suit.
* A jump in a new suit (opener-1♡, opponent-double, you-2♠) shows a good six-card suit.

Sacrifice bids: If your opponents bid to a contract you are confident they can make, it pays to bid to a higher contract that you know you cannot make if the doubled penalty will cost you less than the value of the opponent's score if they play and make their game (or slam). The most profitable time to make a sacrifice bid is with favorable vulnerability. A good example is shown in the following practice deal.

PRACTICE DEAL

Assume that East/West are vulnerable and North/South are not.

Contract: 5♡ Doubled
Opening lead: ♠K

North
♠ 7 5 2
♡ A 8 3
◇ 5 2
♣ A J 10 4 3

West
♠ A K J 9 6 4 3
♡ 6
◇ A 8 3
♣ K Q

East
♠ Q 10
♡ Q 5
◇ K 9 7 6 4
♣ 9 8 7 2

South
♠ 8
♡ K J 10 9 7 4 2
◇ Q J 10
♣ 6 5

West	North	East	South
—	—	—	3♡
4♠	5♡	Pass	Pass
Double	All Pass		

The bidding: West has a very good hand, certainly worth a 4♠ bid over South's 3♡ opening. North judges that the 4♠ contract is unbeatable; he has two defensive tricks (the ♡A if it does not get ruffed, and the ♣A), and his partner made a preemptive bid which implies that he has at most one defensive trick. East-West are vulnerable and they will win 620 if allowed to play and make 4♠ (500 game bonus and 120 for trick-score), while 5♡ doubled should be less expensive. Since North has three hearts and his side is not vulnerable, 5♡ is a good bid. With the cards as shown, 5♡ doubled would be set by two tricks for a minus score of 300—a good result. Also note that East or West may bid 5♠ and they cannot make it (they must lose one heart, one diamond and one club); then the sacrifice bid pays off big—plus 100 rather than minus 620.

The opening lead: The standard procedure is to lead the king from an ace-king combination (exception: lead the ace from a doubleton ace-king).

The play: The opponents cannot be prevented from winning four tricks (one spade, two diamonds and one club), so down two is the best declarer can do.

PART TWO

THE PLAY

THE BIDDING IS OVER.
THE OPENING LEAD HAS BEEN MADE.
THE DUMMY HAS BEEN SPREAD.
WE ARE READY TO PLAY THE HAND.
BUT FIRST

CHAPTER ELEVEN

SUIT COMBINATIONS

In many deals, the key to making a contract depends on how declarer plays a suit combination. Therefore, before getting into how to play the hand, here are some tips on how to play one suit.

Outside of ruffing (covered later in this chapter), there are three ways to win tricks:

> with high cards
> with low cards in a long suit
> by finessing

High cards:

(a) Dummy	(b) Dummy	(c) Dummy
K J 7	K Q 8	J 9 7 3
You	You	You
A Q 3 2	J 7 6	Q 10 4

(a) Four tricks are available, but it is good technique to take the winners in the short hand first—cash the king and jack, then lead to your hand to cash the ace and queen.

(b) Sometimes you must surrender the lead to the opponents before you can win tricks. In this case, lead any honor card to drive out the ace. When you regain the lead you have two tricks.

(c) This time you must drive out two high cards before you can win any tricks. Lead the queen to drive out the ace (or king). When you regain the lead, play the ten to drive out the king (or ace). The jack and nine in dummy are now good tricks.

Low cards in a long suit: A surprisingly large number of tricks are won with low cards, simply because all of the higher cards in the suit have been played. You must keep track of the played cards or you will not realize it when the low cards become good tricks. This does not mean that you should rack your brain trying to remember every card in every suit in every deal. But any suit that offers a chance to win tricks with long cards deserves your utmost attention.

One reason many players have trouble keeping track of the played cards is that they use a more complicated method of counting than is necessary. *The simple method is to count the opponents' cards, not yours*: first, determine how many cards the opponents have in the suit between them—by subtracting the number you have in your hand and dummy from 13. Then subtract one each time a defender plays a card from that suit. This leaves you with an up-to-date total of how many unplayed cards the defenders have in the suit.

(d) Dummy	(e) Dummy	(f) Dummy
A K Q 2	A 8 7 6 5	A 8 7 6 5
You	You	You
5 4 3	K Q 2	K 3 2

(d) There are six cards missing. If you cash the ace, king and queen and see both opponents follow suit throughout (the suit divides 3-3), you can win a fourth trick with the two. The chance to win a fourth trick is not good. *When you are missing six cards, the odds favor that they will not divide evenly. The most likely division of six cards is four-two.*

(e) There are five cards missing. If you cash the king, queen and ace and the suit divides 3-2, you can win two more tricks with dummy's long cards—five tricks in all. The chance to win five tricks is good. *When you are missing an odd number of cards, the odds are strongly in favor that they will divide as evenly as possible (the most likely division of three cards is 2-1, of five cards it is 3-2, and of seven cards it is 4-3).* Note that the order in which you cash your high cards can be important for reasons of communication: the first two plays should be the king and queen. Then, when you win the third trick with the ace, the lead will be in dummy so you can cash the long cards. If you won the third trick in your hand with the king or queen, you would have to play another suit to get the lead in dummy (and that is sometimes impossible). A good general rule: *when running a long suit, cash the high cards in the short hand first.*

Now suppose one defender shows out on the second lead of the suit; it divides 4-1. You may still win a fourth trick in the suit. After cashing the king and queen, cash the ace and lead a low card; concede the fourth trick to the defender with the high card. Dummy's fifth card is now good.

(f) Here again, two extra tricks are available with long cards if the missing five cards divide 3-2. But this time you must give up a trick along the way. It is sometimes best to give up the trick before cashing the top cards, so suppose you lead the suit and play low cards from both hands. When you regain the lead, cash the king first and then the ace so the lead will be in dummy. If the suit has divided 3-2, the two remaining low cards in dummy are now good.

The finesse: The concept of finessing involves the rotation in which the four players play to a trick—the lead, second-hand, third-hand and fourth-hand. You can win a trick with a card that is not high if the player who holds the higher card (or higher cards) has already played to the trick. Since a finesse is an attempt to win a trick with a card that is not high, in most cases *the right play is to lead toward that card.* For example:

(g) Dummy   (h) Dummy   (i) Dummy
A Q   A 7 4   K J

You   You   You
9 5   Q 8   7 3 2

(g) The ace and the queen are the highest and the third highest cards is the suit, and your goal is to win a trick with the queen. You will succeed if West (your left-hand opponent) has the king by leading a low card from your hand toward the ace-queen. West must play a card to the trick before dummy. After he plays a low card you will play the queen and win the trick unless East, who has not yet played to the trick, has the king; a fifty-fifty chance.

(h) Which player would you prefer to have the king? How would you play to win a trick with the queen? If East has the king, you can win a trick with the queen by leading a low card from dummy *toward the queen:* if East plays the king, play low; if he plays low, play the queen. Note that there is no chance to win a trick with the queen by leading it. If West has the king he will cover the queen.

(i) Sometimes finessing involves guesswork. If the ace and queen are divided—West has one honor and East the other—you must make a winning guess to make a trick. First lead a low card from your hand. Suppose that West plays low (your troubles are over if he plays the ace); if West has the ace, the winning play is the king; if West has the queen, the winning play is the jack (which will force out East's ace and set up the king as a good trick to be won later).

(j) Dummy	(k) Dummy	(l) Dummy
K Q 2	A K 10	A J 10
You	You	You
7 5 4	9 7 6	7 5 4

(j) Your goal is to win two tricks with the king and queen. To succeed you must find West with the ace—a fifty-fifty chance. Lead from your hand: if West plays the ace, play low from dummy; if West plays low, win with the queen and return to your hand in another suit and repeat the finesse. Consistent with what you have read so far, you must lead *toward* the high cards with which you hope to win tricks.

(k) The best chance to win a third trick in this suit is to take a "double finesse"—to finesse against two high cards. Lead from your hand toward dummy with the intention of playing the ten unless West plays an honor. The queen and jack can be divided four ways—West has both, just the queen, just the jack, or neither one. You will not win a trick with the ten unless West has both the queen and jack; the odds are three-to-one against it.

(l)   Here is another example of the double finesse. Your aim is to win a second trick with the jack or ten. Lead low from your hand and finesse the ten (unless West plays an honor card). Suppose East wins dummy's ten with the king or queen. When you regain the lead, repeat the finesse by leading from your hand again and finessing the jack. The missing king and queen can be divided in four ways: West has both, just the king, just the queen, or neither one. You will win a second trick unless East has both the king and queen; the odds are three to one in your favor.

Sometimes there are two or three lines of play and you must choose the one that gives you the best chance to make your contract—the percentage play. Remembering the odds for a double finesse will help you to choose the best line: the odds are three to one *against* a double finesse working if you must find one defender with two specific high cards (as in "k"); the odds are three to one *in favor* of a double finesse working if you must find one defender holding one of two specific high cards—as in "l."

In the first six illustrations the correct way to finesse was to *lead toward the high card (or cards) with which you hope to win a trick.* It is *sometimes* right to lead a high card to take a finesse. In the next three examples, the goal is to win three tricks:

(m) Dummy   (n) Dummy   (o) Dummy
     A 5 4   A J 9   A J 3

     You   You   You
     Q J 10   Q 7 6   Q 5 2

(m)   Lead the queen, jack or ten from your hand. If West covers with the king you have three tricks. If he does not cover, play low from dummy. If you win that trick (the finesse works), repeat the finesse. As long as West has the king you can win three tricks.

(n)   The odds are about three to one against it, but your best chance
      to win three tricks is to take a double finesse and hope that West
      has both the king and ten. Lead the queen. If West covers with
      the king, win with the ace, lead another suit to return to your
      hand, and again lead toward dummy, intending to finesse the
      nine. (If West has the king and ten, the double finesse will also
      succeed if your first play is a low card to the nine; but that is
      technically wrong because then you would be limited to one
      trick if East held both the king and ten.)

(o)   Now that the nine and ten are both missing, leading the queen
      will limit you to two tricks no matter how the cards divide. If
      East has the king the finesse will fail; if West has the king he
      will cover the queen, leaving you with J 3 opposite 5 2. When
      considering whether or not to lead an honor card to take a
      finesse, ask yourself this question: if the honor is covered, what
      will I have left? If you don't like the answer, don't lead the
      honor. So the correct play with this combination to win three
      tricks (although chances are slim) is to lead low from your hand
      and finesse the jack. If you win the trick, cash the ace and hope
      that West was dealt a doubleton king.

When to finesse, and when to play for the drop: When you have
length in a suit, it may be better to play to drop a missing high card
than to take the finesse.

(p) Dummy	(q) Dummy	(r) Dummy
8 7 6 5 4	10 9 7 6	K J 5 4
You	You	You
A Q J 10 9	A K J 5 4	A 10 9 8

(p)   Lead from dummy. If East follows suit with a low card, take the
      finesse; do not play the ace. When the only missing high card is
      the king and you have ten cards (or fewer) in the combined
      hands, take the finesse. Simple arithmetic tells you that the
      fifty-fifty chance offered by a finesse is better than hoping there

is a singleton king when three cards are missing. If there were 11 cards in the combined hands the odds are slightly in favor of playing the ace—playing for the king to drop.

(q) When the only high card that is missing is the queen and you have nine cards in the combined hands, cash one top honor; if both opponents follow suit, the odds are slightly in favor of cashing the remaining top honor—play for the queen to drop. With the cards shown, cash the ace or king and if both opponents follow suit, then cash the second high honor. If West does not follow suit to the first lead you know that East has the queen and will take the marked finesse.

(r) When the only high card that is missing is the queen and you have eight cards (or fewer) in the combined hands, the best chance to avoid losing a trick is to cash one high honor and, if the queen does not drop, take the finesse. When the ace and king are in different hands as shown above, you have a "two-way finesse" and must guess which way to play. If you think East has the queen, cash the king first and finesse through East. If you think West has the queen, do the opposite—cash the ace first and then finesse through West.

There is an old saying about whether to play for the drop or take a finesse when the queen is missing: "Eight ever, nine never." In other words, you should always finesse when you have eight cards in a suit and are missing five to the queen; but you should never finesse when you have nine cards in a suit and are missing only four to the queen. It is rarely right to break this rule with eight cards because the odds are heavily in favor of the finesse. But the odds are only very slightly in favor of playing for the drop with nine cards, so it is often right to break the rule and finesse if you have learned something about the opponents' distribution from the bidding or early plays. More about this later.

Safety Plays: Here are two illustrations which show how to play a suit combination to guard against a bad break:

(s)   Dummy   (t)   Dummy
      A J 7 5 4   K 10 8 3

      You   You
      K 8 6 3 2   A Q 9 4 2

(s)   To guard against West having Q 10 9, begin by leading the king.
      East will show out and you still have the ace and jack in dummy
      behind the queen; you have a marked finesse. If you begin by
      leading the ace and West has Q 10 9, you must lose a trick. If
      the missing cards divide 2-1, or if East has Q 10 9, it does not
      matter whether you play the ace or king first.

(t)   Begin by leading the ace or queen. When missing J x x x, the
      safety play to avoid losing a trick no matter how the suit divides
      is to first cash an honor from the hand holding two honors. If
      either defender shows out on the first lead you learn that his
      partner still has J x x and you can avoid losing a trick by
      finessing. Note that cashing the king first would be a
      mistake—you would lose a trick if West began with J x x x.

CHAPTER TWELVE

NOTRUMP CONTRACTS

Now we are ready to play full deals, and the first eight are notrump contracts. In each deal you will be South, the declarer; North the dummy; West the left-hand opponent (the opening leader); and East the right-hand opponent.

A notrump contract is usually a race. The opponents start out by leading a long suit. They try to develop and win enough tricks to beat the contract before declarer can develop and win enough tricks to make it. Analyzing the opening lead is part of the strategy in planning the play, so here are a few words about opening leads before going on to the first hand.

[The opening leader must first decide which suit to lead, and then choose the correct card. If his partner has not bid a suit, the usual choice against notrump contracts is from the longest and strongest suit (excluding suits bid by the enemy). If the suit has a three-card sequence headed by the king, queen, jack or ten (i.e., K Q J, Q J 10, J 10 9, or 10 9 8), the correct lead is the top card regardless of the length of the suit. The top card should also be led from holdings of K Q 10, Q J 9, J 10 8, or 10 9 7; in other words, when holding the first, second and fourth card of the sequence.]

Now let's play the first deal:

(1)

Contract: 3NT

Opening lead: ♠Q

```
                    North
                    ♠ A 3
                    ♡ K 9 8
                    ◇ 10 7 4
                    ♣ Q J 10 9 4

                    South
                    ♠ K 9
                    ♡ A Q J 2
                    ◇ K Q J 5
                    ♣ 8 6 3
```

As South, you have a balanced hand with 16 points and open the bidding with 1NT. North, your partner, has a balanced hand with 11 points (ten in high cards and one for the five-card suit), so he raises to 3NT and that ends the bidding.

Count your tricks: West leads the ♠Q, presumably from a four-card or longer suit headed by the queen-jack-ten. Your partner exposes the dummy for all to see, and you are the declarer at a contract of 3NT. *The first thing to do is count the winning tricks in the combined hands; this should be done before you play the first card from dummy.* You have six winners (two spades and four hearts), so you need three more. The next step is to organize a plan to develop the needed tricks. You will still have a spade stopper after you win the first trick with the ace or king, so there is a sure way to make the contract by developing three diamond tricks.

Win the first trick with the ♠A (or ♠K) and lead any diamond honor—the king, queen, jack or ten. If the defender who has the ◊A does not take his ace, continue leading diamonds until he does. The expected lead from the defender with the ◊A is another spade, which you will win with your other high honor. Now you have nine tricks, so cash the rest of your winners to win the race. Here are the four hands:

Contract: 3NT
Opening lead: ♣Q

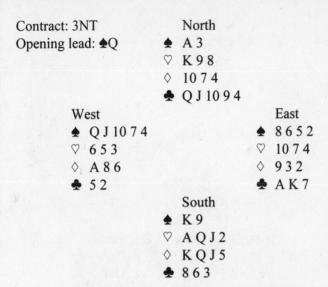

North
♠ A 3
♡ K 9 8
◇ 10 7 4
♣ Q J 10 9 4

West
♠ Q J 10 7 4
♡ 6 5 3
◇ A 8 6
♣ 5 2

East
♠ 8 6 5 2
♡ 10 7 4
◇ 9 3 2
♣ A K 7

South
♠ K 9
♡ A Q J 2
◇ K Q J 5
♣ 8 6 3

It would be a big mistake to cash your second high spade before driving out the ◇A. Since you would have no more spade stoppers, when the opponents get the lead with the ◇A they can win three spade tricks, one diamond and two clubs; setting the contract by two tricks. The general rule at notrump is not to cash your winners until you have established enough tricks to make your contract.

Also, it would be wrong to try to establish the club suit instead of diamonds; you would lose the race because you would have to give up the lead twice to develop the three needed tricks in clubs. When you lead the first club, East would win with the ♣K and lead a spade to knock out your second stopper. When you lead the second club, East would take the ♣A and lead a spade. West would cash three spade tricks and the ◇A for down two.

[Before playing the next deal, more about opening leads: when leading against a notrump contract from a hand with a long suit that is not headed by a three-card sequence, the usual choice of the card to lead is "fourth best"—the fourth highest card in the suit.]

(2)   North
                                       ♠ A J 8 5 3
                                       ♡ Q 6
                                       ◇ 9 7 4
Contract: 3NT   ♣ A K 10

Opening lead: ◇5   South
                                       ♠ 6 2
                                       ♡ A K 9 7 5
                                       ◇ A Q 8
                                       ♣ 9 4 3

West	North	East	South
—	—	—	1♡
Pass	1♠	Pass	1NT
Pass	3NT	All Pass	

Establish winners in a long suit: You reach 3NT on the bidding shown and West leads the ◇5 (presumably the fourth highest from a four-card or longer suit). The diamond lead assures a trick with the ◇Q, so you have eight winners (one spade, three hearts, two diamonds and two clubs). The best chance to establish a ninth is in the heart suit. If the missing hearts divide 3-3, you can run five heart tricks. If the hearts divide 4-2, you can develop a fourth heart trick by giving up one trick along the way. Since you still have a diamond stopper and need only one more trick, you can make your contract if hearts divide no worse than 4-2. A plan has been made, so let's play.

East plays the ◇J on the first trick and you win with the ◇Q. Now lead a heart to the ♡Q, and then cash the ♡A and ♡K. If the missing hearts happen to divide 3-3, the two remaining hearts in your hand are good and you can win ten tricks. But East shows out on the third heart lead, leaving West with the high heart. Now lead a fourth round of hearts, conceding that trick to West. When you regain the lead, you can win a trick with the fifth heart. The four hands:

Contract: 3NT
Opening lead: ◊5

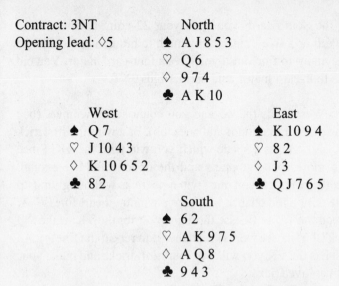

North
♠ A J 8 5 3
♡ Q 6
◊ 9 7 4
♣ A K 10

West
♠ Q 7
♡ J 10 4 3
◊ K 10 6 5 2
♣ 8 2

East
♠ K 10 9 4
♡ 8 2
◊ J 3
♣ Q J 7 6 5

South
♠ 6 2
♡ A K 9 7 5
◊ A Q 8
♣ 9 4 3

The rotation in which you cash your high hearts is important. If you mistakenly cash the ♡A or ♡K first, the second heart trick would be won with dummy's ♡Q and you would be unable to continue leading the suit. With the 4-2 heart break you would be set because you do not have sufficient entries to your hand to establish a fourth heart trick. *As stated earlier: when running a long suit, cash the high cards in the shorter hand first.*

(3)

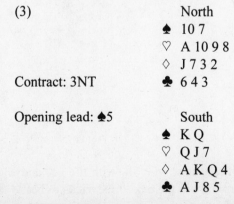

North
♠ 10 7
♡ A 10 9 8
◊ J 7 3 2
♣ 6 4 3

Contract: 3NT

Opening lead: ♠5

South
♠ K Q
♡ Q J 7
◊ A K Q 4
♣ A J 8 5

Holding the South cards you open your 22-point balanced hand with 2NT. Partner's five points are enough to bid game, but first he bids 3♣ (Stayman) to find out if you have a four-card major. You bid 3♢ to deny a four-card major, and partner bids 3NT.

The finesse: West leads the ♠5 and you count seven winners (one spade, one heart, four diamonds and one club). East wins the first trick with the ♠A and returns a spade which you win with the ♠K. Since you have no more spade stoppers and the opponents have enough spades to set the contract, you must win nine tricks without giving up the lead. The only good chance is to take a winning heart finesse. At trick three lead the ♡Q to finesse through West for the ♡K: if the ♡Q wins the trick (the finesse works), lead the ♡J to repeat the finesse. As long as West has the ♡K you will win four heart tricks and make your contract with an overtrick.

Unfortunately, East has the ♡K. The four hands:

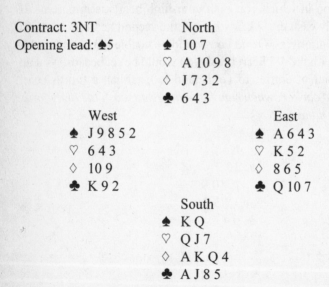

Contract: 3NT
Opening lead: ♠5

North
♠ 10 7
♡ A 10 9 8
♢ J 7 3 2
♣ 6 4 3

West
♠ J 9 8 5 2
♡ 6 4 3
♢ 10 9
♣ K 9 2

East
♠ A 6 4 3
♡ K 5 2
♢ 8 6 5
♣ Q 10 7

South
♠ K Q
♡ Q J 7
♢ A K Q 4
♣ A J 8 5

When you take the heart finesse East will win with the ♡K and lead another spade. His partner will win the next three tricks to beat 3NT. The fate of this contract depends on a successful finesse—a

50-50 chance—but every good player would play the same way and be set when the heart finesse fails. Do not expect to make every contract you reach; making about two out of three is normal.

[This is a good example of why the opening leader should lead from his longest and strongest suit against a notrump contract. If West leads anything but a spade, the contract can be made even if the heart finesse fails. Another interesting point: when a player leads his longest and strongest suit against a notrump contract, his partner, unless he has good reason to do otherwise, must cooperate and return that suit when he is on lead. To beat this contract, East must lead a spade at trick two, and lead another spade later when he wins the lead with the ♡K.]

(4)   North
                                 ♠ A 5 3
                                 ♡ 9 2
                                 ◇ Q 8 5 4
Contract: 3NT   ♣ K 10 8 7

Opening lead: ♡4   South
                                 ♠ K 9 8 2
                                 ♡ A 10 7
                                 ◇ A K 3
                                 ♣ Q J 5

You open your 17-point hand with 1NT and partner raises to 2NT with nine points. This invites you to go to game with a maximum, so you bid 3NT because you have 17 points.

The hold-up play: Against this 3NT contract, West leads the ♡4 (once again, predictably the fourth highest card from a four-card or longer suit) and East plays the jack. You have six winners (two spades, one heart and three diamonds) and the only way to make the contract is to drive out the ♣A and regain the lead before the opponents can win five tricks. If you win the first heart trick and lead a club you will succeed if the missing eight hearts divide 4-4, in which case the opponents can win only three heart tricks. But the contract can be made even if the hearts are divided 5-3 (or worse) if the player with the long hearts does not have the ♣A and you *"hold up" your ♡A until the third round.* Allow East to win the first trick with the ♡J. Assuming the opponents defend well by persisting with heart leads, duck the second heart lead, win the third, and lead the ♣Q or ♣J. The four hands:

Contract: 3NT
Opening lead: ♡4

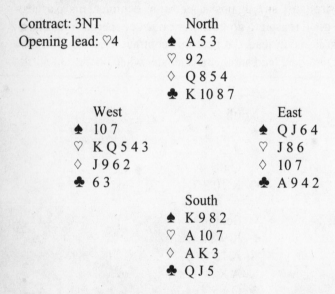

```
                        North
                        ♠ A 5 3
                        ♡ 9 2
                        ◊ Q 8 5 4
                        ♣ K 10 8 7
        West                            East
        ♠ 10 7                          ♠ Q J 6 4
        ♡ K Q 5 4 3                     ♡ J 8 6
        ◊ J 9 6 2                       ◊ 10 7
        ♣ 6 3                           ♣ A 9 4 2
                        South
                        ♠ K 9 8 2
                        ♡ A 10 7
                        ◊ A K 3
                        ♣ Q J 5
```

In this deal good declarer play pays off. East has the ♣A, but when he wins it he has no more hearts to lead; that is if you held up the ♡A until the third round. When you regain the lead you have three club tricks to add to your six winners in the other suits; so you make your contract. If West held the ♣A and five hearts, the contract could not be made whether you held up your ♡A until the third round or not.

[The opening leader should lead the king from K Q 5 4 3 against a trump contract. But this is a notrump contract and West correctly led his fourth-best heart. If the heart suit were headed by king-queen-jack or king-queen-ten, then the king would be the proper lead.]

[Another interesting point about the defense: if East did not play the ♡J at trick one, you could win the trick with the ten. In situations like this, when partner leads a low card and dummy has nothing in the suit, third hand should play his highest card in an effort to win or promote a trick. The rule is "third hand high," but if the suit is headed by two or more equal cards *play the low card of the sequence.* For example: third-hand should play the queen from ♡K Q x, the jack from ♡Q J x, and the ten from ♡Q J 10 x, etc. This strategy for third hand—playing the low card from a sequence—is very important and applies against both suit and notrump contracts. Remember, third hand follows with the *lowest* card of an honor sequence, while first hand leads the *highest.* This is explained in more detail in Part Three.]

It is sometimes right to make a hold-up play with the king, *provided the ace has been played.* For example:

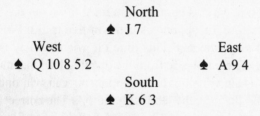

North
♠ J 7

West
♠ Q 10 8 5 2

East
♠ A 9 4

South
♠ K 6 3

West leads the ♠5. If East wins with the ♠A and returns the ♠9, it is safe to hold up at trick two because you have the high spade. Now suppose East does not play the ace.

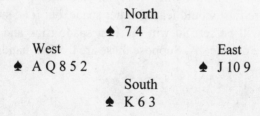

North
♠ 7 4

West
♠ A Q 8 5 2

East
♠ J 10 9

South
♠ K 6 3

Again West leads the ♠5, but this time East plays the ♠9. It is apparent that West has the ♠A because if East had it he would play third-hand high. You should most emphatically take the ♠K; if you do not the opponents will run the first five spade tricks.

(5)   North
                                       ♠ 7 2
                                       ♡ J 6
                                       ◇ K Q 10 5 4 3
Contract: 3NT   ♣ K 10 9

Opening lead: ♠3   South
                                       ♠ A 10 5
                                       ♡ A 8 3
                                       ◇ J 8 2
                                       ♣ A Q J 7

The don't-hold-up play: You open the bidding 1NT and your partner
raises to 3NT. To make this contract you must drive out the ◇A and
regain the lead before the opponents can win five tricks. West leads
the ♠3 and East plays the ♠Q. This time the winning play is not to
hold up your ace. There is a clue from the opening lead that the spade
suit is divided 4-4; in which case the opponents can win only three
spade tricks when they get the lead with the ◇A. The correct card to
lead from a four-card or longer suit is the fourth highest. Since West
led the three and the two is in dummy, it is predictable that West has
a four-card spade suit; if West had more than four cards in the suit and
led his fourth highest, he would still have one or more lower cards in
his hand. It would not matter whether or not you hold up your ♠A if
you could be sure East would lead another spade, but if he switches
to a heart you will be set. So win the first spade trick and lead a
diamond to drive out the ◇A. Suppose these are the four hands:

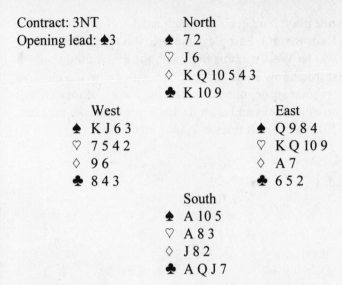

Contract: 3NT
Opening lead: ♠3

North
♠ 7 2
♡ J 6
♢ K Q 10 5 4 3
♣ K 10 9

West
♠ K J 6 3
♡ 7 5 4 2
♢ 9 6
♣ 8 4 3

East
♠ Q 9 8 4
♡ K Q 10 9
♢ A 7
♣ 6 5 2

South
♠ A 10 5
♡ A 8 3
♢ J 8 2
♣ A Q J 7

As you can see the contract is safe if you win the first spade trick. When East gets the lead with the ♢A, only three spade tricks are available for the defense and you still have a heart stopper.

If you duck the first spade trick, East can see a sure way to set the contract by switching to the ♡K, and continuing with the ♡Q if you duck. When he gets the lead with the ♢A, he can win the rest of his heart tricks, giving the defense five tricks (one spade, three hearts and one diamond).

(6)

North
♠ 7 6 2
♡ J 10
♢ A Q 10 9
♣ A J 4 3

Contract: 3NT

Opening lead: ♠Q

South
♠ A 8 5
♡ A Q 9 3
♢ J 6
♣ K Q 10 8

The avoidance play: You open the South hand 1NT and North bids 3NT. West leads the ♠Q, East plays the ♠K, you duck. East returns the ♠3 and you let West win this trick with the ♠9. A third spade is led, East discards a low heart and you win with the ♠A. You have seven winners (one spade, one heart, one diamond and four clubs). You need two more tricks and must decide whether to take the heart or diamond finesse. Which finesse would you take?

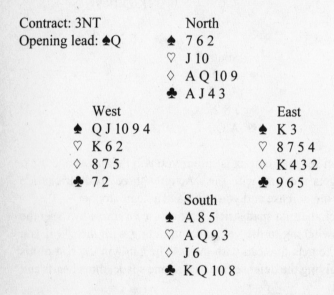

Contract: 3NT
Opening lead: ♠Q

North
♠ 7 6 2
♡ J 10
◇ A Q 10 9
♣ A J 4 3

West
♠ Q J 10 9 4
♡ K 6 2
◇ 8 7 5
♣ 7 2

East
♠ K 3
♡ 8 7 5 4
◇ K 4 3 2
♣ 9 6 5

South
♠ A 8 5
♡ A Q 9 3
◇ J 6
♣ K Q 10 8

Both finesses fail. If you take the heart finesse you will be set because West has two good spades to cash. If you take the diamond finesse you make your contract because East has no more spades. When you take the losing diamond finesse, East will win with the ◇K and lead a heart. Grab your ♡A, *do not finesse*; now that the diamond suit is established you have nine tricks.

This is a typical "danger-hand" situation. West has enough spades left to set 3NT if he gets the lead. His is the danger hand and you must try to develop the tricks you need without allowing him to get the lead. You need only two diamond tricks to make the contract and East is known to have no more spades, the contract is 100 percent safe by taking the diamond finesse whether it works or not.

[There is another good lesson in this deal about third-hand play. The defenders' best hope to defeat 3NT is to drive out your ♠A, establish their long suit and regain the lead before you can win nine tricks. East correctly played the ♠K on the first trick to "unblock." He can well afford to cover his partner's queen with his king since the lead promises Q J 10 (or Q J 9). If he plays low and you hold up your ♠A twice, the second spade trick will be won with his ♠K. Since he has no more spades, he could not drive out your ♠A. The following is a good rule when trying to run a long suit against a notrump contract: *The defender with the shorter suit should save a low card to play last, so his partner can win that trick and continue leading the suit.*]

(7)

Contract: 3NT

Opening lead: ♠6

North
♠ A 7
♡ 9 8 5 4
♢ 8 7 6 3
♣ 6 5 2

South
♠ Q 2
♡ A K Q
♢ A Q 5 2
♣ A K Q 8

The percentage play: You reach 3NT. West leads the ♠6, and you play the ♠7 from dummy, hoping West has the ♠K. East wins with the ♠K and returns a spade to knock out your only stopper. You have eight tricks (one spade, three hearts, one diamond and three clubs), and there are two chances for a ninth trick—the ♢Q if the finesse works, or the ♣8 if the suit divides 3-3. If you play your high clubs and the suit does not divide, you cannot get to dummy to try the diamond finesse. If you finesse the ♢Q at trick three and West has the ♢K, you will lose five tricks (or more) before you regain the lead. Your back is to the wall. What would you do? In situations like this, take the percentage play—the one most likely to succeed. Six cards will divide 3-3 about 36 percent of the time. Is it important to

remember the exact odds? No. What is important to remember is that
when you are missing six cards, the odds are that they will *not* divide
equally—six cards are more likely to divide 4-2 than 3-3. So the
correct play is the diamond finesse, because the fifty-fifty chance
offers better odds that the 3-3 club split. The full deal:

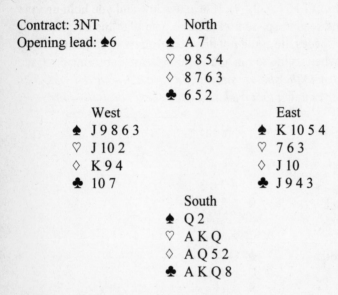

Contract: 3NT
Opening lead: ♣6

North
♠ A 7
♡ 9 8 5 4
◇ 8 7 6 3
♣ 6 5 2

West
♠ J 9 8 6 3
♡ J 10 2
◇ K 9 4
♣ 10 7

East
♠ K 10 5 4
♡ 7 6 3
◇ J 10
♣ J 9 4 3

South
♠ Q 2
♡ A K Q
◇ A Q 5 2
♣ A K Q 8

The ◇K is offside and the clubs do not divide 3-3, so you will be
set. But if you chose the diamond finesse, you played like an expert.

(8)

North
♠ Q 7
♡ 9 8 5 4
◇ 8 7 6 3
♣ Q 5 2

Contract: 3NT

South
♠ A 2
♡ A K Q
◇ A Q 5 2
♣ A K 8 6

Opening lead ♠J

Combine your chances: Against this 3NT contract West leads the ♠J. You correctly play the ♠Q on the first trick, East plays the ♠K and you the ♠A. This deal has the same eight winners as #7, but, because the ♣Q is now an entry to dummy, there are three chances to win a ninth trick: either hearts or clubs divide 3-3, or the diamond finesse works. *You can make 3NT if any one of the three chances works if you play your cards in the right rotation.* How should you play? Answer: first, cash the ♡A, ♡K and ♡Q; if the suit divides 3-3 the fourth heart in dummy is your ninth trick and you have the ♣Q as an entry to get to it. If hearts do not divide, cash the ♣A and ♣K *first* and then the ♣Q; if clubs are 3-3, lead to your ◇A and cash the 13th club. If the clubs do not divide 3-3, the lead is in dummy (your last play was the ♣Q) and you can try the diamond finesse. The four hands:

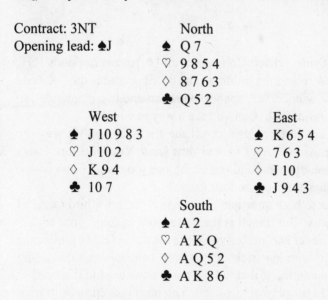

Contract: 3NT
Opening lead: ♠J

North
♠ Q 7
♡ 9 8 5 4
◇ 8 7 6 3
♣ Q 5 2

West
♠ J 10 9 8 3
♡ J 10 2
◇ K 9 4
♣ 10 7

East
♠ K 6 5 4
♡ 7 6 3
◇ J 10
♣ J 9 4 3

South
♠ A 2
♡ A K Q
◇ A Q 5 2
♣ A K 8 6

The only one of the three that works is the 3-3 heart split, but note that you would not have been able to get to dummy to win the 13th heart if you had played the ♣Q before cashing the high hearts.

CHAPTER THIRTEEN

TRUMP CONTRACTS

The next ten deals show a variety of ways to play trump contracts.

(1)

	North
	♠ 8 7
	♡ J 9
	◊ A 9 6
Contract: 4♠	♣ Q 10 5 4 3 2
Opening lead: ♡K	**South**
	♠ A K Q J 10 2
	♡ A 7 6
	◊ K 8 4
	♣ 9

How to count your tricks: You open with 1♠, partner responds 1NT, and you bid 4♠ to end the bidding. The opening lead is the ♡K. You can count nine winners (six spades, one heart and two diamonds), so you need one more trick. Can you see a way to win it?

Before going further, let's count the tricks in another way; *by counting the possible losers in your own hand.* You have four losers (two hearts, one diamond and one club), one too many. Can you see a way to eliminate one of the four losers?

The answer to both questions is the same—ruff the third round of hearts in dummy. But which is the better way to count your tricks? Answer: whichever way makes you more comfortable. My preference is to count the winning tricks at notrump contracts and the losing tricks at trump contracts; that will be the method used in this book.

Now back to the play of this hand. You must concede a heart trick before you can ruff the third round of that suit, so suppose you duck the first trick and, when West continues with the ♡Q, win with your ♡A. Now lead your last heart, ruff it in dummy, and draw trumps. The four hands:

Contract: 4♠
Opening lead: ♡K

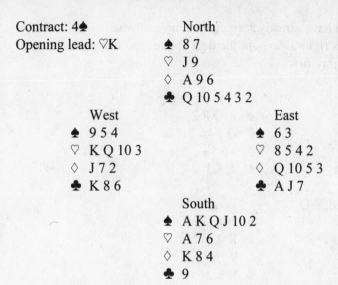

North
♠ 8 7
♡ J 9
♢ A 9 6
♣ Q 10 5 4 3 2

West
♠ 9 5 4
♡ K Q 10 3
♢ J 7 2
♣ K 8 6

East
♠ 6 3
♡ 8 5 4 2
♢ Q 10 5 3
♣ A J 7

South
♠ A K Q J 10 2
♡ A 7 6
♢ K 8 4
♣ 9

[Before leaving this deal, is there a defense to beat this contract? Answer: yes, an original trump lead, followed by a second trump lead when you concede a heart trick—with no trumps left in dummy, you cannot ruff a heart. However, the ♡K is the logical choice and most experts would lead it. Often the opening lead makes or breaks a contract and the winning choice is not obvious.]

Another question: is there a safer game contract? Yes, 3NT, but South cannot be blamed for not bidding it with such a good spade suit and a singleton club.

When to draw trumps: A trite saying from the old days in England: "Ten thousand Englishmen are walking the streets of London with empty pockets because they didn't draw the trumps" Possibly a better one: "Twenty thousand Englishmen are walking the streets of London with empty pockets because they drew the trumps too soon."

There is no question that in most deals it is right to draw the missing trumps as soon as possible to prevent the opponents from ruffing one of your good tricks. Sometimes, however, there is work to be done in the other suits before you draw the trumps, and at other times you should never draw any trumps, as you will see in deals that follow. You have already seen one example of when you should not draw trumps right away—in the deal above, you had to ruff a heart loser in dummy first.

(2)   North
                                             ♠ K Q 8 2
                                             ♡ Q J 4
                                             ◇ J 6 5
Contract: 2♠   ♣ A 8 3

Opening lead: ♣Q   South
                                             ♠ J 10 9 5 3
                                             ♡ K 7
                                             ◇ 9 7 4
                                             ♣ K 6 2

Discard a loser: North opens the bidding with 1♣, you respond 1♠ and then pass when partner raises to 2♠. The opening lead is the ♣Q and you can count six losers—one spade, one heart, three diamonds and one club—one loser too many. You cannot prevent the opponents from winning three diamond tricks and two major-suit aces, so the key is not to lose a club trick. In which hand would you win the first trick? What would you lead at trick two? Answers: win the first trick in your hand with the ♣K and lead the ♡K; if the ♡K is allowed to win the trick, lead another heart. Your plan is to "discard" your losing club on the third round of hearts, and you must do so before the opponents can establish and win a club trick. The four hands:

Contract: 2♠
Opening lead: ♣Q

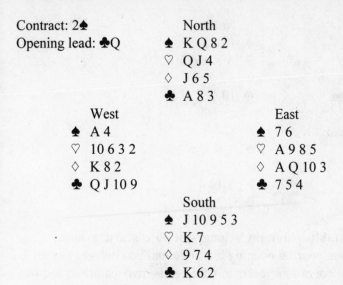

North
♠ K Q 8 2
♡ Q J 4
◊ J 6 5
♣ A 8 3

West
♠ A 4
♡ 10 6 3 2
◊ K 8 2
♣ Q J 10 9

East
♠ 7 6
♡ A 9 8 5
◊ A Q 10 3
♣ 7 5 4

South
♠ J 10 9 5 3
♡ K 7
◊ 9 7 4
♣ K 6 2

Note that if you lead a trump at trick two, you lose the *timing*. West will win with the ♠A and play another club; with the ♣A and ♣K gone, the defense can win a club trick (plus three diamond tricks) when they regain the lead with the ♡A. When the opponents have a high trump and you are in a hurry to discard a loser, do not draw trumps until after you discard your loser.

If you make the mistake of winning the first trick in dummy with the ♣A, you can be set even if you lead the ♡K at trick two. East may hold up his ♡A until the second round and lead a club; then you cannot get to dummy in time to discard your club loser on the third round of hearts.

(3)

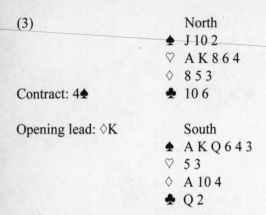

North
♠ J 10 2
♡ A K 8 6 4
◇ 8 5 3
♣ 10 6

Contract: 4♠

Opening lead: ◇K

South
♠ A K Q 6 4 3
♡ 5 3
◇ A 10 4
♣ Q 2

How to establish dummy's long suit to discard a loser: Your
partner raises your 1♠ opening bid to 2♠ and you bid 4♠. The ◇K is
led and you count four losers in your hand—two diamonds and two
clubs. You cannot ruff any of your losers in dummy, but there is an
excellent chance to make the contract by discarding one of your losers
on the heart suit.

After winning the first trick with the ◇A, should you draw all of
the missing trumps? *NO. This time the ♠J and ♠10 in dummy are
needed as "entry cards."* However, it is okay to play one high trump
from your hand, so let's assume that you do so and both opponents
follow suit. At tricks three and four cash the ♡A and ♡K and,
assuming no one ruffs (the odds are better than five-to-one against a
suit dividing worse than 4-2), lead a third heart to ruff in your hand
with a *high* trump. West shows out on the third heart lead, which
means East has one more high heart. So lead to dummy's ♠10 and ruff
a fourth heart in your hand with another *high* trump. The fifth heart in
dummy is now good, so lead to dummy's ♠J and discard any one of
your four losers on the good heart. The four hands:

Contract: 4♠
Opening lead: ◇K

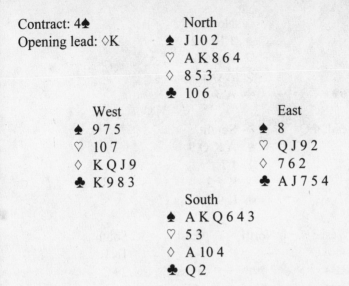

North
♠ J 10 2
♡ A K 8 6 4
◇ 8 5 3
♣ 10 6

West
♠ 9 7 5
♡ 10 7
◇ K Q J 9
♣ K 9 8 3

East
♠ 8
♡ Q J 9 2
◇ 7 6 2
♣ A J 7 5 4

South
♠ A K Q 6 4 3
♡ 5 3
◇ A 10 4
♣ Q 2

If you draw a second round of trumps before ruffing the third heart in your hand you can still make the contract with an overtrick if the missing hearts divide 3-3. But since the suit divides 4-2 you would be set because you wasted one of dummy's entry cards.

As mentioned earlier, when you are trying to win tricks with long cards it is important to keep a mental record of the missing cards in that suit and here is a good hand to illustrate how to do it. First determine that there are six hearts missing—you and dummy have seven between you. Seven from 13 leaves six. *Now count the opponents' hearts, not yours; you never have to count higher than six.* When they both follow suit to the ♡A there are four missing; when they both follow to the ♡K there are two missing; when you ruff the third heart in your hand and West shows out, you know there is still one missing and East has it.

Keeping an accurate count is also important when drawing trumps. Leading one too many rounds of trumps, or one too few, may be fatal.

(4)

Contract: 6♠

Opening lead: ♣Q

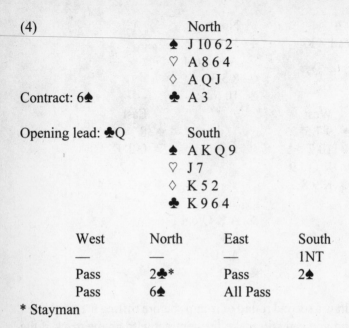

North
♠ J 10 6 2
♡ A 8 6 4
◇ A Q J
♣ A 3

South
♠ A K Q 9
♡ J 7
◇ K 5 2
♣ K 9 6 4

West	North	East	South
—	—	—	1NT
Pass	2♣*	Pass	2♠
Pass	6♠	All Pass	

* Stayman

Avoid overruffs: You reach an excellent contract of 6♠ on the bidding shown, and the opening lead is the ♣Q. You have three losers in your hand—one heart and two clubs. The heart loser is unavoidable, but you can make the contract by ruffing your two club losers in dummy. Since you would not have enough spades left in dummy to ruff two clubs if you draw trumps immediately, win the first two tricks with the ♣A and ♣K (if the missing clubs divide 6-1 and someone ruffs you would be set, but that is very unlikely). Now lead a third club and ruff with dummy's ♠10; you can well afford to ruff with the ♠10 since all of the trumps in your hand are high. Ruffing with a low trump would be a needless risk because East may have been dealt only two clubs and would overruff. Next, play a trump to get the lead back in your hand, lead your last club and ruff it with dummy's ♠J. It is now time to draw the missing trumps, and you must do so *before leading any diamonds*. The four hands:

Contract: 6♠
Opening lead: ♣Q

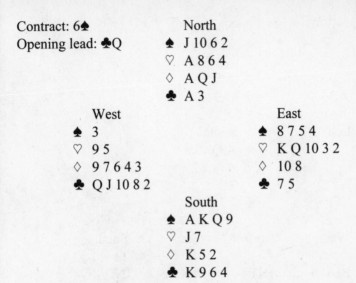

North
♠ J 10 6 2
♡ A 8 6 4
◇ A Q J
♣ A 3

West
♠ 3
♡ 9 5
◇ 9 7 6 4 3
♣ Q J 10 8 2

East
♠ 8 7 5 4
♡ K Q 10 3 2
◇ 10 8
♣ 7 5

South
♠ A K Q 9
♡ J 7
◇ K 5 2
♣ K 9 6 4

Note that East does have a doubleton club; if you had ruffed either club loser with one of dummy's low spades, he would set the contract by overruffing. Also note, after ruffing your club losers, you must cash four rounds of spades to draw all of East's trumps before leading any diamonds. With the cards as shown, East could discard his two diamonds while you are ruffing the third and fourth clubs; in which case he would be able to ruff if you led even one diamond.

This deal demonstrated the advantage of using the Stayman Convention, which led to discovering the 4-4 fit in spades. Twelve tricks are available in a spade contract (by ruffing two clubs), while there are only ten tricks available in notrump.

Sometimes it is necessary to ruff with low trumps, even though you run the risk of being overruffed. For example:

(5)

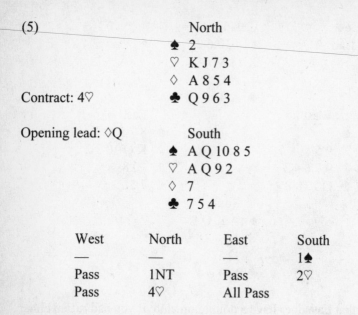

North
♠ 2
♡ K J 7 3
♢ A 8 5 4
♣ Q 9 6 3

Contract: 4♡

Opening lead: ♢Q

South
♠ A Q 10 8 5
♡ A Q 9 2
♢ 7
♣ 7 5 4

West	North	East	South
—	—	—	1♠
Pass	1NT	Pass	2♡
Pass	4♡	All Pass	

The crossruff: West leads the ♢Q against your optimistic 4♡ contract. You have only two winners outside the trump suit, so your best chance to make the contract is to win eight trump tricks by a "crossruff." Since you need eight trump tricks, *the first four ruffs must be made with low trumps* even though there is a danger of being overruffed. Win the first trick with the ♢A, cash the ♠A, and ruff a spade in dummy with the ♡3. Then ruff a diamond in your hand with the ♡2, a spade in dummy with the ♡7, and a diamond in your hand with the ♡9. If no one has overruffed, the contract is now safe by crossruffing with the four remaining high trumps. The four hands:

Contract: 4♡
Opening lead: ◇Q

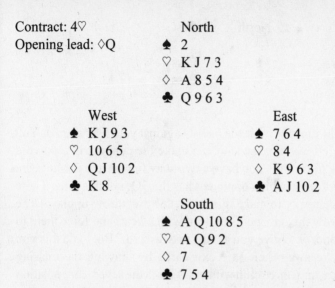

North
♠ 2
♡ K J 7 3
◇ A 8 5 4
♣ Q 9 6 3

West
♠ K J 9 3
♡ 10 6 5
◇ Q J 10 2
♣ K 8

East
♠ 7 6 4
♡ 8 4
◇ K 9 6 3
♣ A J 10 2

South
♠ A Q 10 8 5
♡ A Q 9 2
◇ 7
♣ 7 5 4

Since the defenders were unable to overruff at any point, eight trump tricks are available; but note that if you ruffed with any of your high trumps early you would be set.

[A heart opening lead would limit declarer to seven trump tricks and that would beat this contract. Good players would lead a trump holding the West hand because of the strong holding in declarer's spade suit—it is predictable that declarer will be ruffing spades, and trump leads will reduce the number of ruffs possible.]

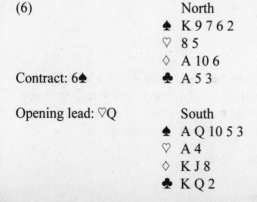

(6)

Contract: 6♠

Opening lead: ♡Q

North
♠ K 9 7 6 2
♡ 8 5
◇ A 10 6
♣ A 5 3

South
♠ A Q 10 5 3
♡ A 4
◇ K J 8
♣ K Q 2

West	North	East	South
—	—	—	1♠
Pass	3♠	Pass	4NT
Pass	5♡	Pass	6♠
All Pass			

The throw-in play: West leads the ♡Q against your 6♠ contract. You have one sure loser, a heart, and can make the contract if you avoid losing a trick to the ◊Q. You have a two-way finesse and it may seem that you must guess which opponent has the ◊Q; not this time. There is a 100 percent way to make this contract by a "throw-in play." The plan is to throw the opponents on lead with a heart and force them to lead a diamond, or to give you a "ruff and discard." But to do this you must first take away their safe exit cards by drawing the missing trumps and cashing three club winners. This is the seven-card position you should reach to execute the throw-in play successfully:

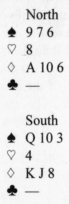

North
♠ 9 7 6
♡ 8
◊ A 10 6
♣ —

South
♠ Q 10 3
♡ 4
◊ K J 8
♣ —

Now lead a heart. If the opponent who wins the trick leads another heart or a club, you eliminate your diamond loser by ruffing in one hand and discarding a diamond from the other; if he leads a diamond, you can be sure of a third diamond trick. The four hands:

Contract: 6♠   North
Opening lead: ♡Q   ♠ K 9 7 6 2
                       ♡ 8 5
                       ◇ A 10 6
                       ♣ A 5 3

West   East
♠ 4   ♠ J 8
♡ Q J 10 6 3   ♡ K 9 7 2
◇ Q 9 7 2   ◇ 5 4 3
♣ 9 8 4   ♣ J 10 7 6

          South
          ♠ A Q 10 5 3
          ♡ A 4
          ◇ K J 8
          ♣ K Q 2

A good time to look for a throw-in play (also called an "endplay")
is when you have a losing trick somewhere and a suit you would
rather have the opponents lead (such as this diamond suit). Before the
throw-in, you must first take away the opponents' safe exit cards. If
you did not draw two rounds of trumps and three rounds of clubs
before leading the heart, a spade or a club lead would not benefit you.

The throw-in play is not easy. So don't fret if you struggled to
follow this one.

(7)   North
                       ♠ J 9 8
                       ♡ A Q 7
                       ◇ Q 4 3
Contract: 4♡   ♣ K 6 5 2

Opening lead: ◇9   South
                       ♠ 10 7 4
                       ♡ K J 10 8 5
                       ◇ A J 8
                       ♣ A 9

West	North	East	South
—	—	1◇	1♡
Pass	3♡	Pass	4♡
All Pass			

Clues from the opening lead: West leads the ◇9. You must lose three spade tricks, so the key to making this contract is to avoid a diamond loser. West led a diamond because his partner bid the suit, and the nine would not be the correct card to lead if he had the king or ten, so East is marked with both of those cards. How would you play to win three diamond tricks? Answer: cover the ◇9 with dummy's ◇Q (this is the key play). East will cover the ◇Q with the ◇K (he cannot gain by playing low) and you take your ◇A. You are left with ◇J-8 over East's ◇10. In other words, you have the highest and third highest diamond and East has the second highest. After drawing trumps, go to dummy and lead a diamond to take the marked finesse.

Contract: 4♡
Opening lead: ◇9

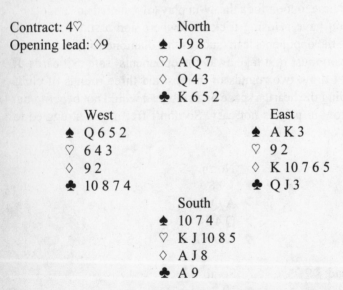

```
                        North
                        ♠ J 9 8
                        ♡ A Q 7
                        ◇ Q 4 3
                        ♣ K 6 5 2
        West                            East
        ♠ Q 6 5 2                       ♠ A K 3
        ♡ 6 4 3                         ♡ 9 2
        ◇ 9 2                           ◇ K 10 7 6 5
        ♣ 10 8 7 4                      ♣ Q J 3
                        South
                        ♠ 10 7 4
                        ♡ K J 10 8 5
                        ◇ A J 8
                        ♣ A 9
```

Note that East also can read that the nine is his partner's highest diamond; he knows that you have the ◇A and ◇J. If you make the mistake of playing a low diamond from dummy on the first trick, he will play low and let you win with the ◊J. Since East would still have the ◊K-10 surrounding dummy's ◊Q, you would have to lose a diamond trick.

(8)   North
                                          ♠ K 9 2
                                          ♡ 8 7 3
                                          ◊ A Q 6
Contract: 4♠   ♣ 10 9 5 4

Opening lead: ♡K   South
                                          ♠ A J 10 8 5 4
                                          ♡ A 2
                                          ◊ K J 9
                                          ♣ 7 3

West	North	East	South
3♡	Pass	Pass	3♠
Pass	4♠	All Pass	

Clues from the bidding: West leads the ♡K and you win the first trick with the ♡A. You have three sure losers (one heart and two clubs), so you will be set if you lose a spade trick. This is a case where it is desirable to draw the trumps right away. How would you play the trump suit? Answer: cash the ♠K and, assuming both follow suit and the ♠Q does not drop, lead a spade from dummy and take the finesse.

The rule "eight ever, nine never," (described earlier) says that with nine cards you should never finesse, but this assumes that you have no information about the opponents' distribution. Here, the bidding is very revealing. West opened the bidding with a preemptive bid of 3♡, so the missing eight hearts are probably divided seven for West and one for East. West was dealt six cards in the other three suits while East was dealt 12. The are six chances that West has the ♠Q and 12 chances that East has it. The odds are about two-to-one that East has the ♠Q (or any one missing card outside the heart suit). The four hands:

Contract: 4♠   North
Opening lead: ♡K   ♠ K 9 2
                                ♡ 8 7 3
                                ◊ A Q 6
                                ♣ 10 9 5 4

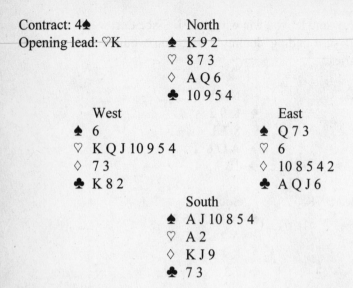

          West   East
          ♠ 6   ♠ Q 7 3
          ♡ K Q J 10 9 5 4   ♡ 6
          ◊ 7 3   ◊ 10 8 5 4 2
          ♣ K 8 2   ♣ A Q J 6

                                South
                                ♠ A J 10 8 5 4
                                ♡ A 2
                                ◊ K J 9
                                ♣ 7 3

This time the percentage play works, East has the ♠Q and you
make the contract. It is possible that West has ♠ Q x and you would
be set if you took the spade finesse, but the odds are against it. All this
arithmetic may be too much for you at this stage of your game, but
there is a simple rule to follow when there are two ways to play a suit
combination and you are trying to decide which defender has a certain
missing high card, usually the queen: *the player with shortness in one
or more of the other suits is a favorite to have the missing high card.*

(9)   North
                                ♠ Q 9 3
                                ♡ 8 7 5 4
                                ◊ A K 10 2
Contract: 4♠   ♣ 10 6

Opening lead: ♡2   South
                                ♠ K J 10 8 5 2
                                ♡ A K
                                ◊ 7
                                ♣ Q J 9 4

West	North	East	South
—	—	1♡	1♠
Pass	2♠	Pass	4♠
All Pass			

Clues from the bidding: West leads the ♡2 and prospects look very good—you have only three losers (one spade and two clubs). *But before playing you should always analyze the opening lead and review the bidding.* East bid 1♡, and West led the ♡2. This tells you that the hearts are divided 6-1. East has at least a five-card suit to open the bidding 1♡; in this case he has six because West led the two; something he would not do if he had a doubleton (standard procedure is to lead the high card from a doubleton). Consider what will happen if you lead a trump at trick two: East will win the ♠A and lead a heart for his partner to ruff— that will set the contract. You must recognize that your second high heart is a *loser.* Can you see a way to prevent the ruff? Answer: cash the ◊A and ◊K to discard your high heart, then lead a trump. East will win the ♠A and lead a heart, but now you have no hearts in your hand and can ruff with a high trump. The rest is easy: draw the missing trumps, conceding two tricks to the ♣AK.

Contract: 4♠
Opening lead: ♡2

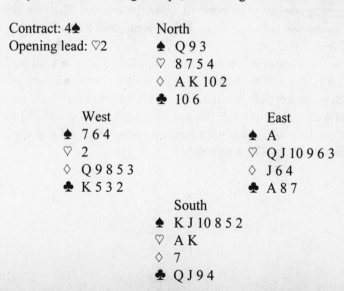

North
♠ Q 9 3
♡ 8 7 5 4
◊ A K 10 2
♣ 10 6

West
♠ 7 6 4
♡ 2
◊ Q 9 8 5 3
♣ K 5 3 2

East
♠ A
♡ Q J 10 9 6 3
◊ J 6 4
♣ A 8 7

South
♠ K J 10 8 5 2
♡ A K
◊ 7
♣ Q J 9 4

(10)   North
                                        ♠ A 7 4
                                        ♡ J 6 3
                                        ◇ 10 9 8
Contract: 4♠   ♣ A 7 5 2

                                        South
Opening lead: ♡K   ♠ K Q J 10
                                        ♡ 7
                                        ◇ A K Q J 3
                                        ♣ 9 8 4

The seven-card trump suit: You always hope to land in an eight-card trump suit, but it is inevitable that you will occasionally wind up playing a hand with seven trumps—only one trump more than the enemy. Against the 4♠ contract, West leads the ♡K and, on the surface, everything seems rosy. You have only three losers in your hand (one heart and two clubs), but you must draw all of the opponents' trumps before you can cash your diamond winners. The most likely division of six cards is 4-2, so you will probably need to keep all four spades in your hand to draw the trumps. The rule is *hoard the trumps in the long hand*. This is especially true when you have only seven of them.

Suppose West wins the first trick with the ♡K and follows with the ♡Q. If you ruff you will not be able to draw the trumps unless the suit divides 3-3, so *do not ruff*; discard a losing club instead—a "loser on a loser". If a third heart is led, discard your other losing club. If a fourth heart is led you can ruff with dummy's ace—the hand with the shorter trump holding. The four hands:

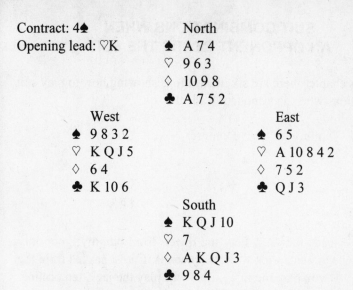

Contract: 4♠
Opening lead: ♡K

North
♠ A 7 4
♡ 9 6 3
◊ 10 9 8
♣ A 7 5 2

West
♠ 9 8 3 2
♡ K Q J 5
◊ 6 4
♣ K 10 6

East
♠ 6 5
♡ A 10 8 4 2
◊ 7 5 2
♣ Q J 3

South
♠ K Q J 10
♡ 7
◊ A K Q J 3
♣ 9 8 4

If you mistakenly ruff any of the heart leads in your hand, West will have one trump more than you; he cannot be prevented from winning a spade trick and will set the contract. If you still have four trumps in your hand when you get the lead, you will be able to draw all of West's trumps and win ten tricks (four spades, five diamonds and one club). You were fortunate this time that there was a way to make the contract, but there is something you should always do when you play a hand with only seven trumps—WORRY.

CHAPTER FOURTEEN

SUIT COMBINATIONS WHEN
AN OPPONENT LEADS THE SUIT

In this chapter there are six illustrations showing how to play suit combinations when an opponent leads the suit.

(a)	Dummy	(b)	Dummy	(c)	Dummy
	Q 3		Q 3		K 7
	You		You		You
	A 8 5		A 10 5		J 8 5

(a)   West leads the four. Play the queen from dummy; your only chance to win a trick with the queen is if West has led from the king. If you play the three, East will play the jack, ten or nine. Then you cannot win a trick with the queen no matter which defender has the king.

(b)   Again West leads the four. This time you have the ten in your hand and there is a sure way to win two tricks by playing low from dummy. If East's third-hand play is a low card, you can win a trick with the ten. If East plays the jack, win with the ace and you will eventually win a second trick with the queen in dummy opposite the ten-five in your hand. If East plays the king, win with the ace and your queen is good. If your first play is the queen from dummy, you will be limited to one trick if East has the king and West has the jack.

(c)   West leads the two. Play low from dummy and you will win one trick no matter which card East plays. If East plays low, win with the jack; if he plays the queen, you will eventually win a trick with either the king or jack; if he plays the ace, the king is high. Note that if your first play is the king you would not win a trick if East has the ace and West the queen.

	(d) Dummy	(e) Dummy	(f) Dummy
	A 10 5	A J 3	J 7 4
	You	You	You
	K 3 2	K 9 2	A K 8

(d) West leads the queen, more than likely from queen-jack. Play low from dummy and win with the king. If West has the jack, a third trick is available by leading from your hand and finessing the ten.

(e) West leads the four. Play low from dummy. If West has the queen, or if East has the queen and ten, you would get the same result whether you play low from dummy or the jack. It is when West has the ten and East the queen that you gain a trick by playing low—East must play the queen or allow you to win the first trick with the nine.

(f) West leads the nine. When the opening lead is a high spot card, especially the nine, it is usually the top of a worthless suit. In this layout, East is marked with the queen and ten. You can win three tricks in the suit by covering the nine with the jack. Assuming East covers with the queen and you win with the ace, you are left with king-eight behind East's ten and can win a trick with the eight by leading from dummy and finessing. Note that East can read the opening lead as his partner's highest card in the suit as well as you can. If you mistakenly play low from dummy, so will East and you will be limited to two tricks.

IN REVIEW
Tips for the Declarer

* Declarer's goal is to make his contract (ignore the possibility of overtricks unless the contract is safe).
* After the opening lead and before playing a card from dummy, count your tricks. At notrump contracts count the winning tricks in the combined hands; at a trump contract count the losing tricks in one hand—usually your own.

* While planning your play, analyze the opening lead and review the bidding to see if there are any clues about the missing high cards and distribution.

* When running a long suit, cash the high cards in the shorter hand first. For example: with K Q x x opposite A J x, cash the ace and jack first.

* Do not expect to make every contract you reach. If you do make every contract, your bidding is much too conservative.

* Do not lead an honor card to take a finesse unless you will be happy with the result if the honor is covered.

* Do not take a finesse which may jeopardize your contract until you are sure there is no better line of play.

* When you have a two-way finesse for a missing queen or jack, play the defender with shortness in one or more of the other suits for the missing honor.

* A hold-up play by declarer (to refuse to win a trick with a high card the first and/or second time a suit is led) is often a good technique. This is especially true against notrump contracts because it may block the opponents' communication—by exhausting one defender's hand of all the cards he has in the suit, so he will not be able to lead that suit later.

* Think twice before drawing trumps. Sometimes it is wrong to draw trumps right away.

* When one defender can set your contract if he gets the lead while the other defender cannot, make every effort to keep the danger hand out of the lead.

* When two or three lines of play to make your contract are available but you can try only one, choose the one that offers the best chance—the percentage play. However, before choosing one line, make sure you cannot try both (or all three if three are available). Two chances are better than one.

PART THREE

THE DEFENSE

Unlike declarer play, defense is a partnership game. While your goal is to set the contract, you can seldom do it alone. Many of the leads and plays you make are to guide your partner's defense, and vice versa; as you shall read in the following pages:

CHAPTER FIFTEEN

OPENING LEADS, AND SUBSEQUENT LEADS

WHICH CARD TO LEAD

The opening leader must first decide which suit to lead, and then choose the proper card in that suit. Deciding which suit to lead is a matter of judgment, while choosing which card to lead is routine and will be explained first.

From a doubleton: From any two-card suit (A K, A J, Q 4, 9 2, etc.), always lead the higher card.

From a three-card sequence: If the suit has a "three-card sequence" headed by the king, queen, jack or ten (i.e., K Q J, Q J 10, J 10 9 or 10 9 8), lead the top card of the sequence regardless of the length of the suit. Similarly, if the suit is headed by the king, queen, jack or ten and you have the first, second and fourth card of a sequence (for example., K Q 10, Q J 9, J 10 8 or 10 9 7), lead the top card regardless of the length of the suit. These suit combinations are desirable choices for an opening lead.

From a two-card sequence: If a suit has a two-card sequence headed by the king, queen, jack or ten, lead the top of the suit if it is three cards long (K Q 2, Q J 3, J 10 4, 10 9 5). With a four-card or longer suit, headed by a two-card sequence, the card to lead depends on whether the hand is played in a trump contract or notrump. The top card is usually best against trump contracts, but lead "fourth best"—the fourth highest card in the suit—against notrump contracts (excluding slams). For example: From K Q 8 5 4, the right card to lead is the king against a trump contract, or the five against notrump.

From an ace-king combination: If the hand is played in a trump suit, always lead the king from any suit containing the ace and king, except lead the ace from a doubleton ace-king.

Against notrump contracts there is no set formula for which card to lead. It is *sometimes* better to lead fourth best, and sometimes better to lead the king. For example, it is usually right to lead the four from A K 8 4 3, but to lead the king from A K J 2 or A K 10 4.

From an inside sequence (also called interior sequence): An inside sequence is one in which you have a higher card in the same suit that is not in sequence (such as A J 10 6, K 10 9 8). Leads from these holdings are fairly common against notrump contracts, but doubtful choices against trump contracts. However, when you do decide to lead the suit, the right card to lead against both notrump and trump contracts is the *high card of the sequence*; even if it is only a two-card sequence. For example: lead the jack from K J 10 9 7 or K J 10 3; lead the ten from K 10 9 8 or Q 10 9 4; but if the suit includes the ace, (e.g., A Q J 9, A J 10 3, A 10 9 8 3), lead the top card of the sequence at notrump, or lead the ace if there is a trump suit. *Do not underlead an ace on opening lead against a trump contract.*

From a three-card or longer suit with no sequence: When leading from a three-card suit headed by the king, queen, jack or ten (but not in sequence), lead the lowest card (lead the five from: K J 5, Q 9 5, J 9 5, 10 6 5). From a three-card suit headed by the ace (e.g., A 8 3), lead the lowest against a notrump contract, but lead the ace if there is a trump suit. Although underleading an ace when on opening lead versus a trump contract is not recommended, it is sometimes acceptable to underlead the ace of trump.

When leading from a four-card or longer suit headed by one or two honors not in sequence, lead "fourth best"—the fourth highest card in the suit (lead the four from Q 8 5 4 2 or K J 5 4). If the suit is headed by an ace (such as A J 8 6 3), lead fourth best versus notrump, but lead the ace if there is a trump suit. It is often right to lead from a suit headed by the ace at notrump, but poison at suit contracts.

Leads from suits such as K J 5, Q 10 8 3, etc. often give declarer a trick to which he is not entitled. So shy away from leading suits with unguarded honor cards versus trump contracts unless partner has bid the suit, or you are in a hurry to establish tricks (explained later).

From three small cards (9 6 4, 7 6 5, etc.), lead the top card against notrump contracts, but lead your lowest if there is a trump suit. Leading the lowest from three small cards against a trump contract is a new idea, but a good one because most experts do it; in the old days the top card was recommended.

With a four-card or longer suit that has no honor cards, lead fourth best (lead the three from 9 7 5 3 2 or 6 5 4 3). Exception: a fourth best opening lead at notrump is usually from a suit containing one or more honors, and partner is encouraged to return the suit. Therefore, if you want to discourage partner from returning a suit, lead the highest card from a worthless four-card suit. For example, lead the eight, from 8 6 5 3; but lead the second highest, the seven, from holdings such as 9 7 5 3 or 10 7 5 3—because your nine or ten might be valuable.

WHICH SUIT TO LEAD

The opening lead is the only play that must be made before dummy is exposed, which makes choosing the suit to lead a challenging task for everyone, even the experts. The guides to help you make a winning choice are the nature of your hand (some suit combinations make better leads than others), and the bidding. For example, it is usually right to lead a suit bid by your partner, and usually wrong to lead a suit bid by your opponents. The tactics for leading against notrump contracts are different from trump contracts, so they are introduced separately.

Against notrump contracts: When nothing in the bidding has suggested otherwise, the general rule used to determine which suit to lead against notrump contracts below the slam level is to lead your longest and strongest suit. If the contract is a notrump slam, choose the safest lead, the one least likely to give declarer a trick.

Against trump contracts: When there is a trump suit, declarer can usually take tricks by ruffing after a suit has been led once or twice. Therefore, you must depend on high cards and trumps to win tricks, rather than long cards as is often the way at notrump contracts. A good lead is from a suit that will not jeopardize a trick and may win or promote tricks quickly—such as A K 2, K Q J, Q J 10 9. However, you may not have one of these attractive holdings, and even if you do, the bidding may indicate a different lead; such as a suit bid by partner, a short suit (a singleton or a doubleton hoping to get a ruff), a trump, or from suit combinations that would normally be frowned upon—such as K J 7 3, A Q 5 4.

Illustrations of how to decide which suit to lead are coming up. First let's look at how leads after trick one differ from opening leads.

LEADS AFTER TRICK ONE

Leading a new suit: When you read about opening leads you saw that selecting *which card* to lead was routine. Here we are concerned with leads at trick two and later. Now you can see dummy and one or more tricks have been played. This additional information sometimes indicates that you should lead a different card than was recommended for the opening lead. For example: it may be right to underlead an ace against a trump contract, or to make a strange lead like the king or jack from K J x.

Another difference is that spot card leads are used to indicate whether you have any high cards in the suit (rather that your length), by leading "low from strength" and "top of nothing." For example: lead the four from K J 7 4 3, Q 10 7 4 or K 6 4 (as you would on opening lead), but lead the eight from 8 7 5 4 3, 8 6 5 4 or 8 6 4. If you are making an opening lead against a trump contract, the four is the recommended lead from all of these holdings, even though you have no honor; if you lead the eight and follow with a lower card it shows a doubleton. The next two deals show the value of leading low from strength, and the highest card from a worthless suit.

(1)

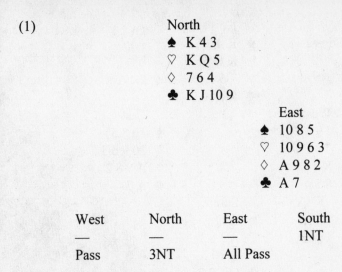

North
- ♠ K 4 3
- ♡ K Q 5
- ◇ 7 6 4
- ♣ K J 10 9

East
- ♠ 10 8 5
- ♡ 10 9 6 3
- ◇ A 9 8 2
- ♣ A 7

West	North	East	South
—	—	—	1NT
Pass	3NT	All Pass	

Lead low from strength: Partner leads the ♠2, a low card is played from dummy, you play the ♠10 and declarer wins the first trick with the ♠Q. He leads a low club to the ♣J and you take your ♣A. There is no chance to beat the contract by returning partner's suit. Aside from the fact that his ♠2 lead showed a four-card suit, he has at most five points (you can see 20 high-card points between your hand and dummy and declarer has 15-17 for his 1NT opening). Concluding that the only chance to win five tricks if partner's few high-card points are in diamonds, you should lead the ◇2. Here are the four hands:

Contract: 3NT
Opening lead: ♠2

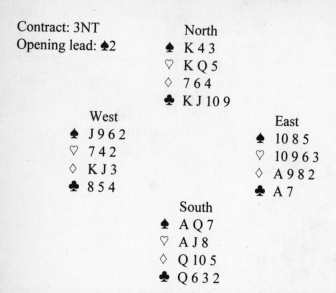

North
♠ K 4 3
♡ K Q 5
◇ 7 6 4
♣ K J 10 9

West
♠ J 9 6 2
♡ 7 4 2
◇ K J 3
♣ 8 5 4

East
♠ 10 8 5
♡ 10 9 6 3
◇ A 9 8 2
♣ A 7

South
♠ A Q 7
♡ A J 8
◇ Q 10 5
♣ Q 6 3 2

Declarer plays the ◇10 on your ◇2 lead and partner wins with the ◇J. Your lead of the two showed that you have the ace or queen—low from strength—so partner should return the suit; first the ◇K and then the ◇3. This nets the defense four diamond tricks and beats the contract. If your partner mistakenly leads the ◇3 before cashing the ◇K, the contract cannot be set. Partner would win the third diamond trick and have no way to get to your hand—you would "go to bed" with the setting trick. Remember the rule: when defending against a notrump contract, save a low card in partner's long suit to play last so you do not block the suit. Note that if you lead anything but a diamond at trick three declarer has nine tricks (three each in spades, hearts and clubs).

(2)

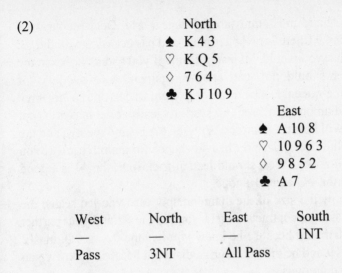

North
♠ K 4 3
♡ K Q 5
◇ 7 6 4
♣ K J 10 9

East
♠ A 10 8
♡ 10 9 6 3
◇ 9 8 5 2
♣ A 7

West	North	East	South
—	—	—	1NT
Pass	3NT	All Pass	

Lead top of nothing: Again your partner leads the ♠2, you cover dummy's ♠3 with the ♠10, and declarer wins the trick with the ♠Q. A club is led to dummy's ♣J and you take your ♣A. As in the last hand you should switch to a diamond, but this time lead the ◇9—top of nothing—to tell partner you have no diamond honors in the suit.

Contract: 3NT
Opening lead: ♠2

North
♠ K 4 3
♡ K Q 5
◇ 7 6 4
♣ K J 10 9

West
♠ J 9 6 2
♡ 7 4 2
◇ K J 3
♣ 8 5 4

East
♠ A 10 8
♡ 10 9 6 3
◇ 9 8 5 2
♣ A 7

South
♠ Q 7 5
♡ A J 8
◇ A Q 10
♣ Q 6 3 2

Partner's hand and dummy are the same as #11. Declarer plays the
◊10 on your ◊9 (there is no better play) and partner wins with the ◊J.
Knowing that you would not lead the nine if you had an honor in the
suit, partner should not lead another diamond into the jaws of
declarer's ace-queen. Declarer has only eight tricks (one spade, three
hearts, one diamond and three clubs) so any lead partner makes except
a diamond will beat the contract. With the ♠A behind the ♠K, and the
◊K behind the ◊A Q, declarer has no chance for a ninth trick. If you
are wondering what West should lead at trick four, the ♠J is a good
choice with the ♠Q and ♠10 gone.

Notice how the size of the diamond spot card you led sealed the
fate of the last two contracts: in #11 you led the ◊2 and your partner
returned a diamond because he knew you had the ◊A or ◊Q; in #12
you led the ◊9 and he did not return a diamond because he knew you
had no high diamonds.

Returning partner's suit: When you decide to return a suit originally
led by partner, it is important to lead the right card. If you began with
three cards in the suit, *lead back the higher of the remaining two*; with
A 7 3, win with the ace and return the seven. If you began with four
cards or more, *return the fourth best of your original holding*; with A
9 6 3 2 or A 9 6 3, win with the ace and return the three. Here are two
examples:

(3)

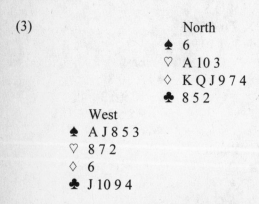

```
                         North
                      ♠  6
                      ♡  A 10 3
                      ◊  K Q J 9 7 4
                      ♣  8 5 2
            West
         ♠  A J 8 5 3
         ♡  8 7 2
         ◊  6
         ♣  J 10 9 4
```

West	North	East	South
—	—	—	1NT
Pass	3◊	Pass	3NT
All Pass			

You lead the ♠5 (fourth best from your longest and strongest suit), partner wins with the ♠K and declarer plays the ♠4. Partner returns the ♠9, declarer plays the ♠10, and you win with the ♠J. How are the missing spades divided? Answer: partner began with ♠A 9 x and declarer with ♠Q 10 x x. Partner denied holding the queen when he won the first trick with the king, and you can tell that he does not have more than three spades because he would not return the nine if he had four; from K 9 7 2, he would have returned his lowest—the two. (**NOTE:** It is possible that partner has two spades—♠A 9—but that is unlikely since declarer would have five and he never bid the suit. Further, the contract cannot be set if partner has only two spades.)

Now back to the play. You know that declarer still has ♠Q 7, or ♠Q 2, so it is wrong to lead another spade at trick three—it would give declarer a trick with the ♠Q and then you cannot beat the contract even if partner has another trick. Your only hope is if partner can get the lead to return a spade through declarer's ♠Q before he can win nine tricks. Lead the ♣J and you will beat the contract if partner has the ♣A or the ◊A. The four hands:

Contract: 3NT   North
Opening lead: ♠5   ♠ 6
                             ♡ A 10 3
                             ◇ K Q J 9 7 4
                             ♣ 8 5 2

    West   East
♠ A J 8 5 3   ♠ K 9 2
♡ 8 7 2   ♡ J 9 6 4
◇ 6   ◇ 8 5 3
♣ J 10 9 4   ♣ A 6 3

                             South
                             ♠ Q 10 7 4
                             ♡ K Q 5
                             ◇ A 10 2
                             ♣ K Q 7

After you win the second trick with the ♠J, partner is left with the
♠2, declarer with the ♠Q 7, and you with ♠A 8 3 (note that you have
the highest and third highest remaining spades). Partner will win your
club lead with his ♣A and lead the ♠2, giving you three more spade
tricks to set the contract two. If you return anything other than a club
at trick three, declarer makes his contract.

In the following layout your hand and dummy's are the same, but
declarer's and East's hands have been changed.

(4)   North
                             ♠ 6
                             ♡ A 10 3
                             ◇ K Q J 9 7 4
                             ♣ 8 5 2
    West
♠ A J 8 5 3
♡ 8 7 2
◇ 6
♣ J 10 9 4

Again the contract is 3NT. You lead the ♠5 and partner wins the first trick with the ♠K, but this time he returns the ♠2, declarer plays the ♠10 and you win with the ♠J. Your partner would not have returned the two if he had been dealt three spades, so he began with four spades (unless he has just two, in which case there is no hope of beating the contract). Declarer began with three spades and is now down to the lone queen, so cash the ♠A and win the first five spade tricks. If you mistakenly lead the ♣J at trick three, or anything other than the ♠A, declarer will win the remaining 11 tricks. The four hands:

Contract: 3NT
Opening lead: ♠5

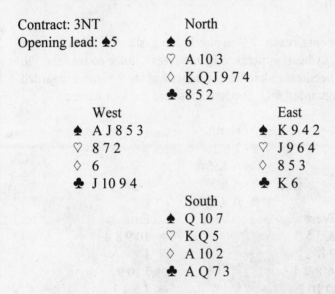

North
♠ 6
♡ A 10 3
◇ K Q J 9 7 4
♣ 8 5 2

West
♠ A J 8 5 3
♡ 8 7 2
◇ 6
♣ J 10 9 4

East
♠ K 9 4 2
♡ J 9 6 4
◇ 8 5 3
♣ K 6

South
♠ Q 10 7
♡ K Q 5
◇ A 10 2
♣ A Q 7 3

Note that when you cash the ♠A your partner must make a good play. He must play the ♠9 under your ♠A to unblock. Otherwise he would win the fourth trick with the ♠9 and block the suit; declarer would make the contract.

CHAPTER SIXTEEN

PASSIVE AND AGGRESSIVE DEFENSE

PASSIVE DEFENSE

When there is no hurry to get your tricks, choose a passive opening lead—the one least likely to give away a trick. For example:

(1)	West	West	North	East	South
♠	K J 5 3	—	—	—	1♡
♡	9 8	Pass	3♡	Pass	4♡
◇	A 8 7 4	All Pass			
♣	Q 10 2				

The opponents reach 4♡ on the bidding shown. What is your opening lead? A heart appears to be the safest choice so lead the ♡9. It would be a needless risk to lead or underlead the ◇A, the unguarded ♠K, or the unguarded ♣Q. Suppose these are the four hands:

```
                    North
                 ♠  7 6 2
                 ♡  A K 5 4
                 ◇  K 6 3
                 ♣  A 9 8
     West                        East
  ♠  K J 5 3                  ♠  10 9 8 4
  ♡  9 8                      ♡  J 7
  ◇  A 8 7 4                  ◇  J 10 9
  ♣  Q 10 2                   ♣  7 5 4 3
                    South
                 ♠  A Q
                 ♡  Q 10 6 3 2
                 ◇  Q 5 2
                 ♣  K J 6
```

Any lead except a heart gives declarer a trick that he could not win if he led the suit himself. A spade lead gives him a trick with the ♠Q; a diamond lead allows him to win a second diamond trick (first a trick with the ♢Q, and later a trick with the ♢K); and a club lead gives him a trick with the ♣J. Suppose you lead a heart and, after drawing two rounds of trumps, declarer cashes the ♣A and then leads to his ♣J. You win this trick with the ♣Q and are on lead again. What would you lead? Lead another club; *avoid breaking a new suit.* This defense gives declarer no help whatsoever, and that is what passive defense is all about. Similarly, if declarer draws trumps and takes the spade finesse, you should win with the ♠K and return another spade.

AGGRESSIVE DEFENSE

When the bidding indicates that dummy has a long and strong suit, or after the dummy is exposed and you see that it has one, you had better take any tricks you have in the other suits before you lose them. *Lead from strength—attack!* If you have no safe lead (such as the king from A K x or K Q J; or the queen or Q J 10), lead away from an unguarded king or queen, or lead an ace. For example:

(2)

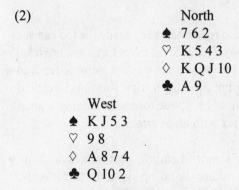

```
                        North
                        ♠ 7 6 2
                        ♡ K 5 4 3
                        ♢ K Q J 10
                        ♣ A 9
           West
           ♠ K J 5 3
           ♡ 9 8
           ♢ A 8 7 4
           ♣ Q 10 2
```

Again, the contract is 4♡. Not sensing any urgency to win tricks, you again lead the ♡9. But when dummy is exposed you see that it has a strong diamond suit; given time, declarer may discard one or more losers on the long diamonds. You must change tactics and try to win tricks before declarer discards his losers. Suppose declarer draws two

rounds of trumps and leads a diamond at trick three. Win with your
◇A and *lead the ♣3.* You can see that declarer has nine sure tricks
(five hearts, three diamonds and one club); if he has the ♠A he has
ten. Your only chance is if partner has the ♠A.

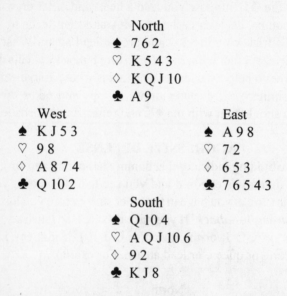

North
♠ 7 6 2
♡ K 5 4 3
◇ K Q J 10
♣ A 9

West
♠ K J 5 3
♡ 9 8
◇ A 8 7 4
♣ Q 10 2

East
♠ A 9 8
♡ 7 2
◇ 6 5 3
♣ 7 6 5 4 3

South
♠ Q 10 4
♡ A Q J 10 6
◇ 9 2
♣ K J 8

Partner wins with the ♠A and returns another spade (he too can see
the strong diamonds in dummy). The defense takes three spade tricks,
and that sets the contract. Be sure to see that passive defense leads to
disaster: if you lead anything but a spade at trick four, declarer will
regain the lead and discard two of his spade losers on dummy's good
diamonds and make his contract with an overtrick.

When not to lead partner's suit: Leading partner's suit is an
aggressive lead because you usually wind up winning tricks early.
Aside from the fact that it is usually the winning choice, you will have
a very unhappy partner if you do not lead his suit and it is wrong.
Unless you have a good reason to do otherwise, *lead your partner's
suit;* and it is almost always right to lead the same card that you would
lead if he did not bid the suit. The next deal shows a rare case where
there is a good reason to do otherwise.

(3)	West	West	North	East	South
♠ 9 6 3		—	—	1♡	1♠
♡ 10 8 5		Pass	4♠	All Pass	
◇ 7					
♣ Q 10 9 5 4 2					

Short-suit leads: Another type of lead to win tricks early is a singleton (or sometimes a doubleton), in the hope of getting a ruff. In this deal the opponents reach 4♠ after your partner opened the bidding with 1♡. The best opening lead is the ◇7. If partner has the ◇A or a high trump, he can get the lead to give you a ruff or two before declarer can draw your trumps. Since partner opened the bidding and is known to have several high cards, the chances that he will get the lead in time are excellent. Suppose these are the four hands:

Contract: 4♠
Opening lead: ◇7

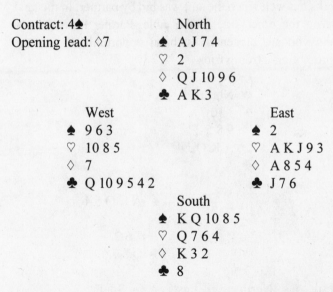

North
♠ A J 7 4
♡ 2
◇ Q J 10 9 6
♣ A K 3

West
♠ 9 6 3
♡ 10 8 5
◇ 7
♣ Q 10 9 5 4 2

East
♠ 2
♡ A K J 9 3
◇ A 8 5 4
♣ J 7 6

South
♠ K Q 10 8 5
♡ Q 7 6 4
◇ K 3 2
♣ 8

Partner wins the first trick with the ◇A and returns a diamond for you to ruff. He certainly should know that you have a singleton diamond; why else would you decide not to lead the suit he bid? You lead a heart at trick three, hoping that partner has the ♡A. As you can see, he does, so he wins that trick and leads another diamond for you to ruff. You win the first four tricks to set the contract. Note that if your opening lead had been a heart, there would be no chance to beat the contract; even if partner cashes the ◇A and leads another diamond you can get only one ruff; partner cannot regain the lead.

Singleton leads are good when you have the "right" trump holding (such as A x x or x x x), and when you believe there is a good chance to get partner on lead before declarer can draw your trumps. Singleton leads can damage the defense if the lead exposes partner's holding in the suit, and may work to declarer's advantage. Do not lead a singleton if you have the wrong trump holding (for example, K Q 10) because you can win trump tricks without ruffing, and do not lead a singleton if you think there is little or no chance to get partner on lead.

An opening lead from a doubleton may enable you to gain a trick by ruffing. Although it is not as promising as the lead of a singleton, it usually works out well when the suit was bid by partner. In the next deal you are on the other side of the table. Partner leads from a doubleton and you are presented with an opportunity to set the contract by promoting a trump trick.

(4)   North
                                       ♠ J 10 7
                                       ♡ 9 8 5 2
                                       ◇ A K Q J 4
                                       ♣ A

                                                   East
                                                   ♠ A K Q 5 4
                                                   ♡ 3
                                                   ◇ 7 6 2
                                                   ♣ Q 8 7 6

West	North	East	South
—	1◇	1♠	2♡
Pass	4♡	All Pass	

The trump promotion play: Your partner leads the ♠9, the ♠10 is played from dummy. You win with the ♠Q and take the ♠A and ♠K.

Partner follows suit to the second spade and discards the ♣2 on the third. You need one more trick. What is the only source of tricks left? Trump tricks. Lead a spade; you may promote a trump for partner.

Contract: 4♡
Opening lead: ♣9

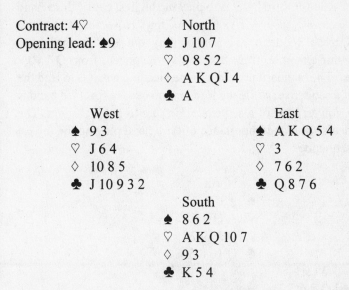

```
                    North
                    ♠ J 10 7
                    ♡ 9 8 5 2
                    ◇ A K Q J 4
                    ♣ A
     West                         East
     ♠ 9 3                        ♠ A K Q 5 4
     ♡ J 6 4                      ♡ 3
     ◇ 10 8 5                     ◇ 7 6 2
     ♣ J 10 9 3 2                 ♣ Q 8 7 6
                    South
                    ♠ 8 6 2
                    ♡ A K Q 10 7
                    ◇ 9 3
                    ♣ K 5 4
```

Partner has the trump holding you were hoping for, so your fourth spade lead promotes his ♡J for the setting trick. If declarer does not ruff the fourth spade lead with the ♡A, K or Q, partner will ruff with the ♡J. If declarer does ruff with a high trump, partner will discard a diamond or club; this will leave him with a sure trump trick—♡ J 6 4 behind declarer's ♡ A K 10 7. [Getting back to the opening lead, note that declarer can win all 13 tricks with any lead but a spade.]

The ruff and discard (also called a "ruff and sluff"): It is wrong to lead a suit in which both declarer and dummy are void if declarer may gain a trick by ruffing in one hand and discarding a loser in the other. In deal #4 declarer was given a ruff and discard when the fourth round of spades was led. In this case it was good defense, because you could see by looking at the dummy that declarer had no possible losers other than in the trump suit—a ruff and discard could not help him, but offered a chance to promote a trump trick for your side.

CHAPTER SEVENTEEN

THIRD-HAND PLAY

When your partner leads a low card and dummy has no honor in the suit, the rule for third hand is to play the highest card, "third-hand high" (for example, from K 10 x play the king). However, if your suit is headed by a sequence of honors play the lowest card of a sequence—for example, from K Q x play the queen, from Q J 10 x play the ten. The standard procedure when leading a suit is to lead the *top* card of a sequence, while the standard procedure for third hand is to play the *lowest* card of a sequence. Be sure to get it straight. The next two deals show the importance of third hand playing the lowest card of a sequence.

(1)

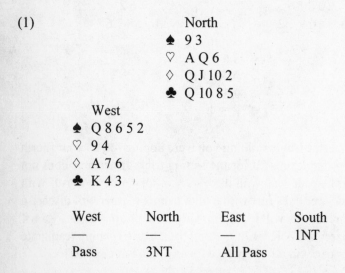

North			
♠ 9 3			
♡ A Q 6			
◇ Q J 10 2			
♣ Q 10 8 5			

West
♠ Q 8 6 5 2
♡ 9 4
◇ A 7 6
♣ K 4 3

West	North	East	South
—	—	—	1NT
Pass	3NT	All Pass	

You lead the ♠5 (fourth best from your longest and strongest suit), partner plays the ♠J, and declarer the ♠A. Before reading further, what did you learn about who holds the missing spade honors? Answer: declarer has both the king and ten; if partner held the king and jack he would have played the king (third hand high); if he held the jack and ten he would have played the ten (the lower card of the

220

sequence). Now suppose declarer leads the ◇K at trick two and you win with the ◇A. What do you lead? Answer: a heart seems best, but any lead except a spade will beat the contract. The four hands:

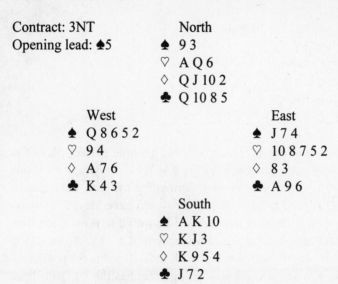

Contract: 3NT
Opening lead: ♠5

North
♠ 9 3
♡ A Q 6
◇ Q J 10 2
♣ Q 10 8 5

West
♠ Q 8 6 5 2
♡ 9 4
◇ A 7 6
♣ K 4 3

East
♠ J 7 4
♡ 10 8 7 5 2
◇ 8 3
♣ A 9 6

South
♠ A K 10
♡ K J 3
◇ K 9 5 4
♣ J 7 2

Declarer has eight tricks (two spades, three hearts and three diamonds). If you lead another spade when you regain the lead with the ◇A, he will win a ninth trick with the ♠10. It all boils down to analyzing partner's third-hand play. His play of the jack denied the king and ten. Knowing that declarer has those cards, you should realize that a spade lead into the jaws of the king-ten would give away a trick.

Suppose you do lead a heart at trick three. Declarer's only chance for a ninth trick is in the club suit. When he leads a club, your partner should win with the ♣A and lead the ♠7. If declarer plays the ♠10, win with your ♠Q and lead another spade to clear the suit. Declarer should cash his eight winners and settle for down one. If he leads another club, you can set him two tricks by winning with the ♣K and cashing the rest of your spades.

(2)

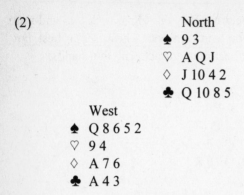

                                    North
                                    ♠ 9 3
                                    ♡ A Q J
                                    ◇ J 10 4 2
                                    ♣ Q 10 8 5
                        West
                        ♠ Q 8 6 5 2
                        ♡ 9 4
                        ◇ A 7 6
                        ♣ A 4 3

Again you lead the ♠5 against 3NT. This time partner plays the ♠10 on the first trick, and declarer the ♠A. What did you learn about the missing spade honors? Answer: partner has the jack, but declarer has the king. If partner had the king he would have played it—third hand high—and if declarer had ♠A K J he would have won the first trick with the jack, not the ace. Now back to the play. At trick two declarer leads the ◇K and you win with the ◇A. What do you lead? Answer: the ♠2. Since you know that partner has the ♠J, your lead will not give away a trick and will help to establish your spade suit.

Contract: 3NT
Opening lead: ♠5

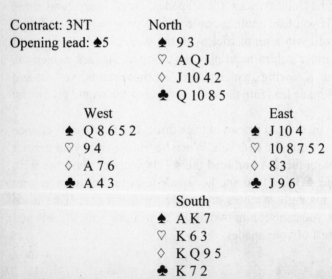

North
♠ 9 3
♡ A Q J
◇ J 10 4 2
♣ Q 10 8 5

West
♠ Q 8 6 5 2
♡ 9 4
◇ A 7 6
♣ A 4 3

East
♠ J 10 4
♡ 10 8 7 5 2
◇ 8 3
♣ J 9 6

South
♠ A K 7
♡ K 6 3
◇ K Q 9 5
♣ K 7 2

Partner plays the ♠J on your second spade lead, and will lead another spade if declarer holds up his ♠K. In either case your spade suit is established and declarer has only eight tricks (two spades, three hearts and three diamonds). He may cash all or any part of his eight winners, but he must eventually lead a club and you will win with the ♣A and run the rest of your spade tricks to set the contract.

Do you see from the last two hands how important it is for third hand to play the lowest card of a sequence? In #1 you learned that declarer had both the king and ten and that it was wrong to lead another spade. In #2 you learned that your partner had the ♠J and that it was right to lead another spade.

When there is an honor card in dummy, there is a difference in third-hand strategy. If third hand has a card that outranks an honor in dummy, it is often wrong to play third hand high unless the honor card is played from dummy. For example: suppose partner leads a low card and the dummy has Q x x. If a low card is played from dummy, it is obvious that you should play the ten from K J 10, or play the jack from K J x; only if the queen is played from dummy should you play the king. What is your third-hand play in the next two deals?

(3)   North
             ♠ K 5 2
             ♡ K 10 4
             ◇ Q 8 3
             ♣ 9 7 6 3

                       East
                  ♠ A 4 3
                  ♡ 7 6 3
                  ◇ A 10 5
                  ♣ K J 8 2

South opens the bidding with 1♡ and North raises to 2♡ to end the bidding. Against the 2♡ contract, your partner leads the ♠J, declarer plays the ♠2 from dummy, and it is up to you. Which spade do you play? Answer: the ♠3 or ♠4. Partner's lead of the jack denies the queen and promises the ten (and hopefully the nine). Declarer has the

♠Q and will win two spade tricks if you go up with your ace, but will win only one spade trick if you let him win the first trick with his queen. Suppose this is the full deal:

Contract: 2♡
Opening lead: ♠J

North
♠ K 5 2
♡ K 10 4
◇ Q 8 3
♣ 9 7 6 3

West
♠ J 10 9 6
♡ 8 5
◇ J 9 7 2
♣ A 10 4

East
♠ A 4 3
♡ 7 6 3
◇ A 10 5
♣ K J 8 2

South
♠ Q 8 7
♡ A Q J 9 2
◇ K 6 4
♣ Q 5

Declarer has six losers (two spades, two diamonds and two clubs), and will lose them all unless the defense slips. After declarer wins the first trick with the ♠Q, his ♠K is sandwiched between partners spade holding, the ♠10 9 6 and yours, the ♠A 4—he cannot avoid losing two spade tricks.

(5)

North
♠ J 4 3
♡ A Q 9
◇ J 10 8 2
♣ A Q 7

East
♠ K 10 8
♡ J 10 7 6
◇ K 4
♣ 9 8 3 2

West	North	East	South
—	1◊	Pass	2NT
Pass	3NT	All Pass	

Partner leads the ♠2, which reveals that he has a four-card suit (if he had five or more spades he would lead fourth best, not his lowest card) and declarer therefore has three spades. The ♠3 is played from dummy and it is up to you. Which spade do you play? Answer: the ♠10. This saves a trick if declarer has A Q x or A x x; note that playing the eight is wrong because declarer might have A 9 x. If declarer has Q x x, it does not matter whether you play the king or ten, declarer can always win one trick in the suit. So the ten is the right play, but the king would be right if the jack had been played from dummy. Suppose these are the four hands:

Contract: 3NT
Opening lead: ♠2

```
                      North
                      ♠ J 4 3
                      ♡ A Q 9
                      ◊ J 10 8 2
                      ♣ A Q 7
      West                              East
      ♠ Q 7 5 2                         ♠ K 10 8
      ♡ 8 5 3                           ♡ J 10 7 6
      ◊ A 9 6 5                         ◊ K 4
      ♣ 10 4                            ♣ 9 8 3 2
                      South
                      ♠ A 9 6
                      ♡ K 4 2
                      ◊ Q 7 3
                      ♣ K J 6 5
```

Declarer has eight top tricks (one spade, three hearts and four clubs). If you mistakenly play the ♠K on the first trick, declarer will win with the ♠A and dummy will be left with ♠J 4 behind partner's ♠Q 7 5 and cannot be prevented from winning a ninth trick with the ♠J. Once you play the ♠10 the contract is doomed; if declarer ducks, continue leading spades until the ♠A is driven out. If declarer tries to get a ninth trick by setting up diamonds, the defense can win five tricks—three spades and two diamonds.

There are other holdings that dummy might have which will make it wrong to play third-hand high. For example: if partner leads a low card and a low card is played from a dummy holding A J x, Q x x or A Q x, in all three cases you should play the ten from K 10 x. When you have an honor in dummy "surrounded," such as K J x or K 10 x over Q x x, playing third-hand high is wrong unless the honor is played from dummy. However, when partner leads a low card and a low card is played from a dummy holding x x x, or A x x (no queen or jack), you should play third hand high—play the king from K 10 x.

The Rule of Eleven: A useful gimmick to help third hand play is the "Rule of Eleven," *but it only applies when partner has led fourth best.* If you subtract the value of the card partner led from 11, it tells you how many higher cards are held by the other three players. Since you can see your hand and dummy, you know how many higher cards declarer has. Sometimes this information is useful. For example:

(6)

North
♠ K 6 2
♡ K 7 5
♢ A K Q 10 9
♣ K 8

East
♠ A J 9 5
♡ A 9 8
♢ 6 4 3
♣ J 3 2

West	North	East	South
—	1◇	Pass	1NT
Pass	3NT	All Pass	

West leads the ♠7. He is presumably leading his fourth-best spade, so subtract seven from 11 to learn that there are four cards higher than the seven held between dummy, you and declarer. You can see all four—the ♠K in dummy and the ♠A J 9 in your hand. Declarer has no spade higher than the seven. Now suppose declarer plays the ♠2 from dummy on the first trick. Which spade would you play? Answer: the ♠5, the only play to beat the contract. The four hands:

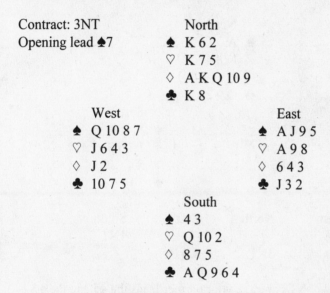

Contract: 3NT
Opening lead ♠7

North
♠ K 6 2
♡ K 7 5
◇ A K Q 10 9
♣ K 8

West
♠ Q 10 8 7
♡ J 6 4 3
◇ J 2
♣ 10 7 5

East
♠ A J 9 5
♡ A 9 8
◇ 6 4 3
♣ J 3 2

South
♠ 4 3
♡ Q 10 2
◇ 8 7 5
♣ A Q 9 6 4

Partner will win the first trick with the ♠7 and lead another spade through dummy's ♠K. The defense will win the first five tricks—four spades and one heart. Note that if you play the ♠Q on the first trick, which would be tempting if you did not know that declarer has no higher card than the seven, the contract cannot be set. It is true that this defense would fail if partner led the ♠7 from ♠Q 10 7, ♠Q 8 7 or ♠7 4 3, but with this bidding it is unlikely that he would lead from any of these three-card holdings and you cannot beat the contract no matter what you do if he did.

The declarer can also use the Rule of Eleven. In this deal he sees only one card higher than the seven (dummy's king), so he knows that East has the three missing higher cards. Although this information is useless to declarer in this case, it sometimes helps him to make the right play.

The unblocking play: When you (or partner) have a long suit that you hope to run to beat a notrump contract, the partner with the *shorter* holding should save a low card to play last, to avoid blocking the suit. For example:

(7)

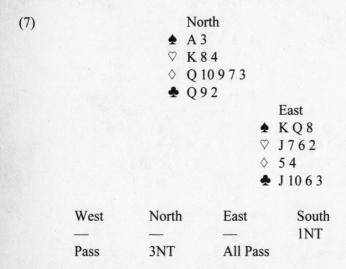

North
♠ A 3
♡ K 8 4
◇ Q 10 9 7 3
♣ Q 9 2

East
♠ K Q 8
♡ J 7 6 2
◇ 5 4
♣ J 10 6 3

West	North	East	South
—	—	—	1NT
Pass	3NT	All Pass	

Against this 3NT contract, your partner leads the ♠J and the ♠3 is played from dummy. How do you defend? Answer: win the first trick with the ♠Q and lead the ♠K. You know from partner's lead of the jack that he has the ten and nine, so you must unblock. The four hands:

Contract: 3NT   North
Opening lead: ♠J   ♠ A 3
                       ♡ K 8 4
                       ◊ Q 10 9 7 3
                       ♣ Q 9 2

West   East
♠ J 10 9 6 2   ♠ K Q 8
♡ 10 5 3   ♡ J 7 6 2
◊ A 8   ◊ 5 4
♣ 7 5 4   ♣ J 10 6 3

                       South
                       ♠ 7 5 4
                       ♡ A Q 9
                       ◊ K J 6 2
                       ♣ A K 8

Declarer has only seven winners outside the diamond suit, so he will lead a diamond after winning the second trick with the ♠A. If you unblocked, your partner will set the contract by taking his ◊A and cashing three more tricks with ♠10 9 6. If you did not unblock, you are left with the ♠K or ♠Q in your hand, you must win the third spade trick. Since you have no more spades and partner has no way to get the lead, declarer will make his contract with an overtrick. (If partner led a low spade you should still play your honors quickly, save the eight and *hope* partner has the jack.)

CHAPTER EIGHTEEN

SECOND-HAND PLAY

The second person to play to a trick often has a problem deciding whether to play second-hand high, or second-hand low. If your goal is to limit declarer to as few tricks as possible in the suit, think about how many tricks declarer will win in the suit, rather than how many you will win. For example:

(1)

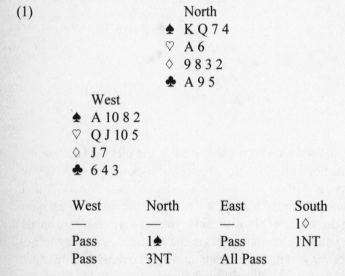

North
♠ K Q 7 4
♡ A 6
♢ 9 8 3 2
♣ A 9 5

West
♠ A 10 8 2
♡ Q J 10 5
♢ J 7
♣ 6 4 3

West	North	East	South
—	—	—	1♢
Pass	1♠	Pass	1NT
Pass	3NT	All Pass	

You lead the ♡Q and declarer wins the first trick in his hand with the ♡K. Then he leads a low spade and you should duck, second hand low. Declarer wins in dummy with the ♠K, leads to his ♣K, and leads a second spade toward dummy. You cannot prevent him from winning a trick with the ♠Q sooner or later, so duck again and let him win this trick with the ♠Q or he will make his contract. The four hands:

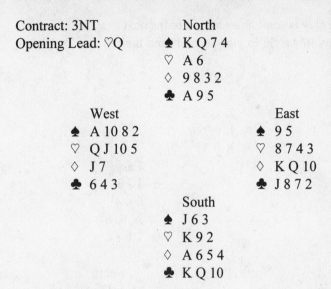

Contract: 3NT
Opening Lead: ♡Q

North
♠ K Q 7 4
♡ A 6
◇ 9 8 3 2
♣ A 9 5

West
♠ A 10 8 2
♡ Q J 10 5
◇ J 7
♣ 6 4 3

East
♠ 9 5
♡ 8 7 4 3
◇ K Q 10
♣ J 8 7 2

South
♠ J 6 3
♡ K 9 2
◇ A 6 5 4
♣ K Q 10

Outside the spade suit declarer has six tricks (two hearts, one diamond and three clubs). His only chance to make his contract is to win three spade tricks. Note that if you went up with the ♠A the first or second time the suit was led, declarer would win three spade tricks with the king, queen and jack. But if you duck twice he can win only two tricks with the king and queen—you are left with ♠A 10, and declarer with the lone ♠J. Only if declarer leads the ♠J should second hand play the ♠A.

Second hand low is most often the right thing to do, and sometimes you must do so without hesitation. For example, declarer leads a low card, you have A x x x, and dummy has K J. If you play low *in tempo* declarer must guess whether you have the ace or queen—he may play the jack and lose two tricks. If you study for a while and then play low, declarer will reason that you were trying to decide whether or not to play your ace; he will go up with dummy's king. (If you are thinking it would be clever to hesitate without the ace you are wrong; that would be cheating.)

Of course it is not always right to play second hand low, and it may be necessary to do some thinking before you decide. Yes, second-hand play is sometimes tough! In the next deal, see if you can figure out why it is right to play second hand high.

(2)

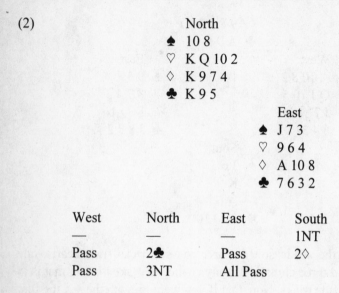

North
♠ 10 8
♡ K Q 10 2
♢ K 9 7 4
♣ K 9 5

East
♠ J 7 3
♡ 9 6 4
♢ A 10 8
♣ 7 6 3 2

West	North	East	South
—	—	—	1NT
Pass	2♣	Pass	2♢
Pass	3NT	All Pass	

Partner leads the ♣6, you play the ♠J, declarer wins with the ♣K and leads a heart to dummy's ♡K. At trick three, the ♢4 is led and you should play the ♢A. Can you figure out why this is one of the exceptional times when it is right to play second-hand high? The clues come from the bidding and the opening lead. Take all the time you need. Answer: declarer's 2♢ bid (response to Stayman) showed no four-card major—so he has two or three spades which means your partner has five or six.

Partner's opening lead was obviously his fourth best. By using the Rule of Eleven, subtracting six (the card your partner led) from eleven, you find out that there are five spades higher than the six held by dummy, you and declarer. You can see four of them between your hand and dummy, so declarer was dealt only one higher card and he has already played it on the first trick. Therefore, your partner's current spade holding is A Q 9 x (or A Q 9 x x). If you go up with the ♢A and lead a spade, partner will run four spade tricks and set the contract. The four hands:

Contract: 3NT
Opening lead: ♠6

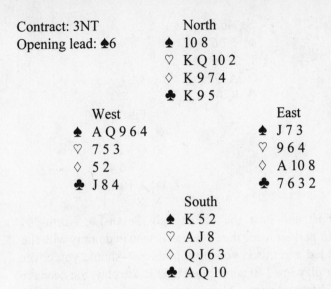

North
♠ 10 8
♡ K Q 10 2
◊ K 9 7 4
♣ K 9 5

West
♠ A Q 9 6 4
♡ 7 5 3
◊ 5 2
♣ J 8 4

East
♠ J 7 3
♡ 9 6 4
◊ A 10 8
♣ 7 6 3 2

South
♠ K 5 2
♡ A J 8
◊ Q J 6 3
♣ A Q 10

Declarer has eight tricks (one spade, four hearts and three clubs). His only chance for a ninth is in diamonds. So, even though he has no more spade stoppers, his play of leading a low diamond from dummy is a good one—he is trying to steal a trick. Many players are brainwashed into playing second hand low without thinking; declarer is hoping that you are in that category. If you do not take your ◊A he will win with the ◊Q and run like a rabbit with his nine tricks.

Cover an honor with an honor: Another old rule for second-hand play which has merit is to cover an honor with an honor; the purpose is to promote some lower card into a trick for your side. For example, if the queen is led from a dummy holding of Q x x, it is obvious to play the king from K J 10 in order to promote the jack and ten, but you should also play the king from K x x as it will promote a trick for your partner if he has the jack or ten (if declarer has A J 10, you cannot win a trick whether you cover the queen or not). Although covering an honor with an honor is usually the right play, you should not do so when there is no chance to promote a trick. In the next deal there are two examples, one showing when you should cover the honor, and the other showing when you should not:

(3)

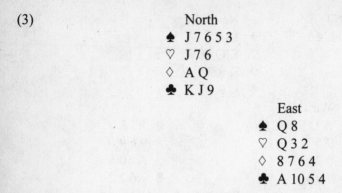

North
♠ J 7 6 5 3
♡ J 7 6
♢ A Q
♣ K J 9

East
♠ Q 8
♡ Q 3 2
♢ 8 7 6 4
♣ A 10 5 4

You are East and hear the bidding go: South-1♠, North-3♠, South-4♠. Your partner leads the ♢J which is won in dummy with the ♢A. The ♠J is led and this is your first problem—should you cover. with the ♠Q or play low? At some point later in the play, the declarer will lead the ♡J from dummy. Should you cover the ♡J with the ♡Q or play low? Answers: you *should not* cover the ♠J, but *should* cover the ♡J. The four hands:

Contract: 4♠
Opening Lead: ◊J

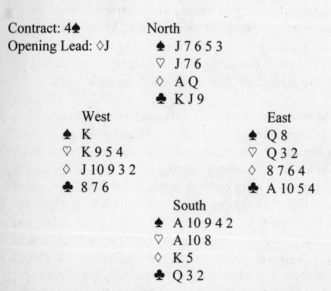

North
♠ J 7 6 5 3
♡ J 7 6
♢ A Q
♣ K J 9

West
♠ K
♡ K 9 5 4
♢ J 10 9 3 2
♣ 8 7 6

East
♠ Q 8
♡ Q 3 2
♢ 8 7 6 4
♣ A 10 5 4

South
♠ A 10 9 4 2
♡ A 10 8
♢ K 5
♣ Q 3 2

You will lose your spade trick if you cover the ♣J with the ♣Q. Seven spades are in sight and declarer's opening 1♠ bid showed at least five, leaving partner with one (or none). So there is no chance to promote a trick for your side by covering the jack.

The heart suit is a different story. If you cover the ♡J with your ♡Q, declarer will win with his ♡A and cannot win any more heart tricks; partner is left with ♡ K 9 behind declarer's ♡ 10 8. If you fail to cover, declarer will finesse and allow partner to win the trick with the ♡K. This leaves him with ♡ A 10 behind your ♡ Q 3 and he can win a second heart trick with the ten by finessing. If declarer's hearts were the ♡A 10 9, he could win two heart tricks whether you covered or not, but covering the ♡J with the ♡Q is right because it might save a trick and cannot lose.

Another time when it is wrong to cover an honor with an honor is when the lead is from two touching honors. For example, if the queen is led from a dummy holding of Q J x and you have K x x, do not cover the first time, but do cover the second honor if it is led later.

There is much more to be learned about second-hand play, but this brief explanation should help you to decide what to do. I might add that when you have a high card in a suit and decide to play second-hand low, do it fast or you will "tip your mitt."

CHAPTER NINETEEN

ATTITUDE SIGNALS

When partner makes a lead and the card you play cannot possibly win or help to promote a trick, your play is a signal to encourage or discourage partner from leading that suit. If you want partner to lead the suit again, play "high-low;" play the highest card you can spare without jeopardizing a trick, with the intention of playing a lower card next. If you wish to discourage partner from leading the suit, play "low-high;" play your lowest card first. Attitude signals are also used when discarding—when you have no more cards in the suit being led—no matter which hand leads to the trick. But they are *not* used when leading a card, and they are *not* used when following to a suit led by the declarer (you do not have to tell partner whether or not you want a suit led when the declarer is already leading it).

(**NOTE:** The attitude signal is easy to learn and should be played by all bridge players. There are other forms of signals, notably "count signals" and "suit-preference signals," but they are too advanced for this book.) Here are three examples of attitude signals:

(1)

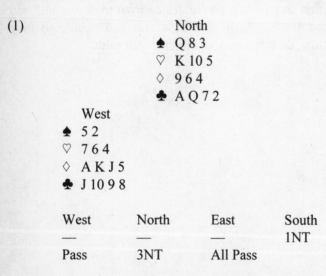

```
                    North
                    ♠ Q 8 3
                    ♡ K 10 5
                    ◇ 9 6 4
                    ♣ A Q 7 2
       West
       ♠ 5 2
       ♡ 7 6 4
       ◇ A K J 5
       ♣ J 10 9 8
```

West	North	East	South
—	—	—	1NT
Pass	3NT	All Pass	

The discouraging signal: This time you are West and your first decision is what to lead! Leading the king from an ace-king combination is usually a great lead, so the ◊K is clearly your best choice. Your partner follows to the first trick with the ◊2 and declarer plays the ◊7. Since partner played the two to discourage you from leading the suit again (an indication that he does not have the ◊Q), you should switch suits. The most attractive lead at trick two is the ♣J (top of a four-card sequence). Here are the four hands:

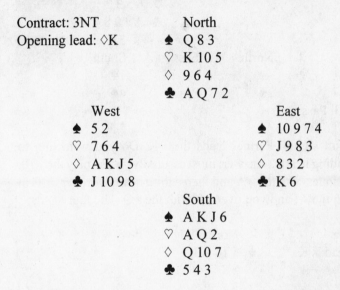

Contract: 3NT
Opening lead: ◊K

North
♠ Q 8 3
♡ K 10 5
◊ 9 6 4
♣ A Q 7 2

West
♠ 5 2
♡ 7 6 4
◊ A K J 5
♣ J 10 9 8

East
♠ 10 9 7 4
♡ J 9 8 3
◊ 8 3 2
♣ K 6

South
♠ A K J 6
♡ A Q 2
◊ Q 10 7
♣ 5 4 3

Declarer has eight tricks (four spades, three hearts and one club). If you lead a diamond at trick two, he can score a ninth trick with the ◊Q. Any lead except a diamond will beat the contract, but a club is the best choice because it is less likely to give away a trick than a spade or a heart. So you lead the ♣J and, in an effort to win a ninth trick, declarer will probably finesse the ♣Q (although it does not matter what he does). When partner gets the lead with the ♣K, he will return a diamond through declarer's ◊Q 10. You will win three more tricks with ◊A J 5, and that will set the contract by one trick.

(8)

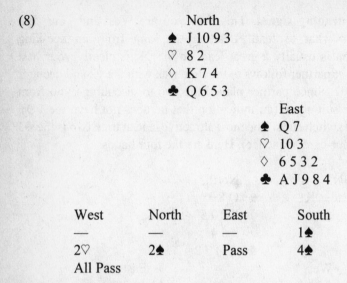

West	North	East	South
—	—	—	1♠
2♡	2♠	Pass	4♠
All Pass			

The come-on signal: Partner leads the ♡K. Do you want him to continue leading hearts? Answer: most assuredly yes, so play the ♡10. Partner continues with the ♡A and then a third heart. Declarer ruffs in dummy with the ♠J and you overruff with the ♠Q. The four hands:

Contract: 4♠
Opening Lead: ♡K

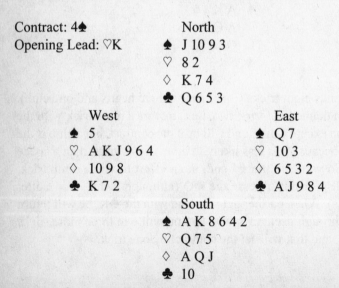

Declarer must lose a club in addition to the first three tricks for down one. Playing high-low with a doubleton is correct when you anticipate ruffing the third time the suit is played. In this case, your high-low with a doubleton heart led to winning a trick with the ♠Q. If partner does not lead the third heart, the contract cannot be set.

(3)

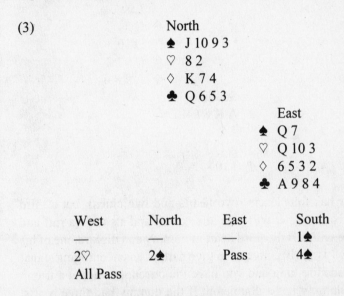

North
♠ J 10 9 3
♡ 8 2
◊ K 7 4
♣ Q 6 5 3

East
♠ Q 7
♡ Q 10 3
◊ 6 5 3 2
♣ A 9 8 4

West	North	East	South
—	—	—	1♠
2♡	2♠	Pass	4♠
All Pass			

Beware the ruff and discard: Once again your partner leads the ♡K against a 4♠ contract and you are in a position to give a signal. Which heart would you play? Answer: the ♡3. If you play the ♡10 and then follow with the ♡3, partner will think you have a doubleton, as in the previous hand, and lead a third heart, which would be a disaster! The four hands:

Contract: 4♠
Opening lead: ♡K

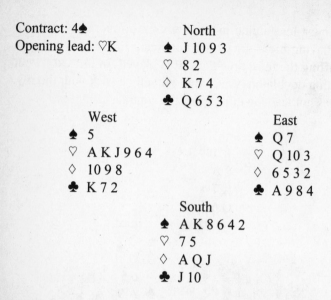

North
♠ J 10 9 3
♡ 8 2
◇ K 7 4
♣ Q 6 5 3

West
♠ 5
♡ A K J 9 6 4
◇ 10 9 8
♣ K 7 2

East
♠ Q 7
♡ Q 10 3
◇ 6 5 3 2
♣ A 9 8 4

South
♠ A K 8 6 4 2
♡ 7 5
◇ A Q J
♣ J 10

Declarer has four losers (two hearts and two clubs), but a third heart lead from partner will give him "a ruff and a sluff" (a ruff and discard). He will ruff the third heart in dummy and discard one of his club losers. It is fairly common to give partner an encouraging signal when he leads the king and you have the queen; but not at a trump contract if dummy has a doubleton. If the dummy had three hearts, signaling with the ten would be appropriate.

Signals with honor cards: Consistent with attitude signals, honor-card signals apply only when the card you play cannot win or promote a trick. In other words, you are following suit when a higher card has already been played to the trick, or you are discarding. The signal is made by playing the top card of a sequence headed by the king or queen, and sometimes by the jack. For example, if any of the other three players has played the ace, play the king from K Q J 10, or the queen from Q J 10 9.

When partner leads the king, you can afford to signal with the queen from Q-J-x because he is known to have the ace and your side will still have the two top cards in the suit. This is the most common and useful honor signal. Here is an example:

(4)

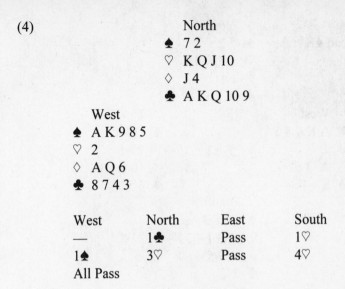

North
- ♠ 7 2
- ♡ K Q J 10
- ◇ J 4
- ♣ A K Q 10 9

West
- ♠ A K 9 8 5
- ♡ 2
- ◇ A Q 6
- ♣ 8 7 4 3

West	North	East	South
—	1♣	Pass	1♡
1♠	3♡	Pass	4♡
All Pass			

You lead the ♠K against this 4♡ contract and partner signals with the ♠Q. Looking at this dummy, you can predict declarer's line of play. When he gets the lead he will draw the trumps and then run the clubs to discard any losers he has on dummy's club suit. So your only chance to beat the contract is to win the first four tricks—two spades and two diamonds. If declarer has the ◇K, which is probable since he bid twice and the only two high cards you cannot see are the ♡A and the ◇K, the first diamond lead must come from your partner. So *underlead* your ♠A at trick two. The four hands:

Contract: 4♡
Opening lead ♠K

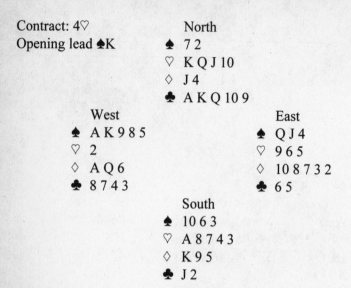

North
♠ 7 2
♡ K Q J 10
◇ J 4
♣ A K Q 10 9

West
♠ A K 9 8 5
♡ 2
◇ A Q 6
♣ 8 7 4 3

East
♠ Q J 4
♡ 9 6 5
◇ 10 8 7 3 2
♣ 6 5

South
♠ 10 6 3
♡ A 8 7 4 3
◇ K 9 5
♣ J 2

Partner will win the second trick with the ♠J and return a diamond through declarer's ◇K. This is the only way to win four tricks. *Note that partner's play of the ♠Q guarantees the jack (or singleton queen).* If he has a doubleton queen, he must play the low card; if he plays the queen, his partner might think he has the jack and underlead the ace.

CHAPTER TWENTY

DISCARDING

When declarer leads a suit in which you have no more cards, the fate of the contract may depend on your discards. How would you discard in the following deal?

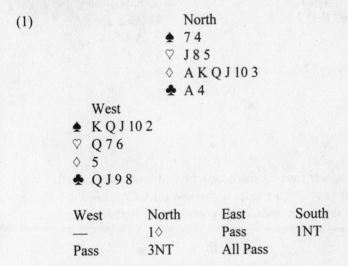

(1)
```
                        North
                     ♠ 7 4
                     ♡ J 8 5
                     ◊ A K Q J 10 3
                     ♣ A 4
        West
     ♠ K Q J 10 2
     ♡ Q 7 6
     ◊ 5
     ♣ Q J 9 8
```

West	North	East	South
—	1◊	Pass	1NT
Pass	3NT	All Pass	

North can contribute seven tricks if his partner can get the lead before the defense can collect five tricks, so his 3NT bid is a good gamble.

You lead the ♠K against 3NT. Declarer wins with the ♠A and plans to cash six diamond tricks. Keeping in mind that your goal is to beat the contract one trick, which five discards would you make as he runs his diamonds? Answer: anything except a spade. You can see that declarer has eight tricks (one spade, six diamonds and one club). If he has the ♡A or the ♣K, he has nine tricks. Your only chance to beat the contract is if partner has both of those cards and *you never discard a spade*. The four hands:

Contract: 3NT
Opening lead: ♠K

North
♠ 7 4
♡ J 8 5
◇ A K Q J 10 3
♣ A 4

West
♠ K Q J 10 2
♡ Q 7 6
◇ 5
♣ Q J 9 8

East
♠ 9 6 5 3
♡ A 10 4 2
◇ 8 2
♣ K 7 5

South
♠ A 8
♡ K 9 3
◇ 9 7 6 4
♣ 10 6 3 2

After declarer runs six diamonds, he will lead a heart. Partner will take his ♡A to return a spade. If you saved four spades, the contract will be set; if you discarded one, you threw away the setting trick.

(2)

North
♠ J 2
♡ A 7 3
◇ A Q 8 5
♣ K 9 8 6

East
♠ K Q 8
♡ 9 2
◇ 10 7 6 2
♣ Q J 5 4

West	North	East	South
—	1◇	Pass	1♡
Pass	2♡	Pass	4NT
Pass	5♡	Pass	5NT
Pass	6◇	Pass	7♡
All Pass			

After using Blackwood to find out that his partner has two aces and one king, South bids a grand slam. The opening lead is the ♠10, the ♠2 is played from dummy, you play the ♠8 and declarer the ♠A. Declarer then leads three rounds of trumps; partner follows suit twice and discards a spade on the third. Before you make a discard, ask yourself: "Why is declarer leading trumps after all of the missing ones have been drawn? Why doesn't he put his cards on the table and claim his grand slam?" Answer: he obviously has a potential losing trick and is going to run his long suit to give you a chance to make a faulty discard. What should you do in this situation? Answer: *take your time* and try not to make any mistakes, especially against a grand slam.

Now back to the play. Your partner discards a spade on the third trump lead, what do you discard? Answer: discard the ♠Q. What do you discard on the fourth trump lead if your partner and dummy both discard a spade? Answer: Discard the ♠K. *Keep the dummy covered*—keep equal length with dummy's long suits. There are eight cards left and the dummy and you both have four diamonds and four clubs. If declarer leads any more hearts, follow dummy's discards—if a club is thrown from dummy, you throw a club; if a diamond is thrown from dummy, you throw a diamond. The four hands:

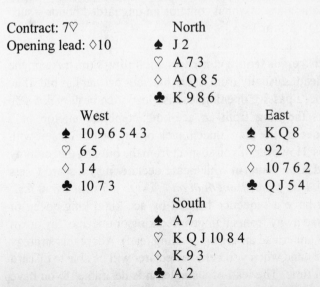

Contract: 7♡
Opening lead: ◊10

North
♠ J 2
♡ A 7 3
◊ A Q 8 5
♣ K 9 8 6

West
♠ 10 9 6 5 4 3
♡ 6 5
◊ J 4
♣ 10 7 3

East
♠ K Q 8
♡ 9 2
◊ 10 7 6 2
♣ Q J 5 4

South
♠ A 7
♡ K Q J 10 8 4
◊ K 9 3
♣ A 2

The only losing trick in declarer's hand is a spade. If you discard a diamond before dummy does, he can discard his losing spade on dummy's fourth diamond. If you discard a club before dummy does, he can play ace, king and ruff a club to establish dummy's fourth club for a discard. Note that partner's lead of the ♣10 promised the ♣9, so, once the ♠J is discarded from dummy, it is safe to discard your ♠K.

IN REVIEW

Opening leads versus 1NT, 2NT or 3NT contracts: The best opening lead is usually a suit that has been bid by your partner. If partner has not bid a suit, and excluding suits bid by the declarer, it is generally right to lead from your longest and strongest suit. Lead the top card of a three-card sequence if it is headed by the king, queen, jack or ten. Without a three-card sequence, the most common lead is fourth best—the fourth highest card in the suit.

Opening leads versus 6NT or 7NT contracts: Choose the lead least likely to give declarer an unearned trick. Lead the top of a three-card sequence, or from a three-card or longer suit with no honors. Shy away from leading a suit which contains an unguarded honor—such as K x x x x, Q x x x or J x x.

Opening leads versus trump contracts, including slams: Again the best opening lead is usually from a suit that your partner has bid. If he has not bid one, a passive opening lead is most often best: pick a safe lead—such as the king from an ace-king combination; top of a sequence headed by the king, queen, jack or ten; or from a suit with no honor cards. However, if you suspect from the bidding that dummy has a long and strong suit (in which case declarer may discard losers in other suits), *lead from strength in an effort to get your tricks fast:* if you do not have a sequence headed by ace-king, king-queen or queen-jack, lead away from an unguarded king or queen or lay down an ace (do not underlead an ace on opening lead). Adopt this strategy throughout the hand when you believe declarer will be able to discard losers if given time. The lead of a singleton is desirable if you have the right trump holding and there is a good chance that partner will be able to get the lead and give you a ruff before declarer can draw your trumps. If you suspect that declarer will be using dummy's trumps for ruffing, lead a trump.

Return partner's suit: When your partner has made an opening lead against a notrump contract, return his suit at your first opportunity unless you have a very good reason to do otherwise. Which card you lead is important, as it helps partner to determine how many cards you have in the suit. If you began with three cards, lead back the higher of the remaining two—from A 7 4, win with the ace and return the seven. If you began with four cards or more, lead back the fourth best from your original holding—from A 8 6 3, win with the ace and return the three.

Lead a new suit: Since the defenders can see whether or not the dummy has a long suit on which declarer may discard losers, they can exercise more skill in selecting which suit to lead at trick two and later than they can on opening lead. If it appears that declarer will not be able to discard any losers, make a passive lead—the one least likely to jeopardize a trick. If dummy has a long and strong suit on which he may discard losers, make an aggressive lead—lead from strength in an effort to get your tricks quickly. The correct card to lead is not always the same as it would be for the opening lead and there is no formula to follow; sometimes you just have to study dummy and reason it out. However, one important strategy is to lead "low from strength," and "top of nothing."

Beware the ruff and discard: Do not lead a suit in which declarer and dummy are both void if declarer may gain a trick by ruffing in one hand and discarding a loser in the other. However, *if you are sure declarer has no more losers outside the trump suit*, giving a ruff and discard cannot hurt and it may promote a trump trick for your side.

Third-hand play: When your partner leads to any trick, play your highest card (third hand high) if your goal is to win the trick, or to promote a trick; but if your suit is headed by two or more equal high cards, play the *lowest* of equals (for example, from Q J x, play the jack; from J 10 9 x, play the nine). If dummy has an honor card in the suit your partner leads and you have a higher honor, do not necessarily play third hand high. For example: if a low card is played from a dummy holding Q x x, play the jack from K J x, and play the ten from K J 10 or K 10 x; only if declarer plays the queen should you play the king.

The Rule of Eleven: When partner leads fourth best, subtract the value of the card he led from 11 to learn how many higher cards are held by the other three players. Since you can see your hand and dummy, you can tell how many higher cards are held by declarer. For example: partner leads the five, so there are six higher cards held by declarer, dummy and you. If dummy has two higher and you have three higher, declarer has exactly one higher.

The unblocking play: One way to beat contracts (especially notrump) is to win tricks in a long suit. When your partner has the long suit, it is sometimes important to "unblock" to get out of his way. This is done by saving a low card in his suit to play last. For example, if partner leads the king and you have A 8 in the suit, play the ace first and return the eight; that way partner can continue leading the suit and win whatever tricks are possible.

Second hand low: Inexperienced players tend to play their high cards prematurely. When you are second hand, the general rule is to play *low* unless you can think of a good reason to do otherwise.

Cover an honor with an honor: This is another second-hand rule. In most cases it is right to cover an opponent's honor card with your honor card, the purpose being to promote some lower card into a trick for your side. There are exceptions.

Attitude signals: When third hand plays a card that has no chance to win or promote a trick, the size of the card he plays is a signal. He plays the highest card he can spare if he wants his partner to lead the suit again (the beginning of a high-low signal), or plays his lowest card to discourage partner from leading the suit again (the beginning of a low-high signal). These signals are also used when discarding, no matter which hand led to the trick. They are *not* used when leading a card, or when following to a suit led by the declarer.

Signals with honor cards: Once again, assuming that the card you play has no chance to win or promote a trick (a higher card in the suit has been played by any player or you are discarding), if you have a sequence headed by the king or queen and wish to signal your partner, play the top card of the sequence. For example, if the ace has been played, signal with the king from K Q J 10, or with the queen from Q J 10 9. When partner leads the king and you have Q J x (no ten), it is usually right to signal with the queen because your side still has the two top cards in the suit—the ace and jack.

Discarding: Many a contract is fulfilled because a defender makes a careless discard. So *take your time* when a suit is being led in which you have no more cards; try not to throw away a card that will give declarer an extra trick. Tend to keep equal length with dummy's long suits, or length in suits bid by declarer, and observe partner's discards and signals.

APPENDIX

Here you will read about the Procedures and Scoring for Chicago Bridge and Duplicate Bridge, the Proprieties, and a simplified version of The Laws of Contract Bridge.

CHICAGO BRIDGE

The most popular variation of bridge played today is "Chicago" (four-deal bridge). The following pages explain how to play and score Chicago bridge; there is also a brief description of both "rubber" and "duplicate" bridge.

To get started, here is a typical scoring sheet. You can make one by simply drawing a horizontal and vertical line to form a cross on a sheet of paper. The scorekeeper puts all of his plus scores on the left side of the vertical line, and all of his minus scores (his opponents' plus scores) on the right.

WE   THEY

Four-deal bridge: A "round" of Chicago bridge consists of four deals, one by each player in clockwise rotation. A deal passed out does not count; the same dealer deals again.

The wheel: The "wheel" is used to keep track of who dealt first and the rotation of the deal. The scorekeeper draws a diagonal cross at the top of the scoresheet and then writes the number "1" in the position of the first dealer, then successively (clockwise) 2, 3 and 4 as each dealer's turn comes up. In the diagram, the player keeping this score dealt first, the player on his left dealt 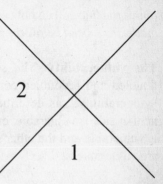 the second hand, and the scorekeeper will write a "3" in the next space when it becomes his partner turn to deal.

Trick score: When declarer wins enough tricks to fulfill his contract, he wins points for each trick in excess of six. This "trick score" varies, depending on whether the contract was played in notrump, a major, or a minor. The formula is as follows:

Notrump	Major Suits	Minor Suits
1NT = 40	1♠ or 1♡ = 30	1♢ or 1♣ = 20
2NT = 70	2♠ or 2♡ = 60	2♢ or 2♣ = 40
3NT = 100	3♠ or 3♡ = 90	3♢ or 3♣ = 60
4NT = 130	4♠ or 4♡ = 120	4♢ or 4♣ = 80
5NT = 160	5♠ or 5♡ = 150	5♢ or 5♣ = 100
6NT = 190	6♠ or 6♡ = 180	6♢ or 6♣ = 120
7NT = 220	7♠ or 7♡ = 210	7♢ or 7♣ = 140

Note the easy pattern for remembering trick-score values: notrump counts 40 for the first odd trick (the seventh trick won by declarer's side) and 30 for each additional; spades and hearts always count 30; and diamonds and clubs always count 20.

There is a difference between the score for tricks *bid and made* and tricks *not bid and made*. The latter are called "overtricks." Tricks bid and made are scored *below the line* (meaning the horizontal line on the scoresheet) and contribute toward game. Overtricks are scored *above the line* and do not contribute toward game. *Only tricks bid and made are scored below the line. All other scoring goes above the line.*

The vulnerability: The score for game bonuses, slam bonuses, doubled and redoubled contracts, and undertricks, depends on the "vulnerability;" as described below. On the first deal of the four, neither side is vulnerable; on the second and third deals, dealer's side is vulnerable and the other side is not; on the fourth deal, both sides are vulnerable.

Bonuses for games: Game bonuses are awarded for 100 points or more of trick score *below the line.* Note in the trick-score table that bids of 3NT, 4♡, 4♠, 5♣ and 5◇ are required to reach 100 points; they are the minimum game contracts. There is a bonus of 300 points for bidding and making a nonvulnerable game, and a bonus of 500 points for bidding and making a vulnerable game. These bonuses are entered on the scoresheet at the time the game is made. Since there are four deals, it is possible to win from zero to four games.

Part-score (or partial): Any score of less than 100 points below the line is call a "part-score" and contributes toward game in the later deals, but any game scored (by either side) wipes out all previous part-scores. Under no circumstances can a part-score be carried over from one game to the next.

   Part-scores made in the first three deals carry over to the next deal. For example, if you have a part-score of 60, a bid of one notrump or two of any suit will give you game if you make it; it would be foolish to bid higher unless you think you can make a slam. But a part-score made on the fourth deal cannot be carried over, so a 100 point bonus is awarded for making a part-score *on the fourth deal only.*

Bonuses for slams:	Not Vulnerable	Vulnerable
Small slam (any six bid)	500	750
Grand Slam (any seven bid)	1000	1500

Bonuses for honor cards: At the end of each deal, bonuses are awarded for being dealt certain combinations of honor cards *in one hand*. If one player holds all five honor cards (A K Q J 10) *in the trump suit*, his side receives a bonus of 150 points—called "150 honors." If one player holds any four of the five honor cards *in the trump suit,* his side receives a bonus of 100 points—called "100 honors." If one player holds all four aces and *the contract is played in notrump,* his side receives a bonus of 150 points—called "150 aces."

The score for making doubled and redoubled contracts: When a contract is doubled, the score for tricks bid and made is doubled; when the contract is redoubled, the score for tricks bid and made is multiplied by four. Only the "trick score" is doubled (or redoubled), and if it adds up to 100 points or more a game bonus is awarded.

The score for doubled and redoubled overtricks depends on the vulnerability. When not vulnerable, each *doubled* overtrick is worth 100 points; when vulnerable, each is worth 200 points. When not vulnerable, each *redoubled* overtricks is worth 200 points; when vulnerable, each is worth 400 points.

Also, there is a 50-point bonus for making a doubled contract, and a 100-point bonus for making a redoubled contract.

Undertricks: When declarer fails to win the number of tricks required by his contract, his side loses points for each "undertrick." When not vulnerable, the penalty for each undertrick is 50 points; when vulnerable, the penalty for each is 100 points.

If the contract is doubled and declarer is not vulnerable, the penalty is 100 for the first trick, 200 for the second and third tricks, and 300 for each additional trick: down one = -100; down two = -300; down three = -500; down four = -800; down five = -1100, etc.

If the contract is doubled and the declarer is vulnerable, the penalty is 200 for the first trick and 300 for each additional trick: down one = -200; down two = -500; down three = -800; down four = -1100; down five = -1400, etc.

If the contract is redoubled, the penalty for undertricks is always exactly twice the amount of the doubled penalty.

After four deals have been played: The scores are totaled and the difference is entered on a score sheet, and then the players change partners for the next rubber.

HOW CHICAGO BRIDGE IS SCORED

	We	They
(1)	30	
(1)	60	
(2)	1370	
(3)		780
(4)	160	
	1620	780

Deal 1: The wheel shows that your left-hand opponent dealt the first hand; neither side was vulnerable. You and your partner bid 2♠ and made three. Your score is 60 below the line, and 30 above.

Deal 2: Your partner dealt the second hand, your side was vulnerable and your opponents were not. You bid 6◊ and won 12 tricks for score of 1370—750 slam bonus, 500 game bonus, and 120 trick score. Note that since a new horizontal line is drawn, all of your scores can be entered as one figure—it is not necessary to write 120 below the line and 1250 above the line.

Deal 3: Your right-hand opponent dealt the third hand, his side was vulnerable and your side was not. They bid 4♠ and won 12 tricks with

100 honors for a score of 780—500 game bonus, 180 for tricks, and 100 for honors.

Deal 4: You dealt the fourth hand, both sides were vulnerable. You bid 2♡ and won eight tricks for a score of 160—60 for trick score and 100 for making a part-score on the fourth deal.

Your side wins—1,620 to 780. Your net score is 840 points, but it is rounded to the nearest 100 to make an eight-point rubber.

RUBBER BRIDGE

In case you get involved in a game of rubber bridge, the scoring is the same as for Chicago bridge, except: (1) If a deal is passed out, the next player in turn deals the next hand; instead of the same player. (2) The rubber ends when one side has scored two games, rather than when four deals are completed. (3) Instead of giving bonuses for games at the end if each deal, a bonus is given to the winning side at the end of the rubber: 700 points if the other side has not scored a game, or 500 points if the other side has scored a game. (4) A side is not vulnerable if it has not scored a game, and is vulnerable if it has scored a game.

DUPLICATE BRIDGE

The scoring for duplicate bridge is the same as Chicago bridge, with three exceptions: (1) Honors do not count at duplicate bridge. (2) Part-scores do not carry over from one deal to the next; a bonus of 50 points is awarded for bidding and making any part-score. (3) The vulnerability is predetermined and shown on the "duplicate board" which is placed in the center of the table and left there until the deal is completed.

Partnerships remain intact throughout the game, but you play against different opponents from time to time. In most cases the North-South pairs remain stationary; the East-West pairs and the duplicate boards (containing the bridge hands) change tables. At the end of each deal, the North player enters the score on a score sheet and the East-West players check for errors.

A tournament director runs the game. He assigns starting positions, distributes the duplicate boards, calls for the players and boards to change tables at the end of each round (most commonly two boards are played each round), and settles any irregularities that may occur.

The most popular form of duplicate bridge is a pair contest scored in "match points." The strategy for match-point scoring is quite different from Chicago bridge. At Chicago bridge the goal is to win as much as you can on each deal. At match points you are actually competing against all the other pairs who hold the same cards as you and your partner (not the pair you are playing against), and the goal is to get a better score than they do. You earn one match point for each pair you beat (it does not matter whether you beat them by ten points or 1000 points), and a half of a match point for each pair that you tie. The maximum number of match points that can be won in one deal depends on how many times the deal is played. For example, if it is played 13 times, 12 is the top score (achieved by getting a better score than all 12 of the other pairs who held your cards), and six is average.

Match-point scoring is all done by the tournament director, or in larger tournaments by a computer, at the end of the game.

Virtually all of the duplicate bridge played in North America is under the auspices of the AMERICAN CONTRACT BRIDGE LEAGUE. If you are interested in becoming a member, their address and telephone are:

American Contract Bridge League
2990 Airways Blvd.
Memphis, TN 38116-3847
Telephone: 800/264-2743, or 901/332-5586

THE PROPRIETIES

Bridge is a game for ladies and gentlemen, so manners and etiquette are important. Below are recommendations for proper conduct.

* Do not pick up any of your cards until the deal is completed.
* Once you have looked at your hand, limit your activity to making calls and plays in your turn. Avoid extraneous general conversation, or discussion of previous deals.

* Make your calls in a normal tone of voice (no earthquake doubles), and do so without undue haste or hesitation. It is impossible for anyone to make every bid in perfect tempo, but no one insists on perfection. Just do the best you can.

* Use the identical wording for each call. For example: "Pass" is proper, not "I Pass," or "No Bid." "Double" is proper, not "I Double," "I Double You," or "I Double Three Spades."

* If you think your partner has given you unfair information, do not take advantage. For example: if your left-hand opponent opened the bidding with 3♠ and your partner takes a long time before he passes (he obviously has a good hand and was considering a bid), you should pass with doubtful values. However, you should bid if your hand is clearly good enough to make a bid if partner had not hesitated. It is not unethical to take advantage of an opponent's hesitation.

* During the play of the hand, do not detach a card from your hand before it is your turn to play. For example, if partner has made the opening lead, do not remove a card from your hand until after declarer has played a card from dummy.

* As dummy, do not exchange hands with partner, walk around the table to see his hand, or glance at an opponent's hand (although many players cannot resist, it is wrong to do this).

* Strive to play your cards in a uniform manner and at a normal pace. It is unethical for partner to take advantage of your hesitation, or the manner in which you play your cards. Hesitating when you have nothing to think about in an attempt to deceive an opponent is cheating.

* Do not express satisfaction or dissatisfaction with a bid or play made by partner. For example, do not frown when partner does not lead the suit you want led.

* Unless asked, avoid offering advice to partner, and especially to the opponents.

* Do not criticize another player for a violation, unless he does so repeatedly. We are all human and sometimes violate the ethics code unintentionally. A friendly attitude toward the other players means more enjoyment for all.

THE LAWS OF CONTRACT BRIDGE

The laws of contract bridge are designed to correct irregularities, not to "punish" any player. Although in a friendly game players pay minimum attention to the laws and dismiss an irregularity without enforcing the rule, ignoring the rules will not bring the fairest solution. It is better to play by the rules. Below is a condensed version covering many of the most common irregularities. There are some variations in the rules for duplicate bridge, but there you have a director to settle any irregularities.

Redeal: A redeal is necessary if before the last card is dealt:
* The wrong player is dealing.
* A card is faced during the deal.
* The cards are incorrectly dealt.

A redeal is necessary if before play is completed it is discovered:
* The pack is incomplete and a missing card (or cards) cannot be found.
* Two hands are incorrect; one player has too many cards, and another too few.

A redeal is not required if:
* The wrong player completed the deal. The deal stands; the player who dealt begins the auction and the player who missed his turn to deal has no redress.
* A player played more than once to a trick, or failed to play to a trick.
* A missing card is found elsewhere, not in a previous trick. It is restored to the deficient hand and revoke penalties may apply.

Review of the bidding: Each player may ask for a review at his turn to bid. This review should be given by an opponent. After the final pass, any player (except dummy) may ask for a review at his first turn to play. Subsequently, no review of the bidding is allowed, but any of the three active players may ask what the contract is.

Changing a bid: There is no penalty if the change is made without pause for thought. When a change is made after some seconds:
* If the original bid was legal and the offender chooses to repeat it, partner must pass one time.
* If the offender substitutes any other legal bid, partner must pass for the remainder of the auction. Lead penalties may apply.

Insufficient bid: When a player makes an insufficient bid, the opponent who calls next may accept it (accidentally or on purpose) by making any bid, double or pass, as though the insufficient bid were legal.

If the next player refuses to accept the insufficient bid:
* The offender may make the bid sufficient by bidding the lowest possible number in the same named suit or notrump. No penalty.
* Make any other legal call. This forces the offender's partner to pass for the rest of the auction, and there may be lead penalties.

Bid out of turn: When a player makes a bid when it is not his turn, the opponent who calls next may accept it (accidentally or on purpose) by making any legal bid, double or pass. The bidding continues as if no irregularity occurred.

If the next player refuses to accept the bid out of turn:
* If the irregularity occurred before the offender's partner's turn to call, that partner must pass throughout the auction.
* If the irregularity occurred at right-hand opponent's turn to call:
    (1) If that opponent passes, offender's legal bid is repeated without penalty.
    (2) If that opponent makes a legal bid, double or redouble, offender may make any legal call. If the call repeats the denomination bid out of rotation, there is a penalty: offender's partner must pass one time. Any other action by offender forces partner to pass throughout the auction and lead penalties may apply.

Pass out of turn: When a player passes out of turn, the opponent who calls next may accept it (accidentally or on purpose) by making any bid or pass. The bidding continues as if no irregularity occurred.

If the next player refuses to accept the pass out of rotation, the penalty depends on whose turn it was to bid:

* If the irregularity occurred before any player has bid or at right-hand opponent's turn to call, offender must pass one time at his next turn.
* If the irregularity occurred after one or more bids have taken place and it was offender's partner's turn to call, offender must pass throughout the auction. His partner may make any legal bid or pass, but he may not double or redouble at that turn.

Card exposed or led during the auction: If a player faces a card during the auction it stays on the table until the auction is closed. If it was an honor card, or a premature opening lead, offender's partner must pass when it is next his turn to call. If the offender becomes declarer or dummy, the card is picked up without penalty. If the offender becomes a defender, the card is a penalty card.

Penalty card (major): Definition: a card of honor rank, or any card exposed during an irregularity (as in leading out of turn, or in revoking and then correcting). Also, when one defender has two or more penalty cards, all such cards become major penalty cards.

Procedure: When a player has a major penalty card, it must be played at the first legal opportunity. If a player has two or more penalty cards that can legally be played, declarer may designate which one is played first.

Penalty card (minor): Definition: A card below the rank of an honor and exposed inadvertently (as in playing two cards to a trick, or in dropping a card accidentally).

Procedure: When a defender has a minor penalty card, he may not play any other card of the same suit below the rank of an honor until he has first played the penalty card. He is allowed, however, to play an honor card instead of the penalty card. He is not forced to discard or lead the minor penalty card at his first opportunity.

Lead penalties: When a defender has the lead while his partner has a major penalty card, declarer may:

* Require or prohibit (for as long as the lead is retained) the lead of the exposed suit. The penalty card is picked up at once. No further penalty.
* Allow that defender to lead any suit. Major penalty card provisions continue to apply.

When a defender first has the lead (including the opening lead) after his partner has made a bid out of turn or an insufficient bid and then changed his call (by bidding a different suit or notrump, doubling, or redoubling), declarer may:

* Require the lead of the suit not repeated.
* Prohibit the lead of the suit not repeated for as long as he retains the lead.
* Require or prohibit the lead of any one specified suit if notrump, double or redouble was the call not repeated.

Lead out of turn by a defender: If a player leads out of turn (including the opening lead) when it was the offender's partner's turn to lead:

* Declarer may accept the lead from the wrong hand.
    (1) The dummy is tabled and declarer plays next (clockwise) to the trick from his hand.
    (2) Declarer spreads his hand on the table and becomes dummy; his partner the declarer. This option is usually accepted when declarer inadvertently begins to spread his own hand and exposes one or more of his cards.
* No penalty if an opponent implied in any way that the wrong hand should lead.

Lead out of turn by declarer: When declarer leads out of turn from his hand or dummy:

* The lead may be accepted by either defender making a statement to that effect, or by the next defender in turn playing a card to the irregular lead.
* The lead may be rejected by either defender if it was a defender's turn to lead or the declarer led from the wrong hand. In either case, he restores the card led in error to his or dummy's hand, and plays a card from the right hand without penalty.

Inspection of a trick: Declarer or either defender may inspect the first trick until his side has led or played to the following trick. Thereafter, until play ceases, tricks may be inspected face down only to account for a missing or surplus card. If a trick with the wrong number of cards is discovered, it is inspected face up. The player having the wrong number of cards is held responsible.

Revoke: Any active player may ask someone who has failed to follow suit whether he has a card of the suit led, in order to prevent a revoke. Dummy may ask only declarer. If a player withdraws a played card to follow suit, thus correcting a potential revoke, the withdrawn card becomes a major penalty card. Other players in turn may change cards played after the retraction. Declarer's withdrawn card is never a penalty card.

Procedure after an established revoke: A revoke becomes established when the offending side plays to the next trick. If the offending side won the trick on which the revoke occurred, that trick and one more trick (if a subsequent trick is won), will be transferred to the other side. If the nonoffending side won the revoke trick, and the offending side won any more tricks after the revoke, one trick is transferred. In addition, if a trick is won after the revoke by the offending side with a card he could have legally played to the revoke trick, an additional trick is transferred.

If the revoke penalty fails to transfer the number of tricks that would have been won had the revoke not occurred, the nonoffending side shall receive these tricks.

There is no penalty for a revoke if:

* The offending side did not win the revoke trick or any thereafter.
* The revoke was made by failing to play a card from dummy or a penalty card.
* The revoke occurred on the twelfth trick. Correct it without penalty.
* Attention was first called to the revoke after the cards were mixed together.

Claims and concessions: Declarer makes a claim by putting his hand face up on the table and stating a proposed line of play. The defenders face their cards on the table and analyze the claim. If they accept the claim, the cards are thrown in. If they do not accept, the hand is played out. Declarer may not take a finesse unless it has previously succeeded, or an opponent has shown out in the suit, nor may he draw any outstanding trumps if this was not mentioned in the proposed line of play. Any doubtful point is resolved in favor of the defenders.

A defender's claim is treated in a similar fashion, but the other defender is not permitted to make an unusual play which would benefit his side because he saw his partner's hand.

Scoring corrections: Forgetting to enter the score for honors, or for an incorrect addition, may be corrected before the net score for the rubber is agreed upon. However (unless all four players agree), no correction may be made as to the number of tricks taken in a previous deal once the bidding of the next hand has started.

GLOSSARY

ABOVE THE LINE: The place to score undertricks, overtricks and bonuses—everything except trick-score.

AMERICAN CONTRACT BRIDGE LEAGUE (ACBL): A national organization of bridge players in North America.

ARTIFICIAL BID: A bid to ask for or give information, but not related to the length of the suit actually bid. There are many: cue-bids, responses to Blackwood, Stayman, etc.

ASKING BID: An artificial bid asking partner to tell you something about his hand, rather than telling him something about your hand. The two most common are Blackwood (asking about aces and kings) and Stayman—asking about four-card major suits.

ATTITUDE SIGNAL: A card played by a defender to encourage, or discourage, his partner from leading a suit. The usual method is to play high-low to encourage a lead (a "come-on" signal), and to play low-high to discourage a lead.

AUCTION: The bidding.

AVOIDANCE PLAY: A play made to keep a dangerous opponent from getting the lead.

BACK SCORE: The summary sheet on which the results are credited to the winners and debited against the losers.

BALANCED HAND: A hand containing no singletons or voids and at most one doubleton; the possible distributions are 4-3-3-3, 4-4-3-2 and 5-3-3-2. A hand with 5-4-2-2 or 6-3-2-2 distribution is a "semi-balanced hand." Any other distribution is an "unbalanced hand."

BELOW THE LINE: The place to score tricks bid and made (trick score). All other scoring goes above the line.

BID: An offer to win a specified number of tricks in a specified suit or notrump.

BIDDING: The phase during which all bids are made—the auction.

BLACKWOOD CONVENTION: A bid of 4NT asking partner how many aces he holds.

BLOCKING: A play that prevents the running of an established suit.

BODY CARDS: Intermediate cards—nines and tens.

BONUSES (scored above the line): Awards for bidding and making a game or slam, for holding four or five honors in one hand in the trump suit, for holding all four aces in one hand at a notrump contract, or for making a doubled or redoubled contract. Also, at Chicago bridge for making a part-score on the fourth deal, or at duplicate bridge for making a part-score on any deal.

BOOK: For declarer, the first six tricks taken. For the defenders, one trick shy of the number needed to defeat the contract.

BREAK: How the missing cards in a suit are divided between the opponents. A bad break means lopsided distribution (such as five missing cards dividing 4-1); a good break means even distribution—such as five missing cards dividing 3-2.

CALL: Any bid, double, redouble or pass.

CARD READING: Deducing information about the opponents' hands from their bidding and played cards.

CASH: Play a winning card.

CHICAGO BRIDGE: Four-deal bridge, named for the city in which it originated.

COMPETITIVE BIDDING: Auctions in which both sides enter the bidding.

CONDONE: To forgive an irregularity by an opponent. For example, if the declarer leads from the wrong hand and the next defender in turn plays to the trick, the lead out of turn is condoned; no penalty.

CONTRACT: The final bid in the auction, with the obligation to win a specified number of tricks.

CONVENTION: A specific agreement between partners to give an unusual meaning to a bid or defensive play.

COUNT SIGNAL (not for beginners). A way to show your length in a suit to partner. Most common usage is to play high-low with an even number of cards, or low-high with an odd number.

COVER: To play a higher card to the trick than the one played by your right-hand opponent.

CROSSRUFF: To ruff back and forth between two hands.

CUE-BID: A forcing bid in a suit that is not intended as the trump suit. It is most often a suit that has been bid by an opponent, but may be an unbid suit if another trump suit has already been agreed. In many cases it is a slam try showing control in the bid suit, but is also used for other reasons—to show a stopper, or to ask partner's help in deciding the denomination or how high to bid.

DEAL: Distribute the 52 cards into four hands of 13 cards each. The cards are dealt one at a time, face down, in a clockwise rotation beginning with the player on dealer's left and ending with the dealer.

DECLARER: The partner who made the first bid in the denomination named in the final contract. Declarer plays both his and dummy's cards.

DEFENDER: Either opponent of declarer.

DEFENSIVE BIDDING: All the bidding by the side which did not make the opening bid.

DEFENSIVE TRICK: A card, or combination of cards, that will win a trick when defending a contract.

DENOMINATION: The suit or notrump named in a bid.

DISCARD: Play a card which is not in the suit led and is not a trump.

DISTRIBUTION: The way the 13 cards in a hand are divided among the four suits, or the way the 13 cards of a suit are divided among the four players.

DOUBLE: A call that increases the scoring value for undertricks, trick score and overtricks (see penalty double, takeout double).

DOUBLE DUMMY: Play a hand while looking at all four hands.

DOUBLE FINESSE: Finesse against two missing cards.

DOUBLE JUMP: A bid two levels higher than necessary.

DOUBLETON: A holding of exactly two cards in a suit.

DRAW TRUMPS: Lead trumps until the opponents have no more.

DROP: Capture an opponent's high card by playing a higher card.

DUCK: Play a low card when holding a higher card which could win, or might win, the trick.

DUMMY: Declarer's partner; also the hand he places face up on the table.

DUPLICATE BOARD A device with four pockets to keep the four hands intact, for duplicate play.

DUPLICATE BRIDGE: A form of bridge where each hand is played at one or more other tables.

DUPLICATION OF VALUES: Wasted values in a suit, such as A-Q opposite K-J (with the four top honors only two tricks are available), or K x x opposite a singleton—in many cases the king is useless.

ECHO: A high-low signal.

ENDPLAY: See throw-in play.

ENTRY: A way to gain the lead in a particular hand. Careful and effective use of entries is one of the basic arts of card play.

EQUALS: Two or more cards of the same suit which are adjacent in rank. For example, the king-queen-jack are equals; or, if the queen has been played, the king-jack are equals.

ESTABLISHED SUIT: A suit that has been set up so that it now has all winners.

EXIT: Leading a card that compels an opponent to win the trick.

EXPOSED CARD: A card played or shown in an illegal way, and subject to penalty.

FALSE CARD: One played to deceive the opponents.

FINAL BID: The last bid in the auction—the contract.

FINESSE: An attempt to win a trick with a card that is not high, which will succeed if the missing higher card (or cards) is favorably located.

FIT: Usually refers to a good trump suit contained between two hands; it also means that the distribution of high cards in two hands blends well together.

FIVE-CARD MAJORS: An opening bid of 1♡ or 1♠ showing a five-card or longer suit.

FLAT HAND: Balanced distribution (4-3-3-3 or 4-4-3-2).

FOLLOW SUIT: Play a card in the suit that was led.

FORCING BID: A bid to force partner to bid again.

FOURTH BEST: A lead of the fourth highest card in a suit.

FOURTH HAND: In bidding, the player on dealer's right. In play, the last player to play to a trick.

FREAK HAND: One with fantastically wild distribution of the suits, such as 8-3-1-1, or 7-5-1-0.

FREE BID: A bid made after partner's bid has been overcalled by right-hand opponent.

GAME: A contract which, if made, will score 100 points or more below the line. The minimum game contracts are 3NT, 4♠, 4♡, 5◊ and 5♣.

GERBER CONVENTION: A bid of 4♣ asking partner to show the number of aces he holds.

GRAND SLAM: A contract to win all 13 tricks.

HAND: The cards held by one player; also, the complete deal of 52 cards.

HOLD UP: To postpone taking a sure winner in an opponent's suit.

HONOR BONUSES: Five trump honors in one hand = 150 points. Four trump honors in one hand = 100 points. Four aces in one hand at a notrump contract = 150 points.

HONOR CARD: Any ace, king, queen, jack or ten.

HONOR TRICK: A high card, or combination of high cards, that can (or might) win a trick the first or second time the suit is led.

HUDDLE: A long pause before making a bid or play.

INSUFFICIENT BID: A bid that is not higher than the last valid bid and therefore illegal.

INVITATIONAL BID: One that encourages, but does not command, partner to bid again.

JUMP BID: Any bid that skips one or more levels of bidding.

JUMP SHIFT: A single jump in an unbid suit—either a response to an opening suit bid, or a rebid by opener after a response to his opening suit bid.

KIBITZER: A spectator.

LEAD: Play the first card to a trick; the first card played.

LEAD-DIRECTING DOUBLE: A double intended to help partner select the best opening lead.

LEVEL: The number of "odd tricks" stated when bidding.

LIFE MASTER: A high ranking achieved by players in the ACBL.

LIMIT BID: A bid that gives a precise description of the values held—such as an opening 1NT bid which describes the strength of a hand within three points.

LONG CARDS: Cards left in a player's hand after all others in that suit have been played.

LONG SUIT: One in which you hold more cards that any other player, at least four.

LOSER: A card which cannot win a trick.

MAJOR SUIT: Spades or hearts.

MAKE: Fulfill the contract.

MASTERPOINT: The unit used by the ACBL to rank tournament players.

MATCH POINT: A unit used for scoring at duplicate bridge.

MAXIMUM: A hand having the highest value for the bid made; for example, an opening 1NT with 17 points.

MINIMUM: A hand having the lowest value for the bid made; for example, an opening 1NT with 15 points.

MINOR SUIT: Clubs or diamonds.

MISDEAL: An irregularity in dealing, which requires a new deal by the same player.

NEGATIVE RESPONSE: A bid to deny strength when partner has made a forcing bid; e.g., a 2◇ response to a 2♣ opening bid.

NEW SUIT: A suit that has not been bid previously.

NONCOMPETITIVE BIDDING: Auctions where one side does all of the bidding.

NOTRUMP: A bid to play without a trump suit.

ODD TRICK: Any trick in excess of six won by declarer.

OFFSIDE: A card that is in an unfavorable position; a finesse against it will lose.

ONE-OVER-ONE: A bid of one in a suit in response to partner's bid of one in a suit.

ONSIDE: A card in a favorable position; a finesse against it will win.

OPENING BID: The first bid of the auction.

OPENING LEAD: The lead to the first trick.

OPTIONAL DOUBLE: A double leaving it up to partner's judgment whether to bid or pass.

OVERBID: A bid for more tricks than one can expect to win.

OVERCALL: The first bid by a side after an opponent has opened the bidding.

OVERRUFF: Play a higher trump after the trick has already been ruffed.

OVERTAKE: To cover partner's high card, usually with the next-higher card; the purpose being to get the lead, or to unblock.

OVERTRICK: A trick won by declarer in excess of the number of tricks required by his contract.

PACK: The 52-card deck.

PARTIAL: Part-score.

PART-SCORE: A trick score of less than is necessary for game, less than 100 points.

PASS: The necessary call when a player chooses not to make a bid, double or redouble.

PASSED HAND: A player who had the chance, but chose not to open the bidding.

PASSED OUT: Said of a deal in which all four player pass in succession.

PENALTY: Points lost through failure to fulfill a contract. A levy sometimes imposed on a side for a violation of the rules.

PENALTY CARD: A card illegally exposed by a defender. The usual penalty is to leave the card face up on the table and to play it at the first legal opportunity.

PENALTY DOUBLE: A double made with the expectation of beating the contract.

PLAY: The act of contributing a card to a trick; the card played; the entire period in which the 13 tricks are played.

POINT COUNT: A method of hand evaluation for high cards and distribution.

POST-MORTEM: A discussion of a previous hand, wherein a player suggests an alternate bid and/or play.

PREEMPTIVE BID: A bid made at a high level in a long suit to make it more difficult for the opponents to compete.

PREFERENCE: A bid in partner's first suit when he has shown two.

PROPRIETIES: Standard of behavior governing the conduct of the players.

PSYCHIC BID: A bid made to mislead the opponents, rather than to describe a hand.

PUMP: Shorten declarer's trump holding by forcing him to ruff.

QUICK TRICK: See honor trick.

RAISE: A bid in the same denomination as partner's last bid; to make such a bid.

REBID: The second bid by a player; or to bid the same suit twice.

REDOUBLE: A call made after an opponent doubles. It multiplies (by two) the scoring value of a doubled contract for tricks bid and made, overtricks and undertricks.

RENEGE: See revoke.

REQUIREMENT: The minimum holding needed for a bid.

RESCUE BID: A bid in a different suit after partner has been doubled for penalty.

RESPONDER: The partner of the opening bidder.

RESPONSE: A bid made in answer to a bid or takeout double by partner.

REVALUATION: Upgrading or downgrading the worth of your hand based on the previous bidding.

REVERSE BID: A nonjump rebid in a new suit at the two-level that ranks higher than one's first-bid suit.

REVIEW: A restatement of all previous calls, in sequence, given on request.

REVOKE: Fail to follow suit when able to do so.

ROTATION: The clockwise order for dealing, bidding and playing.

RUBBER BRIDGE: The old-fashioned game, in which a rubber is completed when one side wins two games.

RUFF: Play a trump when a different suit has been led.

RUFF AND DISCARD (SLUFF): Lead a suit at a trump contract when both the declarer and dummy are void, thus allowing declarer to ruff in one hand and discard a loser in the other.

RUFFING FINESSE: In a suit contract when one hand has a sequence of high cards (such as K-Q-J) and the other hand is void, lead one of the honors: if second hand covers, ruff; if second hand plays low, discard a loser.

RULE OF ELEVEN: When the fourth highest card is led from a long suit, subtract the value of the card led from 11 to find out how many higher cards are held by the three players excluding the leader.

SACRIFICE BID (or SAVE): Bidding a contract that you do not expect to make; the purpose being to cut your losses. If doubled and set, the amount you lose will be less than if the opponents were allowed to play and make their contract.

SAFETY PLAY: Play a suit in such a way as to guard against a bad break, thus reducing or eliminating the risk of being set.

SECOND HAND: In bidding, the player on dealer's left. In the play, the second player to play to a trick.

SEMI-BALANCED HAND: 5-4-2-2 and 6-3-3-2 distribution. See Balanced Hand.

SEQUENCE: Two or more cards adjacent in rank.

SET: Defeat the contract.

SHAPE: The distribution of the suits in a hand.

SHORT MINOR: An opening bid in a three-card club or diamond suit.

SHOW OUT: Fail to follow suit.

SHUT-OUT BID: A preemptive bid.

SIDE SUIT: Any suit that is not trump. Typically, a long suit other than trump in the declarer's hand.

SIGNAL: A play, or series of plays, by a defender, to convey information to partner.

SIGN-OFF BID: A bid requesting partner to pass.

SINGLETON: An original holding of exactly one card in a suit.

SKIP BID: Jump bid.

SLAM: A contract to win 12 or 13 tricks.

SLUFF: Discard.

SMALL SLAM: A contract to win 12 tricks

SOLID SUIT: A long suit that has no losers.

SPLIT HONORS: Second-hand play of an honor card from a sequence when following suit.

SPOT CARD: Any card below the ten.

SQUEEZE: Lead a card that compels an opponent to discard a winner or unguard a suit.

STANDARD AMERICAN: The bidding system practiced and recommended for the average American bridge player, which excludes most bidding conventions.

STAYMAN CONVENTION: An artificial bid of 2♣ in response to 1NT, or 3♣ in response to 2NT, asking the notrump bidder to bid a major suit if he can, or to bid diamonds if he cannot.

STOPPER: A card, or combination of cards, which will prevent the opponents from running tricks in a long suit.

STRIP: Deplete the cards in a suit from your hand and dummy (or in some cases from the enemy hands), in preparation for a throw-in play.

SUIT: One of the four groups of 13 cards in a deck. The four suits are spades ♠, hearts ♡, diamonds ♢ and clubs ♣.

SUIT-PREFERENCE SIGNAL (not for beginners): A signal sometimes used when leading, following suit or discarding, to tell partner which of the *other* suits you want him to lead.

SUPPORT: To raise partner's suit; also, any cards that will be useful if the hand is played in partner's long suit.

SWITCH (or shift): After winning a trick, to lead a different suit.

TAKEOUT DOUBLE: A double which asks partner to bid.

TEMPORIZING BID: A forcing bid in a suit not intended to be trump. The subsequent bid will clarify the strength of the hand and which trump suit (or notrump) is preferable.

TENACE: Two honor cards not in sequence, such as A Q x or K J x.

THIRD-HAND: In bidding, the dealer's partner. In play, the leader's partner.

THROW-IN PLAY: An endplay, in which an opponent is thrown into the lead and forced to make a play that helps declarer.

TOP OF NOTHING: The lead of the highest card from a worthless suit.

TOUCHING: Cards in sequence such as king-queen or jack-ten, or suits in sequence such as spades-hearts, hearts-diamonds, or diamonds-clubs.

TRAP PASS: To pass right-hand opponent's bid when you have a strong hand and length in his suit, hoping that you get a chance to make a penalty double later.

TRICK: Four played cards, the lead followed by one card from each of the other three hands in clockwise rotation.

TRICK SCORE: The value of the odd tricks when a contract is made.

TRUMP: The suit named in the final bid, or any card of that suit. To play a trump card on the lead of another suit—to ruff.

TRUMP ECHO (not for beginners): A high-low signal in the trump suit to show possession of a third trump.

TWO-CLUB OPENING BID: A very strong bid, artificial and forcing.

TWO-OVER-ONE: A bid of two in a lower-ranking suit in response to partner's opening bid of one in a suit.

TWO-SUITER: A hand with at least five cards in one suit, and at least four cards in another.

TWO-WAY FINESSE: A suit combination in which a finesse may be taken through either opponent.

UNBALANCED HAND: One containing a very long, or a very short suit. See Balanced Hand.

UNBLOCK: To get rid of a high card in a short suit. The purpose is to enable partner to maintain (or get) the lead so he can cash his winners in the suit.

UNDERBID: A bid for fewer tricks than the value of the hand warrants.

UNDERLEAD: Lead a low card when holding one or more winners, usually in a trump contract.

UNDERTRICK: Each trick by which the declarer fails to fulfill his contract.

UNUSUAL NOTRUMP OVERCALL: An overcall in notrump, usually at the two-level, showing length in the two lowest-ranking unbid suits.

UPPERCUT: To ruff with a high trump, forcing declarer to overruff with a higher trump, thus promoting a trump winner for partner.

VOCABULARY OF BIDDING: Fifteen words: the numbers one through seven, the four suits, notrump, double, redouble and pass.

VOID: A holding of no cards in a suit.

VULNERABILITY: The score for game and slam bonuses, overtricks and undertricks is higher when a side is vulnerable than when it is not vulnerable. At Chicago Bridge the vulnerability for the four deals is determined by who dealt: first deal, neither side is vulnerable; second and third deals, the dealer's side is vulnerable; fourth deal, both sides are vulnerable. At duplicate bridge the vulnerability is predetermined and shown on the duplicate boards.

WEAK JUMP OVERCALL: A jump bid in a suit over an enemy bid which shows a weak hand with a long suit.

WEAK TWO-BID: An opening bid of two in a suit (excluding clubs) to show a weak hand with a long suit.

WINNER: A card that can win a trick.

YARBOROUGH: A hand containing no honor cards.